DREW HASTINGS
CHASING DREW HASTINGS

Chasing Drew Hastings

a memoir

—

Drew Hastings

A gallery off photographs related to this memoir can be seen
at www.drewhastings.com/memoirgallery.
Website: www.drewhastings.com
Twitter: @drewhastings

Jacket design by Yinger Design
Front cover photo by PJ Yinger
Back cover photo by Unknown
Author bio photo by Shay Nartker

ISBN 978 1 7358066 1 7 (hardcover)
ISBN 978 1 7358066 2 4 (softcover)
ISBN 978 1 7358066 3 1 (ebook)

Published by Caleb Hill Press
4710 Caleb Hill Road
Hillsboro, Ohio 45133

For Harrison

CONTENTS

Social Insecurity

I woke to the sound of the compressor on my window's A/C unit kicking in. That was my first problem, that I, an *accomplished* fifty-year-old man, was still living with a window A/C unit, tied down by a bungee cord, instead of central air conditioning.

My second problem—I didn't know what time it was. I lay in bed trying to get a feel for it. I couldn't use the sunlight as a gauge because I'd covered my bedroom windows with aluminum foil a while back, but my hunch was that it was somewhere between 8 a.m. and 1 p.m.

I also had a hangover from playing *DOOM* all night—a scary thought, that you could be physically hungover from a computer game. I was addicted to video games long before this cultural malady went mainstream, but then I'd always been ahead of the curve when it came to escapism. I did like to mix it up—sometimes I played cards until dawn in the poker rooms down by LAX. The morning-after effects for both activities were the same: temporary double-vision, a dull, grogginess that made you wonder if you'd had a mild stroke in your sleep, and a barking cough from too many cigarettes.

I lived in a one-bedroom apartment in Hollywood at the corner of Hollywood Boulevard and Curson Avenue. The place was desirable because of its central location, but not desirable enough to have off-street parking.

I was a standup comedian, a good one by most accounts, and those accounts had brought me to Los Angeles twelve years earlier, and a lot had happened since. But in Hollywood it's the stuff that *almost happened* that far outweighs what *did* happen, and that's probably a better increment for measuring one's time here. I got out of bed, coughed my way to the kitchen, and made a pot of coffee. The clock said 11:00. At least I hadn't slept until noon. My cat brushed against my leg and I shook some food from the bag of Kozy Kitten into his bowl.

Carrying an overflowing coffee cup to my desk, I sat down and stared at a small mountain of white stuff piled up. I slurped a sip, and pondered what lay heaped before me, and made a fateful decision. I was determined to sit there until I went through every last bit of it.

I sighed, looked over at my cat, and said, "How did I let all this unopened mail pile up?"

Surely there are as many examples of avoidance behavior as there are people like me to think them up. Not dealing with your mail is one of the classics and, based on the postmarks at the bottom of the mound, I had been avoiding mine for seven weeks.

I needed something in my stomach for this task. I swiveled my chair ninety degrees right so I could get up. Lest you think that my place was expansive enough to contain an actual office, the five-by-eight-foot outdoor balcony had been walled-in on its outside edge by the landlord in the 1970s, thereby creating a "home office," though its value as an IRS deduction far outweighed its functional use. I found scones in the kitchen, poured more coffee, and went back to the small mountain.

I began by sorting it into three piles: Bills, Junk, and Probably Relevant. Normally, I would also have a pile called Magazines, but since I'd let my subscriptions lapse, all I received were postcards like the one from *Archaeology Magazine* that showed a frowny face with the caption "We thought you dug us?" Everyone's a comedian.

I pitched all the junk mail into the wastebasket, then took the stack of bills and threw all of those into the trash as well, only keeping the ones stamped "Disconnection Notice." Those I set aside, knowing I had to pay them today, but I first wanted to open the Probably Relevant, an official looking #10 envelope from the Social Security Administration.

I reached for my letter opener. I've always used one and I bought my first when I was about twenty-two from a stationary store in my hometown of Cincinnati. At the time, I thought letter openers were a very adult thing to own, and the mark of a civilized person. To me, there were two types of people in the world: those who treated their mail with respect, opening it with the neat, surgical precision that a letter deserves, and those who simply forced their index finger into an opening, crudely tearing, ripping, almost sexually assaulting the poor thing.

This letter opener was a small, eight-inch replica of an English broadsword, whose point I deftly inserted into the end of the Social Security envelope. I removed a two-page "Statement of Earnings." I had received a few of these Social Security mailings before, but I'd never bothered to open them. As someone who'd been self-employed since I was nineteen, I viewed Social Security as something I'd never use or need. Social Security was for regular wage earners who were going to be happy with a fixed income in their Golden Years. But me? I was an entrepreneur! My income was virtually unlimited! My absolute certainty—the undeniable *given* in my life—was that my "Later Years," which I guessed would be from my fifties onward, would be somehow assured. I would be "well off," whatever that meant. So certain was Drew Hastings that he would one day own Boardwalk and Park Place that he didn't even bother with the two hundred dollars for passing Go, *Monopoly*'s version of Social Security.

All of this confidence in my success was in spite of the fact that I'd never had an inkling how any of this would come about. I had no blueprint, no plan, and certainly no goals, just this amorphous cloud swirling about my head like the one that swirled around the feet of Charlie Brown's friend, Pigpen. But my cloud wasn't a dirty, fly-ridden, dustbowl. No sir. Mine was a cumulonimbus mix of Midwest optimism, work ethic, and the belief that my creative brand of problem-solving could overcome any obstacle.

But on this day, despite the ongoing distractions of pot, video games, and women, there was a creeping awareness that my Later Years were now the Much Sooner Years, and far scarier still was the notion that something within me had recently changed. A Tumor of Doubt had formed. It was small, but real. It was producing symptoms. For instance, I had started feeling sorry for myself, something alien to every fiber inside me. My "bigger-than-life" personality—an appeal I had always depended on—had been slowly shrinking and I entertained the frightening thought that maybe I was never this kind of person at all. Maybe I only had a "bigger-than-life" *persona* and now it was failing. And if it was just a persona I had developed long ago and used to appeal to friends, comedy audiences, women, and network television execs, then who was the real me and why had I created some façade? To make matters worse, this was all beyond my psychological pay grade. Oh, I had the *ability* to be introspective, but preferred to bury any psychological turmoil in the soothing white noise of my vices.

As I sat there, I began to entertain the idea that whatever information the Social Security Administration had for me might actually be *relevant* to my life someday, and someday soon.

On the first page of the US government's Social Security Statement is a record of all of your earnings from your very first paycheck up to the present—in my case, 1969 to 2004—and it tells you how much money you've made during your life, in two neat columns. They then perform calculations that assume you'll continue earning at your present rate until retirement. It's like an actuarial table analyzing one's success, or lack thereof.

Next comes a short section called "Retirement Eligibility." One sentence in bold type caught my attention immediately: "Based on your earnings history and at your current earnings rate, if you retire at age 62, you will be eligible for $852 a month." I stopped. What exactly did that mean? For a second, it sounded good—$852 every month? Nice!

No. Wait. I went back and re-read it. I lit a cigarette, even though one was still burning in the ashtray. I talked myself through. "*This* is what I'm to be rewarded with based on all the money I've ever made? This is what the government is saying I'm supposed to live on?" I read the next section. This one they'd italicized: "*It is very important to remember that Social Security was never intended to be your only source of income when you retire.*" This admonition didn't even seem like something a governmental agency would normally say. It seemed so . . . opinionated. I imagined one of those 1950s' television dads, his arm around my shoulders, holding a tobacco pipe aloft and looking into the distance: "Now son, it's is very important to remember that Social Security was never intended to be your only source of income when you retire." Except that I never had a 1950s' dad—or a dad in any other decade for that matter.

I made a few calculations. I spent $120 a month on cigarettes, $90 on dry cleaning, $35 on cable. Maybe $150 on gas for the Cadillac. About $80 on pot. Probably $100 at the hair salon. Jesus—I hadn't even figured in food yet! I quit adding.

What had been a vague feeling that things weren't quite working out was suddenly very un-vague and in my face. Other than a few seat-of-the-pants business plans I'd scribbled on the backs of napkins, I'd always winged it. Now the consequences of a lifelong cavalier attitude were staring me in the face. My sophomoric mantra of "I'm going to make it big and people will know my name!" now seemed like some pathetic bumper sticker on a broken-down car on the side of the road.

I got up and went to the kitchen to pour a third cup of coffee, then headed to the bathroom to relieve myself of the first two. I looked in the mirror and saw the same guy that I'd been overly impressed with for years. "Look at me," I said. "I'm tall, articulate, good-looking, male, charismatic, intelligent. Hell, I'm *white*, for Christ's sake."

On the way back to my desk, I noticed the five-bulb light fixture that hung above the dining room table. I considered reaching up and unscrewing three of the bulbs, as though this power-saving move might actually get me caught up financially with some of my friends. I played in a weekly poker game where a few of my buddies casually discussed buying second homes, or whether it made sense to further fund their 401Ks, or move cash to an investment vehicle with better returns. I'd nod and offer comments because I'm well-versed in financial matters. I just never went home and applied this knowledge to my own life.

I could safely state that my friends and acquaintances generally thought of me as smart, funny, and worldly. They all would have agreed that I could tell a great story, that my love life had been large, varied, and enviable. I looked ten years younger than my age and I probably *was* the picture of success. More than a few assumed I came from some wealthy WASP family, an assumption that almost always raised my hackles and prompted me to set them straight: my midwestern background was, in fact, quite humble, I'll have you know.

But in reality, I had $1,800 in a checking account, a 1976 Cadillac Eldorado that was more vintage than valuable, a few antiques, a bunch of Incan artifacts I'd looted out of Peru in the '80s, and 110,000 frequent flyer points from Delta. The Social Security statement lying in front of me and my checking account balance were irrefutable evidence of the life I'd built—or rather, not built.

I picked it up again and looked at the next section titled "Your Earnings Record at a Glance." There were thirty-four rows beginning in 1969 and ending in the previous tax year, 2003. At a glance, all those yearly figures looked like a substantial amount of money. Where was it? I had none of the big expenditures most guys have. No ex-wives, no children. I'd had no parents to care for, no expensive, chronic health issues. There was shockingly little to show for more than thirty years of wheeling and dealing, hustling, and mostly honest hard work.

What really disgusted me was that I'd avoided looking at my life for this long. That I'd been in some bicameral state, like those times when you're driving down the freeway and suddenly aware that you don't remember the last five minutes. You think to yourself, "Damn, I could've slammed into the rear of a car or worse! Where was my mind?" Except that I'd been in this state for years.

I peered at those numbers, as if by looking hard enough I could decipher some solution. Then I opened the big, lower drawer of the desk and fished around until I found an 11" x 17" pad of graph paper. Maybe a visual representation would help. Most men will tell you that our barometer of success, for better or worse, is money. So I reasoned that if I wanted to understand my life, I needed to follow the money.

On the horizontal line across the page bottom, I plotted the years, and then went vertically up the left side and listed dollars at five-thousand-dollar increments. I got as far as 1992 before my eyes went buggy and I had to light another Marlboro Ultra Light.

When I was finished, I found a red fine-point marker and a stainless steel ruler and connected the dots from one year to the next. The lines went up, then down, then down farther, then sideways. Then a long line up again. I made a final red line, connecting 2002 to 2003, and put down the marker, replacing it with a Marlboro. The two hours that had elapsed since I opened the statement was the most time I'd spent examining any aspect of my life in years.

The first thing I noticed was that it didn't look like a chart documenting progress because it had no real pattern. Instead it looked medical, like an EKG printout of someone in cardiac distress. Movement was extreme, unanticipated, and without rhythm. A $3,600 income in '74 that leapt to $17,000 in '75. Then zero two years later, followed by a manic leap to $26,000 heading into the 1980s. This repeated itself over and over. Wild swings from $31K to $0 to $81K, all in the space of three years. Most of these were small businesses I'd started and then shut down after a year or so out of lack of interest or seeing another opportunity that looked more promising.

I slumped in my desk chair, still pondering the chart. I knew that the visual chart of most Americans' work histories would have showed a slow, steady rise upward as the years progressed, representing pay raises, promotions, and savvy career moves. Most likely, only catastrophic illness or divorce would've caused a sudden downward turn. As I stared at my crazed graph, I realized there *was* a pattern. It was in my behavior. The first word that came to mind was *unsustainable*. Mine was a pattern of unsustainability.

For whatever reason, I couldn't stick with anything. I couldn't, or didn't, build on successes—the result being that I often ended up back at square one, or close to it, time and time again. I also knew that were I to make a chart of my love life it would look nearly identical. I became very aware of how quiet it was in the apartment—actually, it wasn't just quiet, it was a silence that prevailed. And that suddenly made me feel very alone.

Sometime in my forties I'd resigned myself to the idea that I was destined to end up alone. Yes, I often enjoyed solitude, but I also didn't want to inflict myself on yet one more woman who was unaware that I was unaware of what a healthy relationship looked like, and so the idea of ever having a family never once formed in my mind. Even by focusing with all my might I could not conjure up a believable picture of me surrounded by a wife and children.

When I was six, my father split. As in, "gone for good." His name, like mine, was also Drew Hastings. I visited my grandparents the following year and when I asked about my dad, they told me that after he left, my father immediately remarried. He had another baby boy, and his new wife said to him, "I want you to forget that you ever had another wife and children, so we'll name *this* baby Drew Hastings. This is the *real* Drew Hastings—not that other one." So by the time I was seven, there were three Drew Hastings: me, the one who left me, and the one who replaced me.

So began a lifelong preoccupation with my name and a hyper-vigilant effort to not only protect it, but ensure its supremacy. You remember that kid who just couldn't help writing his name into wet cement? That was me. It seems like most of my childhood was spent carving my name into trees, park benches, and school desktops. I have an old steamer trunk full of memorabilia I've lugged around my whole life. Inside is a stack of old business cards rubber-banded together. Cards from every venture, scheme, and undercapitalized LLC I've ever gotten, or tried to get, off the ground from 1975 through 1988. The businesses vary, but on every card, my name is front and center.

My first was a janitorial company whose sole assets consisted of a vacuum cleaner and a toilet plunger, but the business card read "Patriot Cleaning: A Drew Hastings Company." It was supposed to make you think I dominated the janitorial market, replacing urinal cakes and refilling sanitary napkin dispensers across the Midwest. This ambition was typical and, as with all my enterprises, business cards were the first and frequently the most significant startup expenditure. An initial order was usually 10,000 cards—the height of optimism—and always with "Drew Hastings" in prominent, raised boldface font.

There was "Hastings Trucking: A Division of Drew Hastings Industries," a one-truck operation. There was "Polo Supplies Inc.: Equestrian Gear from Drew Hastings Limited," a brief venture that came into being after I attended a polo match and saw how much money rich people dropped on horse supplies. These startups, formed on a wing and a prayer, should have had a disclaimer underneath my bold corporate names: "Keeping my head above water since 1977."

In the steamer trunk, along with the business cards, is a large stack of "membership" cards. These consist of any organization I could join for free that issued embossed cards to its members. They usually said something exclusive and status-conferring, like, "This certifies that *Drew Hastings* is a member in good standing." I was a member of the Playboy Club, the National Geographic Society, and a Platinum member of the Columbia Record & Tape Club and the Sierra Club. I had my name prominently displayed on airline frequent flyer cards and casino-issued players' cards. Drew Hastings was giving his data away long before data was data. I imagined future archaeologists squinting excitedly over my excavated cards, muttering, "He must have been some kind of king!"

In my late twenties, my preoccupation with the Drew Hastings brand found a new avenue in monograms. Obsessed, I owned monogrammed shirts, cuff links, towels, and when I pulled cash from my pocket, it was in a monogrammed money clip.

By my early thirties, I knew that if I was going to have "my name in lights and my initials in diamonds," I needed to get serious. One obvious career that seemed tailor-made for me—owning a car dealership. Automobile dealerships were almost always named after their owners. The entire business model was built on name recognition, and the owners had the added benefit of having their name in chrome on the back of the car for everyone to see. But there was just something inherently uncool about *Drew Hastings Chevrolet* on the trunk of a Malibu. A future as a well-known car dealer conjured thoughts of alcoholism, adultery, messy divorces, and missing VIN numbers. Plus, the most I could hope for was local, or at best, regional fame. I imagined local television spots: "Hi! I'm Drew Hastings! Come on down to Hastings Chevrolet, Pontiac, Mazda, GMC for the best deal on . . ." No, If I was ever going to be on television, it was going to be for something bigger than selling cars. I was going to be known for being me.

I'd always been driven, but my ambition was usually overshadowed by my preoccupation—making my name known to the world. The realization of just how much I'd limited other career paths by that misguided priority was sad indeed. I was a middle-aged man whose entire life had been a game of *Chutes and Ladders*. How had it come to this? I knew that if I didn't choose the right path forward, right now, I was going to end up a sad waste of a man. Time, Mr. Hastings, was running out.

All through my life, I'd been stumbling toward whatever I perceived to be success, and always with the feeling that everyone around me had some valuable information that had been withheld from me. What had I missed? Where were all those secrets? Everyone else seemed to hold the key to success while I was merely picking the lock. All I'd ever wanted was to make a name for myself, and yet it seemed I had only fashioned a shell that was starting to crack. It wasn't as if I'd never succeeded at anything—*I had*, numerous times—but success seemed to show up like illness. I had bouts, flare-ups, and outbreaks of success that then went into remission and I had no idea when, or even *if*, I might experience it again.

I turned back to the desk and thought of one of the many quotes I'd collected over the years, "A disease known is half cured." If I was going to make any big changes I had to look back on where I'd come from, where I'd gone off the rails. I opened the desk drawer once more, pulling out a pad of writing paper, lit another cigarette, and got to work.

PART I

The Name Game

CHAPTER 1

Sons of Single Mothers

I fly down to Sarasota to visit my mother. She fell and broke her pelvis last year and since then, I worry about her. She's now eighty-two and I'm sixty-five. At lunch, after some small talk that includes our displeasure with Sarasota's unbridled growth, I ask her about her childhood. She's become a little more open with age, but I still have to refrain from too many questions or she closes up. I ask about her father's occupation in London. He was a draftsman. My mom always tears up when she talks about him. She idolized him and for most of her childhood he was bedridden with tuberculosis. He died when she was ten. I look at her with the tears not quite spilling down her cheeks, and am struck that seventy-five years after his departure, she still gets so emotional. Then I realize that half a century after my father left, I still mourn him. Well, not exactly—I stopped mourning *him* a long, long, time ago—but I still mourn the loss of a *father*. We have that in common, my mom and I.

Even typing the word "father" or "dad" feels alien. The word might as well be "cancer," or some other thing I've never experienced. It's like I had a limb amputated when I was a kid. I learned to operate without it but for a long time there was that feeling of phantom limb syndrome that actual amputees get, where they can still feel pain emanating from the space that their limb once inhabited.

In 1968 I was getting dressed for the annual eighth grade dance at John F. Kennedy Jr. High. I was in my sport coat, staring into the bathroom mirror trying to figure out how to tie a necktie. My mom came in and stood behind me. She put her arms over my shoulders, looking into the mirror in front of us, as we tried to figure out a Windsor knot. Finally we gave up and on the way to the dance my mom made a detour to the shopping center and bought a clip-on. I felt like a fraud in that clip-on. The necktie was the all-American symbol of masculinity and adulthood, but the one dangling from my neck—this make-do affair—felt like an admission I'd never measure up. I resented my mother for not knowing how to tie a tie, for forcing me into this position, but most of all I resented myself for having to rely on her.

I watch my mother move around the kitchen making tea. She seems so frail now, though she would take issue with that if I said it aloud. She won't even let me help her in or out of the car when we drive to Longboat Key for lunch.

My mother is only seventeen years older than me. Both of my parents were young when they met. My father was barely twenty and in the Navy when he met sixteen-year-old Pamela Ann Hewittson-Fisher in London while he was on shore leave. They quickly married, then my mom became pregnant, or maybe it was the other way around. I was born in Casablanca, Morocco, where my dad was stationed, and he brought us to his native Ohio when she was just eighteen. My sister, Karen, was born a year later and then he was gone for good.

Karen and I both agree that we don't remember our mother much until we were about ten. Of course, we recall *having* a mother—she fed us, clothed us, provided for us—we just have a hard time remembering her in specific acts of *mothering*. Mostly what I remember of my mom from those early years was that she was stunningly beautiful—almost identical to Audrey Hepburn—and she spoke with an English accent. She was aloof and unaffectionate, partly because of her personality and partly because she was British, and all of this made her exotic and beyond reach, which left me in awe of her.

"Do you want Darjeeling tea or Constant Comment," she asks.

"Let me have the Constant Comment."

Her resemblance to Audrey Hepburn is not as obvious anymore. Her face looks tired and has those lines that chronic pain produces.

"Sugar or Sweet'N Low?"

"Sugar, thanks."

Even though her accent is all but gone, my mom's Britishness is still, to me, her predominant feature. Her worldview, attitude, and behaviors were shaped by Great Britain, and she brought them along with her to America. To my mother, Ohio was not a state, but a far-flung British colony, like Burma, where it was best not to get too friendly with the native population lest you pick up their bad habits.

"Where in God's name are your shoes?" my mother would shriek in horror, pointing at my feet when I was a kid.

"Mom, everyone in the neighborhood goes barefoot in the summer," I'd explain.

"Well, you're *not* everyone. You look like a street urchin."

"Mom, I'm seven."

"Always an excuse," she'd say, with a dismissive wave of her hand.

Behaving in a "civilized" manner was always of paramount importance.

"Civilized people don't eat their food with their fingers."

"But they're French fries, mom!"

If Karen and I were playing, we'd hear, "Would you and your sister please quiet down and act somewhat civilized!" To her way of thinking, playing cowboys and Indians should be at the same decibel level as coloring in a book. I laugh now, thinking back on our upbringing, but there's no question her Britishness rubbed off on me. Though I'm proudly midwestern, I have what some see as an elitist streak and little tolerance for drama. No wonder my childhood movie idols were John Wayne and Rex Harrison—two vastly different ideas of men.

"Are you parked behind me? Because I need to go to the drugstore to pick up some things," my mom says.

"Yes, but I can drive you over there."

"Well, if you're not too busy . . ."

"Mom. I flew down here to see you—what else am I going to be busy with?"

Beginning when I was thirteen and until I was almost thirty, Mom was involved with a married man. He had a wife and children in another city, and our lives seemed to be dictated by the whims of his availability. When the phone rang, she leapt to answer it. Then it was, "Change into something nice, we're going to dinner with Jim." Or, "Be back here by six, Jim's coming over for dinner." Always spur of the moment and never was it an outing.

Jim never showed any particular interest in me nor I in him. My mom continued that relationship for more than fifteen years and I couldn't help feeling sorry for her—she often seemed stressed and powerless. What's the old saying—"We don't get to choose who we fall in love with." The irony of it was that they had a clandestine affair for many years until Jim got divorced. Then he and mom moved to sunny Sarasota and were married, only to divorce after seven years when my mom found out he was having an affair. I was about thirty-five by then and remember being blown away by the news. I'd watched two people that were hopelessly in love beat the odds, and still it went south. It cemented my already cynical views on love, marriage, and commitment for another twenty years, and my mom has lived by herself ever since.

On the third day of my visit to Mom's, I take her out to dinner, determined to broach the subject of her financial wherewithal and the possibility of her moving. She lives in a large townhome and my sister and I feel she should be somewhere where she's not so alone. I cringe at the idea of bringing this up—she's fiercely independent, it seems even more so since the divorce. And any talk of finances would be awkward. My mother's a very private person. Everything with her is on a "need to know" basis. As children, even my and my sister's most innocuous questions were usually met with some suspicion.

"Mom, what's your middle name?"

"Why in God's name would you ask me something like that?" There were only two types of questions to her way of thinking—stupid ones and ones that we had no business asking. Which is why my mom is now eighty-three and I have no idea how equipped she is for retirement. I don't know if she has eight thousand dollars in a cookie tin or six hundred thousand in an IRA.

I watch her interrogate the waiter about the gluten-free choices. She's still stylish, but I'm unnerved by how she's aged. Part of me still sees her as the stunning beauty that she was and I recall how so many people were sure she was my older sister. But I also see how time has taken its toll. She never got over what happened with Jim. I remember the first couple years right after the divorce she looked like death warmed over. I was really concerned for her at the time but her always-aloof demeanor and sense of privacy didn't allow for more than a conciliatory hug. Slowly our relationship has warmed, but it's not like we're revealing our deepest secrets to each other.

Finally, over dessert, I try to be very nonchalant when I say, "You think you'd ever look at moving to a retirement community?"

"No, I don't think I would," she replies. I'm grateful for that answer because I was convinced it would be, *Well, if you like the idea so much—maybe you should look at moving into one.* Effectively the conversation ends there. I don't even bother asking about her finances.

One day, just a year or so before I turned fifty, I sat upright in bed with the thought, *My mom has never once asked me if I ever plan on getting married.* I then said it out loud just to see if it sounded as odd as it did in my head. It did. Then it dawned on me that she had never asked me if I wanted children. To me, the only thing odder than her never asking me about these things was a man almost fifty years old only now realizing that his mother had never inquired about them. I called two friends and asked them if they thought that it was odd and they most definitely did. I don't think my mother ever really wanted to have kids. I've had that feeling ever since I was about ten. But I'm not going to make that assumption. Women have children for all kinds of reasons. Then again, maybe she never asked because she knew me better than I knew myself. How much does any mother really know her son?

When I was thirteen, I was getting knocked around by two bullies just fifty feet from our apartment door where they'd finally caught up with me—after a mile-long chase during my morning paper route. My mom, hearing the commotion, came out to the second-floor balcony of our apartment and scolded my tormentors in her crisp British accent, "You there. Leave him be! Have you nothing better to do?"

Curled up in a ball on the ground, I thought, *No, Mom, they* don't *have anything better to do!* The two kids looked up at my mom, then down at me and snickered as they walked away. It sounded like Mary Poppins had come to my rescue. Not only was it apparent that I was unable to defend myself, but now that my mother had intervened, it guaranteed that these bullies would double down on the beatings. That evening she said something like, "You need to start standing up to them," a solution that to me was woefully inadequate. Only a man could have helped me with this problem—he could have taught me how to fight, or instilled some confidence, or at least helped me get over my abject fear of these guys. But there was no one. Only my mom with her impotent advice.

By the time I was eighteen, our relationship had grown antagonistic. I no longer saw a mother telling me what to do, instead she was a woman—*a female*—trying to control me. What could she possibly know about the world of men I was entering? And because my teen years were a chronology of risky behaviors and questionable choices, my mom saw me as one prone to bad judgment, and who didn't have the sense to come in out of the rain.

I straightened up in my early twenties and started various business ventures. My mom and I became business partners and grew closer through a shared interest for the first time. We talked daily, and our relationship changed, mostly for the better—but not entirely. The dynamic that had formed between us back when I was a teen continued, and my mother had a conditioned response to anything she disagreed with, which lasted until I was in my fifties. We'd have a disagreement or I'd bring up a suggestion and she'd blurt, "That is the most idiotic thing I've heard in ages." Or, "How could you be so stupid—*what were you thinking*?" Always some variation of the same belittling comments and I always bit my tongue and became defensive.

It didn't occur to her that she was being demeaning, but either my mother continually viewed me as a clueless dolt or she was simply stuck in some chastising loop from those early days. Regardless, I let her continue in that manner for years.

We are having lunch on Siesta Key on the last day of my visit, chatting about elections and the timing of owning marijuana stocks. When I picked her up at her house, we hugged, which is a new thing. My mother has never been particularly affectionate—she used to hug me like I had something sticky on my shirt. But that has changed recently. We've even started ending our phone calls with "I love you," and I no longer sit tensed at how she'll respond to a comment I've made or an opinion I've ventured. There's no defensiveness any more.

These things only came about after an episode in a Lowe's home improvement store. My mom had come up to visit a few years back and was helping me with some ideas for a commercial building that I was renovating. As we walked through Lowe's, I asked her a question about using some light fixtures that I already owned instead of buying new ones. She retorted, "For God's sake! I don't know what's wrong with you that you can't see that those old light fixtures of yours are all wrong! You seem almost incapable of thought sometimes!"

I snapped, turning to my mother and saying in a voice that could be heard three aisles over, "Don't you ever fucking talk to me like that again! I don't know who the fuck you think you're talking to, but I am no longer your fourteen-year-old kid. I'm a fifty-five-year-old man. I wouldn't let *anyone* ever talk to me like that and I'll be goddamned if I'm going to let *you. Is that clear?*"

My mom's eyes welled up with tears—whether out of anger or fear or shame I didn't know. I didn't care. I was so angry that I had let her address me like that for so long and was mortified that people in Lowe's heard her berating me like a child. We were silent all the way back to her hotel and she never spoke to me like that again. It had taken decades for her to see how she spoke down to me, just like it took decades for me to see her differently. How many times had I discounted useful advice or guidance she offered that, had it come from someone else, I would have seen its value immediately? But as I sit here in the sun at lunch on Siesta Key listening to

Mom interrogate yet another waiter about the gluten-free items, I realize that we're finally equals. We respect each other now.

One morning when I was fifteen years old, my mom decided that my long hair was becoming way too hippie-ish and demanded that I go get it cut. I promptly ran away to New York City and hung out with all the other disaffected hippies down on Manhattan's Lower East Side. I was there almost five months before I called home. She sent me a plane ticket.

We got into another argument when I was sixteen and I ran away again, this time to a crash pad in downtown Dayton. I contracted hepatitis, got deathly ill, and my mother got me into Kettering Memorial Hospital and visited me every day after work.

At seventeen, I was busted in Atlanta for selling hallucinogens. I sat in Fulton County jail for a month and a half before I finally broke down and called my mom. She sent me money for an attorney and a way home.

I was a middle-aged man before I realized all she had done for me. The night I did realize it, I called her on the phone and told her how sorry I was for being so ungrateful. I cried and cried and the snot poured from my nose and my face burned with shame and I don't think my mom understood half of what I said before I hung up. Even now, I hate myself for being so unaware, so self-centered, not seeing that she was there for me all along. She was just a teenager when she had me. Christ, when I started junior high school she was still in her twenties.

Another way to tell my mother's story is like this: A seventeen-year-old leaves a dismal post-war London for Morocco. She has a baby that same year and moves to a small town in middle-of-nowhere-America. In spite of a husband who left her with two small children, she managed. At twenty-three, she produced and hosted an acclaimed political television show in Columbus, Ohio. Before she was thirty, she developed the first ad campaigns for Kentucky Fried Chicken and Wendy's restaurants, then went into the corporate world—still a rarity for women in the 1960s—in Dayton, Ohio, and on to successfully run a manufacturing company in Cincinnati. All along, she sacrificed to ensure that my sister and I were in the best school districts possible and had decent clothes to wear. After we were out of the house, she left to try her hand at real estate development in Florida, and ultimately became a well-respected, successful interior designer in Sarasota.

On the flight home I reflect on these last few days with my mom. Maybe it's because we're both older, but for whatever reason, I saw her in a somewhat different light this visit. Over the years, when I've tried to understand my behavior and why I've become the man that I am, it's that empty space, that missing piece—my father—that I look at. Maybe that's human nature—to give too much weight to the missing fragments in our lives, much like a jigsaw puzzle that we discover is short a couple of pieces. All we see is the hole in the puzzle where the missing piece should be, and all of our focus and anguish becomes centered on desperately looking under the table for the lost piece and on the completeness that only having all one thousand pieces of the landscape that's on the cover of the box can bring.

But that focus on the lost piece of my life has been misguided. The who and why of the man I've become is, of course, more about the part that *is* there—my mother—and less about the piece missing.

I've always professed that my mother and I are nothing alike, but as I reflect on her life it's impossible not to see my own. We've both had varied professional successes and profound personal heartaches. We are both survivors of all that life has thrown at us and yet we've been there for each other in our own arms-length, emotionally stilted way. For better or worse, I am my mother's son.

CHAPTER 2

A Book of Quotes

"Don't dig your grave with your own knife and fork," my grandfather said, nodding toward a huge, fat man waddling down the street. "That's the danger of excess, Drew."

"Got it," I said. I was skinny as a rail and nobody else in our family was overweight, but I took everything my grandad told me as gospel. I idolized both him and my grandmother. His name was William Andrew Hastings Sr., and though I'd only seen my dad once since he moved out, Karen and I saw our grandparents often. I hung on his every word and, because he tended to teach me lessons via quotations, I wrote every one of them down in a special notebook. They were usually biblically-oriented or something vaguely agrarian.

"Remember, Drew, always ask a farmer's permission before cutting across his property," he'd say, nodding toward a pasture as we drove by in his big musty-smelling Pontiac DeSoto.

"It is more blessed to give than to receive," he'd say while writing a small check to a charity organization.

"Heed the words of Benjamin Franklin: 'Never a borrower or a lender be.'"

"Energy and persistence conquer all things."

My grandparents lived in Martins Ferry, the oldest settlement in Ohio, first inhabited in 1779. It was a small, grimy coal and steel town on the Ohio river across from Wheeling, West Virginia, and was my favorite place in the world. Aside from my grandparents' home, it was the only connection I had to my father. He was born there, as were my grandparents and their parents before them. I don't think either of my grandparents had ever lived more than twenty miles away from the brick-paved streets of Martins Ferry. It was a blue-collar town where most men worked in the steel mills or coal mines that had been there for one hundred fifty years, creating a patina of coal dust that covered everything if one didn't take great pains to keep it at bay. My grandparents' house was a large, three-story, turn-of-the-nineteenth-century frame house that was worn and tired-looking, like most homes in Martins Ferry. Inside, the floors creaked loudly with every step. They wailed as Karen and I skipped through the parlor, and the stairs moaned when we crept down them. The house made it difficult to have secrets.

Grandma and Grandpa Hastings were of Welsh-Scots-Irish descent, like most of the early Ohio settlers. My grandmother, Blanche, was almost identical to TV's Aunt Bea from *Mayberry*. She didn't have fat so much as a plump thickness that's common to Midwest, middle-aged women, and always smelled of rose water. Grandma Hastings also had a high-strung, worrisome nature. She was often "in a tizzy," as my grandfather would say.

My grandfather, Bill as he was known, was tall and on the lean side like all the Hastings men. He had kindly, pale blue, watery eyes, excellent posture, and walked like he was leading a solemn procession. He worked for Wheeling Steel as a supervisor at the foundry. Though he was humble, I always got the impression he was proud that he wore a tie and worked in the office instead of down in the foundry itself, as I believe our ancestors had. Aside from his notable quotations, he liked me to learn from parables, like the story of Damon and Pythias, a lesson which he once said I should "cleave to my bosom." He was fascinated by history, global and local, and stoked my curiosity about everything.

When I wasn't listening to Grandpa's wisdom, Karen and I were up in their attic. She played with old porcelain dolls with cracked faces and eyes that opened unnaturally. I was addicted to my grandparents' *Reader's Digest* collection. They had thousands of issues stacked everywhere and must have subscribed since the early 1500s. I sat there in the attic reading for hours, blowing the coal dust off the covers and transcribing into my notebook the "quotes for good living."

"A man never stood so tall as when he stooped to help a child."

"A successful person is one who can lay a firm foundation with the bricks that others throw at him."

Throughout their entire house were antiques, from the chairs to the doily-covered tables to the glass curio cabinets. Everything else was knick-knacks, which covered every surface of the house. Figurines, glass bells, memento ashtrays from Niagara Falls that were always full of change, buttons, or safety pins. And displayed prominently between all of those knickknacks were framed photographs. Very few were of my grandparents—they would have considered that to be vain—most were of their two children, my dad and his sister, my Aunt Judy.

Karen and I were always drawn to these pictures of our father, though Karen less so. I studied them, peered at them, looking for answers, I guess. Photos of him sat on their coffee tables, on the shelves of parlor bookcases, and hung on hallway walls. The more current pictures that my grandparents displayed made it feel like he was here regularly—*maybe even just last week!*—even though we knew he lived far away in New York City. Every visit I'd ask my grandparents about my dad. Had they seen him? Was he doing okay?

They would fill in sketchy biographical information, but what I most remember is that every time I asked them if they'd seen him, their reply was always, "Your father said to say he loves you and misses you very much." I would not see my father for more than thirty years, but my grandparents repeated that same line to my sister and me every time we visited them until the day they died.

My grandfather was a deacon and in the choir at the Third Street Presbyterian Church. I still picture him asleep in his recliner, with an open bible in his lap. He neither smoked nor drank, and warned me of the horrors of these vices by pointing out sleeping bums on park benches. "I knew him since high school. He was such a promising boy. Never put liquor to your lips, Drew—you'll end up a wretch." I'd swear to him that I never would, as he muttered to himself, "It's just terrible, terrible, such a waste." I always marveled at how my grandfather was able to remain so pure, so unadulterated. More than anything, I wanted him to be proud of me.

And though my grandfather was my first male role model, we slowly drifted apart. He meant the world to me, but then my world seemed to fall apart. First, my mother re-married. Then my grandmother died when I was nine. My mother divorced. We moved. We moved again. I became a delinquent. I started getting high and then higher. At twenty-one I started a series of small businesses, always counting on my strong work ethic to succeed. But when that wasn't enough, I lied, or cheated, or stole to make it work and the quote I lived by—"the end always justifies the means"—was nowhere in my childhood notebook.

Then, when I was twenty-seven, Karen was in the middle of a divorce from a guy she'd been married to for a couple of years. He had an IQ somewhere around room temperature and was a psychopath, or a sociopath, or both. I once watched him beat a man half to death with his shoe. He started getting psycho with Karen, stalking and threatening her. She was living with me at the time and after he threw a homemade bomb at our apartment door, which luckily failed to detonate, she asked me to stand up to him before he killed her. I didn't. All that paralyzing fear and lack of confidence that I had when confronted by bullies long ago was still there and I made my excuses. I was ashamed beyond words. It was bad enough that her big brother wasn't there to protect her—he hadn't even attempted. It was the opposite of everything my grandfather had always tried to teach me.

I wasn't there when my grandfather died at eighty-six in March of 1982. I was twenty-eight and wrapped up in my own life, trying to start my newest business—a document shredding operation—snorting coke, and chasing girls. I didn't even know he was gone until two months after he'd been buried. I drove from Cincinnati to Martins Ferry hoping to get a few of his things—knickknacks, a piece of furniture, photos—any reminder of what had been the happiest times of my life. But there was nothing. I heard that my father and my Aunt Judy had descended upon his house, grabbing what they wanted, fighting viciously over his belongings, then disposing of everything else at auction.

I went to the cemetery and lay down beside his grave and when my head touched the grass I burst into tears. After the sobbing subsided, the moaning came, like I was some wounded animal. I thought about the story of Damon and Pythias that my grandfather used to tell, the two brothers who were so close, had such a strong friendship, that one offered to die for the other. Through snot and tears I tried to explain my shame—about failing my sister when she most needed me, about my drug use and the wasted nights. And I saw that I wasn't crying for my grandfather, I was crying for me, for the little boy carrying his notebook full of quotes and stumbling through life. All at once I was grateful that my grandfather never saw the man that I didn't turn out to be, and that made me sob all the harder.

CHAPTER 3

Jewboy

There are times in our early life that have outsized impact for the rest of our days. It may have been thirty years ago, but our biases or food preferences, or even physical mannerisms originated there. That period of time could be as short as the week you went to camp when you were ten. When you left you were impacted, influenced. Maybe you made a lifelong friend, or you developed a pathological fear of raccoons. Perhaps you learned to swim in open water and at week's end you left brimming with confidence—or you almost drowned and to this day have nightmares about lungs full of water.

A lot can happen in a week. But the segments of influence can also be longer, months or maybe years. Beginning when I was eight years old there was a very specific four years that affected me in a myriad of ways, and they began when my mother uttered this sentence:

"Marty and I got married while you were away this summer."

That's how I found out I had a stepdad, though at age eight, the closest description of him that I could formulate was *man-who-will-now-live-with-us-and-act-like-my-dad-even-though-I-already-have-a-dad*. This marriage happened in August of 1962, while Karen and I had been at our grandparents' house in Martins Ferry. We were cautiously excited. Mom had been dating Marty for some months and he would bring trinkets and other small gifts when he came to visit. He was dark-haired, and looked like Dean Martin.

"Are we going to be moving?"

"Yes."

"Will we be going to a different school?"

"Yes."

"Where will we be moving?"

"Why do you bombard me with so many questions?"

A few days after the announcement, Mom instructed us to put on our good church clothes since we were going to meet Marty's parents. Marty picked us up and we drove to their house. Though their home was an ordinary one-story ranch house, when I stepped through the front door, I found myself in a strange world—one of a tightknit clan of people, most of whom spoke a different language, who ate exotic foods and had thousands of years of custom, ritual, and strict religious observance governing their everyday lives. Enter the Jews.

Marty stood us in front of two ancient people in matching recliners. "Drew, Karen, these are my parents, your new grandparents, Rose and A.J. Mellman. You can call your grandmother Bubbe, and your grandfather Zayde. Those're their Yiddish names."

"Hello," we mumbled in unison. Then Karen moved over behind our mom. I listened while the adults talked. Marty's parents had accents and they looked perpetually worried. He later told me that they came from Russia. Occasionally Marty and his parents would start arguing in another language, which I later found out was both Hebrew and Yiddish. This language was not like anything I heard in the movies, like French or Spanish, and a lot of the words sounded like the speakers were trying to clear phlegm from their throats. What had Mom gotten us into? The arguing got worse and I tried to sound out and write down a few of the recurring words. That night I asked Marty their definitions.

Meshuggeneh—Marty said this meant a crazy person. His mom and dad had used this word numerous times during our visit.

Shiksa—this was a word I'd heard used a few times. Marty told me it meant "a non-Jewish woman," but the way his mom was using it sounded like it was Hebrew for "Marty what have you done to us?"

Sheigetz—which I was told meant "a non-Jewish male." I wrote it down as loosely meaning "son of a shiksa."

The next day I asked my mother why the Mellmans spoke another language.

"Marty and his family are Jewish."

"What's Jewish?"

"It's just a different religion than ours. They're Jewish and we're Episcopalian."

I didn't give it much more thought. I just assumed that we still had the same God, the same Jesus, and that my earthly record would now be transferred to this new Jewish church. It was easy to be impressed by my new stepfather. Marty was good-looking, wore Sharkskin suits, and always seemed tanned. He could let a lit cigarette hang from one side of his mouth and talk normally without the ash ever falling off, his left eye squinting to keep the smoke out while his right eye looked at you. When his cigarette wasn't in his mouth he held it so naturally it seemed like a sixth finger. He wore jewelry. Gold rings, necklaces, and cufflinks. I'd never seen that stuff on men before. In contrast, Grandpa Hastings might wear a Masonic button on his suit for a special occasion.

Marty quickly started letting me tag along as he attended to his businesses. He owned a used car lot near downtown Columbus with a neon sign announcing "Marty's Used Cars." I was thoroughly impressed that he had his name on a big lit sign. The lot had an office with a desk, and a back room full of junk where an old black man worked on tires and cleaned up the ten or fifteen cars that sat in the lot under the long string of flashing bulbs.

Marty would tell the old man to rearrange the cars, moving some to the front row and others to the rear. He'd look to see who had come in to make their weekly payment on the car they'd financed. Periodically, he'd pull a large wad of money out of his pocket, sometimes giving some to someone who came in or taking money from someone else. A lot of being in business seemed to be about the wad of money that went in and out of his pocket. This was the first habit I picked up from Marty. For the rest of my life I would always carry a large wad of cash in my front pocket.

Marty also owned a jazz place, the 502 Club, which attracted the top jazz musicians from across the US. I'd sip a coke at the bar while Marty counted money at the registers, looked over liquor supplies, and pulled out his wad of cash to deal with whoever he was talking to, which was mostly black dudes who wore sunglasses at night, like Marty. I not only thought Marty was rich, I figured he had to be famous too, since all the ads for his club bore his name: *"Marty Mellman's 502 Club is proud to present Little Stevie Wonder, America's harmonica genius!"* Even if I still missed my father and wondered why I didn't hear from him, Marty Mellman, for better or worse, made him slightly easier to forget.

Curious as I was about the whole Jewish thing, nothing prepared me for the first time that I walked into Marty's church, Agudas Achim synagogue, on the corner of Broad and Roosevelt in the heart of Columbus's Jewish community. Marty put something called a yarmulke—a little beanie-type hat—on my head as we walked in. Everywhere were men in pews, many of them with beards. They were rocking back and forth like crazy people, except that these men were praying. Marty said it was called "davening." All of them wore prayer shawls and prayed aloud in Hebrew. These prayers sounded so *mournful*, seemed less like praying and more like wailing. This was the first time I ever had the feeling of *Other*—that people were not essentially all the same, that all old people were not just variations of my grandparents, and that churches were not basically all the same. I was different from these people and that, in turn, introduced the concept of acceptance and rejection. These Jews were from the tribe of Judah and I was descended from the tribe of Episcopalia.

Marty's family also had a completely foreign dynamic. They all loved to talk—loudly. They were argumentative, they debated, they were excitable. Everyone seemed to have an opinion and everybody seemed to involve themselves in everyone else's business. They waved their hands around when they spoke, which made them seem like they were upset about something even if they weren't. A sharp contrast from the understated WASP way of my mom and her side of the family. With my mother, you spoke when spoken to and what was *not* said often ruled your life. Usually just a withering glance from my mother was communication enough in our household. And these Jewish people seemed so *physical*—kissing, hugging, or worse, pinching your cheeks with both of their hands. My sister and I were not used to these exaggerated displays of affection.

Nothing, though, contrasted our families more than food. Mostly delicious and sometimes beyond gross. Jewish food was heavy. It often smelled weird. Boiled cabbage. Beef tongue. Corned beef, creamed herring, borscht. It was at every gathering in great quantities and usually being forced on me. "Eat! You look like a toothpick, eat!" some new relative or family friend would exclaim. They set out so much food it didn't look like a meal so much as a dare.

The first Christmas after our Jewish immersion, Grandma and Grandpa Hastings drove over from Martins Ferry to pick us up for a week-long visit and they met Marty for the first time. I'm sure that to my grandfather, who was very protective of Karen and me, the sight of Marty peering over lowered sunglasses, a cigarette in one hand and a drink in the other, was a shock.

"So, it's probably been hectic since your mom and Marty got married, and moving to the new house, yes?" asked my grandad, from the driver's seat.

"Yeah! I've been going with Marty around to his businesses and helping him. He has three different places," I shared, excited about all the goings on.

"They don't have Jesus in their church," my sister announced from her seat next to me.

There was a noticeable silence and my grandparents looked at each other.

"Well, I'm sure it will be fine," my grandad said. But the ride was quieter than usual. Marty was the antithesis of the small-town, pious life that my grandparents embodied. It must have been a crushing blow and slowly but surely we would start growing apart.

In the spring of '63 I discovered the Jewish Center, a cultural center that young people attended after school, kind of like a Jewish YMCA. They taught Hebrew, history, and Judaic studies. My new cousins, Harley and Ronnie, went there and I saw this as the fast track to acceptance. These

31

were the go-go years for American Jews. Israel had been founded fewer than twenty years before and I wanted to be in on the ground floor. Well, as much as a nine-year-old Gentile could be. My mother seemed unsure.

"Do you think this will go over with your parents?" my mom asked Marty.

He picked up the phone, because Marty seldom did anything without conferring with his mother. "Hey Mom. What do you think about Drew getting enrolled in the Jewish Center?"

Marty listened to his mother on the phone for a long time.

"What do you mean, 'What's the point?' He wants to learn Hebrew, get involved—"

They seemed to bicker for a while before Marty hung up. My mom looked at him. "That went over like I thought it would."

Regardless, Marty enrolled me in the Center and I started attending after my elementary school let out.

"Did you know that Theodore Hertzl was the father of Zionism and founded the State of Israel?" I announced to my mom and Marty the following month. "'*Eem teerzu ain zo agadah,*' translates to, 'If you will it, it is not a dream.' That's a quote by Hertzl, in reference to his vision for creating a Jewish state." I had bought in to the whole Jewish thing, lox, stock, and barrel. I wrote that quote down in my notebook alongside all the ones from my grandfather. I figured if Hertzl could create an entire Jewish nation out of desert, I could create a Jew out of a skinny Gentile.

The phone rang one Sunday evening. "Drew, Karen, your grandparents are on the phone," my mom called out. We squealed. We hadn't talked to them since Christmas and had so much to tell them.

"Happy Easter, kids!" Grandma and Grandpa Hastings said in unison over the line.

Karen spoke to them first. She didn't share my enthusiasm for the whole Jewish Experience, so seldom spoke of it. I took the phone.

"Guess what! Last week was Passover—in Hebrew it's called *Pesach*—anyway, we smeared blood on our front door and waited for the Angel of Death to come by!"

They asked if we celebrated Easter that weekend also.

"Mom got us Easter baskets but we didn't go to our regular church. We haven't been going there lately."

My grandparents seemed disappointed with that news but changed the subject. We talked a bit more and made plans to go to see them when school was out in June.

"Have you seen Dad or talked to him," I asked at the end of our call.

"Why, he was here just a while back and said he misses you and he loves you very much."

Marty often took me to various businesses belonging to his numerous relatives around town. They all seemed to know each other from way back. "Drew, this is Mr. Schottenstein, my parents knew him back in Minsk. This is Mrs. Goldfarb, my parents knew her back in Russia." It seemed like we were related to all of them. Not just the Mellmans, but also the Greenes, the Schottensteins, the Finks. With these Jews, it was like you were related to millions of people. It was impossible to imagine my stepfather separate from his family. Marty was never just Marty—his family and his Jewishness were completely intertwined in his life. And my mom, sister, and I were engulfed by it. I don't think my mom realized she wasn't just marrying Marty Mellman, she was marrying all the Mellmans and the Whole Jewish Thing.

Marty and I became closer.

"Always be a sharp dresser," he said, adjusting his tie in the mirror. Like my grandfather, Marty had his own quotes for living and I wrote them all down in my notebook. His were not biblical quotes though. Marty's were either fashion or image related. "Don't sit like that. People will think you're a sissy," he'd tell me when I sat in a chair with my legs crossed like David Niven did in the movies.

"American men sit like this." He demonstrated, his ankle resting on one leg and his knee pointing out to the side. It looked clumsy to me, but I did not want to look like a sissy so I wrote it down.

One Saturday morning, we were in the 502 Club. The place was empty as Marty inventoried liquor bottles. "Never let a schvartze run a bar tab over ten dollars," he said as he was counting. A "schvartze" was Hebrew or Yiddish slang for a black person, in the same way that "goyim" referred to non-Jews.

"Why not?" I asked, as I wrote down his advice.

"Because if it's a small enough amount that it's manageable, they'll come up with money to pay it off. If the tab gets too big, then they figure they will never be able to pay it off so they just disappear and start drinking somewhere else."

"I have a quote in my notebook that says, 'Don't throw good money after bad.' Is that like the same thing?" I asked.

"Yeah, kind of like that," Marty said.

Contradictions arose. One day at my elementary school we had Show and Tell. I brought in a menorah and yarmulke, and talked about Jewish customs. For the rest of the school year, some of the kids called me "Jewboy." I laughed it off like I didn't care, but I did, and I wished I'd never brought that stuff to school. My Judaism was finally being recognized—but by all the wrong people.

That year at Christmas in Martins Ferry, our grandparents spoiled us with too many presents, and in the evenings we'd pile into our grandparents' car, driving around Belmont county looking at all the houses decorated with lights, oohing and aahing. It was perfect. Until I opened my big mouth, trying to make conversation.

"Marty says there is no Jesus and they don't believe in Him," I announced at the dinner table.

Grandpa Hastings' already naturally watery eyes got a little waterier. "Well, that's not true. That's just a damned, outright lie," Grandpa said. Grandma nodded in agreement. I had never heard my grandfather, who was such a positive man, raise his voice or cuss. I almost started crying.

Then Karen spoke up. "One day when I was walking home from school I went by a house where some people were moving and there was a pile of stuff by the sidewalk. In the pile was a framed picture of Jesus. He looked so sad and lonely lying there in the pile, so I brought him home with me, but Marty saw the picture in the house and got really mad at me and took the picture and told me to never bring a picture of him in the house again."

Everyone was silent at the table. My little sister didn't realize the tension that she was furthering. I had wanted to tell my grandpa that I was learning Hebrew and Jewish history and all about the synagogue, but I didn't want to upset him any further.

I was the only non-Jewish kid I'd ever seen at the Jewish Center or at the synagogue. I had a crewcut and blue eyes and stuck out like a sore thumb in the sea of dark-haired, mostly brown-eyed kids. I felt self-conscious a lot of the time. They often joked about "the goyim." But there was no way they meant me—*I was doing this Judaism thing a 110 percent.* People in the synagogue sometimes looked at me, not like grownups giving a passing glance at some little kid, but more out of curiosity. "Who is this boy and how did he get in here?" It didn't help that I was always trying to hold my yarmulke on my head as I walked, or worse, chasing it down the sidewalk when it blew off. I tried to keep a positive attitude about it all. My mantra was, "If you're not born a Jew, you just have to work twice as hard at it."

One afternoon I came home from my Hebrew classes and could barely contain myself. "A bar mitzvah! I want to be bar mitzvahed!" I announced to Mom and Marty at dinnertime. Though my mom seemed nonplussed, Marty was all for it. Since Bubbe was the final word on all familial matters, Marty called her after dinner.

"Ma, Drew, he wants to get a bar mitzvah. Yeah. Well, I think it's a good idea. What?— yeah, yeah, well, so what—what do *you* think? Why make like it's the end of the world?" He hung up.

My mom said, "She didn't seem like it was a priority, did she?"

"You know my mom, she's . . . conservative, from the Old Country. She'll be fine." He turned to me. "Don't you worry, you'll get your bar mitzvah."

This was a huge deal to me. It solved so much at once. First and foremost, I would finally fit in. I'd no longer be an outsider, and because Marty wanted this for me, I wanted to make him proud of me. But, mostly, *it would officially make me a Man.*

One day in the fall of '65, Marty asked if I wanted to go outside and throw the football. "Yes!" I said, a little surprised because he wasn't the athletic type, though I'd seen him throw a football once, and he could throw it really far. We went out to the large field behind our house, along the backside of the neighborhood houses.

"Okay, run out for a pass," Marty said, peering into the sun across the long field.

I ran out and turned.

"No, farther," he called, motioning out with his free hand.

I ran farther and stopped, but Marty motioned me on again.

"No, keep going!"

I was almost to the other side of the field. He was very small in the distance and I was a little worried I wouldn't even see the ball, or that it would hurt when I caught it, coming from so far away.

Marty cupped his hand to his mouth and yelled, "Are you ready?"

"Ready!" I yelled back, watching him intently. If I could catch a football at this distance he'd be impressed and so would whoever would be looking out their back windows.

Marty cocked his arm, and leaned his body back like he was going to throw a Hail Mary. Suddenly, he straightened up, cupped his hand to his mouth, and yelled, "Suckerrr!" Then he dropped the ball, turned, and walked back into the house. For a moment, I just stood there, uncomprehending. I looked at the back door, thinking maybe he'd return, that he was just kidding with me. After five minutes I realized that was the joke. *I was the joke.* I walked the length of that field back to the house where Marty was already asleep on the couch, snoring, a drink in his hand. I had no idea why he'd done that to me. My mom and he had been arguing a lot lately but that didn't have anything to do with me.

Two weeks later he talked me into going out again to toss the football, telling me, "This time I'll throw it, I promise." Again, I ran way, way out, and he did the same thing. I didn't know whether to hate him for doing it again or myself for falling for it.

Fall turned to winter and I continued my Hebrew lessons and bar mitzvah classes at the Center, prerequisites for any bar mitzvah candidate. It was odd seeing twelve-year-olds in yarmulkes walking down the hall conversing in Hebrew. A little more than a year from now I'd be thirteen. My bar mitzvah would change everything, and everyone's view of me. I couldn't wait.

A few months later, I started hearing the fights between my mom and Marty. Usually they were in the evening behind the closed door to their bedroom. But one night, the four of us, Mom, Karen, Marty, and I, were sitting at the table having dinner. Suddenly, Marty, who was having words with Mom, slammed his hand down on the table and his heavy wedding ring shattered a dinner plate. He cut his fingers on the edge, and blood sprayed over his steak. The red meat of his cut hand matched his steak and the sour cream on his baked potato turned a bright pink. He wrapped his hand in a towel and drove himself to the ER for stitches while Karen and I finished eating.

Marty must have figured that since us kids witnessed the dinner table outburst, there was no real reason to keep his voice down any longer. From that point on, when he and Mom fought, they didn't bother waiting until they were behind closed doors. We could hear them arguing and screaming at each other regularly. So could the neighbors.

When I wasn't at school, I tried staying focused on my Hebrew lessons. The bar mitzvah was my goal. Maybe it would make Marty proud of me. Maybe he and Mom would stop fighting. I still looked up to Marty, maybe I even loved him, but picturing him as my dad was starting to look cloudy. He had a mean streak that I'd never seen before, and I was more than a little scared of him.

One Saturday I was down at Alum Creek with my friend Andy trying to build a raft.

"Drew! Your stepdad's here!" Andy whispered, pointing up the road.

"Oh shit." I wasn't allowed to be down at the creek, but I never thought anyone would actually come down here checking on me. Yet here was Marty, looking out of place on a gravel road in the woods in his Sharkskin suit and sunglasses, a cigarette dangling from his hand.

"Drewsie, get back to the house. Now," Marty said, in a very casual way, yet I knew I was in big trouble. I hated it when he called me Drewsie, which he had started doing lately. It sounded like he was mocking me, which he was.

Back at the house he told me to come into the bedroom.

"You were told that you weren't allowed at the creek," Marty said, still looking down at me over the top of his sunglasses. He had a very affected way about him, like he was acting in a movie, and when he spoke it was usually measured as if for dramatic effect. "You. Just. Don't. Seem-to-want-to-learn. *Do you, Drewsie?*"

I started sniveling. He sounded menacing. This was the first time I'd ever been in trouble—why was he saying it like I was always a problem? Like he'd been waiting a long time to utter this line? He undid his belt slowly, and pulled it out of his pants, even more slowly, saying it again, "You just don't seem to want to learn."

I really started crying then, begging him not to.

But Marty simply said, "Pull your pants down and turn around."

I did, sobbing and holding both hands over my backside. I pleaded with him not to hit me. Then I got five or six hits with his belt and it hurt bad. When he stopped, I pulled my pants up and ran off to my room, crying. I was upset that I'd done something wrong, that I got caught, and I was humiliated that I had gotten punished with Marty's belt. Especially at the age of twelve. My mom had spanked me once or twice for childish wrongdoings, but this was different. It felt like I'd been violated, like what you did to an animal.

My mom never said anything about the incident except, "Well, you knew you were not allowed at the creek." It felt like things were falling apart. She seemed to work all the time. Marty got lax about getting me to the Jewish Center and I was often late or missed my bar mitzvah lessons. When he and I went over to Bubbe and Zayde's house it felt like they were treating me less like a grandson and more like a guest. And the way Marty introduced me changed.

"Marty, so who's this little guy you have with you?" a friend of his would ask.

The year before, Marty would have said, "This is my son, Drew," but his reply now became, "Oh, this is my wife's boy."

One Sabbath day, I was sitting in shul, looking around the synagogue at all the men praying devoutly. I found myself rocking along with them, trying to keep up with the prayers. Suddenly, I felt like a fool. I was sure they knew I was just mimicking them—that I could take all the Hebrew lessons in the world but I was never going to be one of the Chosen People. I was getting all of the persecution but none of the benefits of being Jewish.

Sometime in early 1966, I think Marty started hitting my mom. They'd have horrible fights in their bedroom at night. I lay in bed and listened to Marty calling my mother all kinds of vile names, then scuffling, my mom crying out. The first time I heard them I cried and put the pillow over my head. The second time, I wished that I was already a man. I'd rush into their bedroom, beat up Marty, save my mom, and be a hero. But I wasn't a man and Marty was scary.

The end came as abruptly as it had started—with one sentence. In March of '66, our mother came into our bedroom in the middle of the night and woke my sister and me. She had us get dressed and pack our suitcases and a couple of boxes, which we loaded into the car trunk, and drove off in a hurry. Though Karen seemed confused about what was going on, I knew. This was like the Jews running from the slavery of the pharaoh and fleeing Egypt. Except we were getting the hell out of Columbus and away from Marty. The three of us rode in the car for a long time and said nothing. I finally blurted out, "Mom, what about my bar mitzvah? It's less than a year away."

"It doesn't matter," she said. "We're not Jewish anymore."

CHAPTER 4

Oneida Victor #2

A t the confluence of the Olentangy and Little Miami Rivers in South Central Ohio, a little creek branches off and inconspicuously makes its way down to the Dayton suburb of Kettering, where it empties into a six-foot sewer pipe behind a strip mall anchored by the IGA grocery store and The Carpet Barn. It was at the headwaters of this creek where, among the half-submerged grocery carts and scraps of soggy carpet remnants, at fourteen, I sought my fortune and adventure.

"Mom, you know who the first great entrepreneurs in America were?" I asked, excitedly reading from a library book.

"I haven't the faintest."

"Trappers! In the early 1700s when America was new, the vast expanse of wilderness leading west was opened up by trappers. They were the first great adventurers—"

"And they were likely killed by savages," she cut me off.

"I'm going to start trapping. I'm tired of working for other people."

"You're fourteen. How can you be tired of working for other people when your only employment has been a paper route?"

Undeterred, I continued reading. "Demand for fur was so high, that by 1868, the market collapsed. Fur bearing animals had been depleted to the point that a trapper could just barely make a living."

"Well, there you go, then," she concluded. "There are no more animals. It's 1968—you'd have to be an idiot to trap now."

In the Kettering of 1968, income opportunities were limited for fourteen-year-olds. You could try to get on as a bagboy at the grocery store, but you had to know someone, or you could go the paperboy route.

I'd had a paper route until the previous month, getting up at 5 a.m. and delivering the *Dayton Journal Herald* on my bike, cruising the suburban darkness. But Ricky Dunning and his minions had routes also, and one morning they'd pummeled me outside my apartment building until my mom chased them off. I loved having a paper route and making my own money but dreaded the thought of being cornered again, so I quit—ashamed that they'd called me a pussy and I had not fought back.

It had been barely two years since my mom, Karen, and I had left Marty. First we moved to the town of Westerville, somewhere north of Columbus, and I remembered little of our year there except living in an apartment building and hanging out with a loser named Jack from school. He had big pouty lips and wore Beatle boots with Cuban heels, had long bangs that fell over his eyes, and smoked cigarettes. He said *fuck* a lot and never carried a book home from school since *homework is for suckers*. We were the same age, but he seemed older and I recognized that he had given up on the world and the world had given up on him, and he both fascinated and scared me. I didn't want to end up like him.

Westerville was also when I met Jim, the married man who Mom dated for the next fifteen or so years and then married. We moved to Kettering in the middle of seventh grade and I was tired of being the new kid in school, which always put me on the bullies' radar. My new best friend was Dave Millard who lived in a house with two parents and was nothing like Jack from Westerville. Dave also trapped, so it seemed like an ideal profession to take up, a more natural path to manhood than a bar mitzvah. Plus, it was a job that would put me out in the woods, far away from suburban teens

41

that wanted to kick my ass at every opportunity. And most of all, trapping seemed glamorous and rugged. I needed to be thought of as rugged if there was a chance that it would keep me from getting my ass kicked, and, as Dave pointed out, the best reason to become a trapper was to impress girls.

"That Cherie girl that you like would probably think it's cool," he said.

Cherie Sherwood. The mere mention of her name made me convulse slightly in a love-struck seizure. She had dark shoulder-length hair, small unintimidating breasts, and a smile that would make a Nazi melt. I was hopelessly in love with her, but to imagine that Cherie might feel the same about me made my face sting with embarrassment. She lived in a big white house with two parents. Her mom baked cookies and stuff. And Cherie was a cheerleader.

We had the same English and history class. I tried to work up the courage to talk to her but it was hard to catch her when she wasn't in the middle of a group of chatty, laughing friends. Sometimes, when the laughing heads parted long enough that she saw me, she'd smile and, because I was fourteen and hadn't yet had the smile permanently knocked out of me, I smiled back.

"Did you tell her I like her?" I asked Dave, not taking my eyes off Cherie as she walked by in the middle of her crowd.

"Yes, I told you three times I did."

"And when you told her what did she say?"

"She said, 'Oh, That's sweet.'"

"Are you serious? That sounds like how she would talk if she was looking down at a puppy!"

"Well, I wouldn't get worked up about it. I heard she's going steady with Trace Trusler."

That shut me up. Trace Trusler was good-looking, didn't wear glasses like I did, lived in a big white house in the same neighborhood as Cherie, his parents were friends with her parents, and he was in a rock band that played at the school dances. Even his name was cool. *Trace.* How could anyone possibly compete with that? Becoming a trapper seemed like it might be my best shot.

I started with a string of eight traps from the local sporting goods store. Dave came over and we scattered the traps about the living room floor. He was reading from a book on trapping I got from the library. "Says here after you skin the animal, you have to stretch it out on a board and scrape all the fat off the pelt, then you let it cure and dry out for a month."

"If you skin animals in the living room, Mom's gonna kill you," Karen warned.

I pictured my mom coming in from work and seeing clouds of flies swarming over bloody animal skins hanging from the balcony.

"You figured out what you're going to trap? Raccoons, maybe?" offered Dave.

"No, I like raccoons. I couldn't kill those."

"How 'bout rabbits? They pay two bucks a pelt plus you get fifty cents for the feet cuz they use them to make keychains."

I shook my head. I once shot a rabbit and remembered watching it flop around in the blood-stained snow and making the most pitiful squeaking sound. It had made me cry.

"Nah, not rabbits."

"Well," Dave said, looking up from the book, "then that leaves muskrats."

Muskrats it was, and once I returned from the wilds, my Schwinn bike loaded down with pelts, the people would stand on their cul-de-sac lawns squinting in the sunlight and pointing excitedly at my success. Especially Cherie Sherwood.

"I gotta go home and finish my history project," said Dave. "My dad and I are making a medieval catapult that actually works!"

"Yeah, I gotta get mine done too."

My project was a six-foot tall Trojan Horse made from chicken wire and papier-mâché. It was on wooden wheels and had a tape recorder inside that played my voice reciting the events of the Trojan War, and was the first creative endeavor of my life. I'd sketched a drawing of how it should look, how a hidden door under the horse's stomach would hold the tape recorder with a speaker wired into its mouth. My mom and I cut and glued papier-mâché strips over the chicken wire for two months whenever she had time after work. It was the first time we'd ever done anything like that together. It felt good to actually *do* something with her even as I felt a certain adolescent resentment at this maternal entanglement. When it was finished, I was quite proud and had to admit that my grand vision would not have come about without her. The day I had to turn the project in, my mom and I realized we'd never thought about how we would get a two-hundred-pound, six-foot Trojan horse to the school and she was very late for work after towing it on its wooden wheels at five miles per hour behind the car.

The following week I set out up the creek to find a trapping spot. The creek started behind the nearby shopping center. Dodging rusted shopping carts and old washing machines, I pressed on upstream, leaving behind the mud-filled pop bottles and familiar suburban backyards, and eventually I even passed the golf course. I followed the creek another twenty minutes until I came to the lands discovered by adventurous real estate developers, their claims marked by stakes driven into the ground, the orange plastic surveyors' ribbons fluttering in the breeze. Finally, I could no longer hear the screams of kids in backyard swimming pools, nor the noise of construction equipment, not even the sound of traffic. Only birds and trickling water.

I carried a .22 rifle with me. I had read that all trappers carried rifles because you didn't know what you might run across out in the untamed wilderness. I also carried my eight traps. My trap of choice was the Oneida Victor #2, a leghold trap considered to be the "Workhorse of the Industry" according to *Trapping Monthly*.

The method for trapping muskrats was simple: you followed the stream and kept your eyes open for "runs." These were smooth paths in the mud on the creek bottom where the muskrat traveled back and forth from his food source to his den, which was usually under the stream bank. You placed the trap under about two feet of water along his run, then drove a stake through a long chain attached to the end of the trap. People usually assume that it's the trap itself that kills its quarry, but the trap merely holds the animal by the leg. The part that kills the muskrat is the drowning, though I didn't want to be there when it happened.

I found several good spots to place my traps. I didn't set them yet—this was just a scouting trip—and planned to come back in a few days to make sure the runs were still being used. I stashed my traps under a log and journeyed home.

The next night I told my mom the news. "The Trojan Horse won first place in the entire school for the history project."

She seemed rather surprised, but said, "That's great. Now if you can just do the same in your other subjects."

"Yeah, okay. So, anyway, thank you for helping me with it."

"You're welcome."

I hoped that my history project had impressed Cherie. This effort was part of a two-pronged attack: woo her with furs and dazzle her with my intellectual prowess. And it seemed to be working—she was noticing me.

"Your horse project was really cool," Cherie said the next day.

"Uh, thanks!" I was thrown. That was the longest sentence she'd ever uttered to me.

"I didn't really think you had something like that in you," she added, smiling.

I knew what she meant. I was becoming somewhat of a delinquent and my teachers regularly said, "Drew, you're A material—why do you keep getting Cs? You can do so much better than this!"

Cherie sounded like she was saying the opposite but I didn't care. She was talking to me and was impressed by my endeavors—these were the kind of genetic markers that women coming into child-bearing age looked for in a mate! Then she scribbled something on her notebook paper and handed it to me. Her phone number.

"Call me this week. We finish dinner about seven, and I can talk after that."

"Okay, cool," I said, trying not to vomit.

That night I sat in front of the phone too paralyzed with fear. *It's almost 7 p.m. She's done with dinner. Oh God it's 7:10 already! Oh no it's 7:27 she may go to bed soon! What if one of her parents answers? Thenwhat? Thenwhat? OhmyGod it's 8:10 I have to call right now or she'll think I don't want to talk to her!*

My little sister walked by my room. "Why are you shaking like that scarecrow in the *Wizard of Oz*?"

I dialed Cherie's number.

Her mother answered. "Hello, Sherwood residence."

I almost hung up. Why didn't she just say "Hello?" I already felt unworthy but managed, "Is Cherie there?"

It came out of my mouth as, "Awwk! Strrunhhnnga—screee"

Mrs. Sherwood replied, "Yes, she's here. May I ask who's calling?"

"Derrrrr."

"Okay, hold on a minute, Drew."

"Errplick."

I don't remember the gist of that phone call. Idiotic, mindless, fourteen-year-old stuff, I'm sure. But it went on for an hour.

I called her three nights that week. During the day, at school, she'd make a point to break away from her gaggle to come over and talk. Which made everyone else talk. All was bliss. And I hadn't even presented her with furs yet!

Monday after school, I hurried out to where my traps were stashed and set each of them in the promising spots. I rushed back toward home, barely getting out of the woods by dusk, following the creek until I arrived behind the shopping center where I spotted the familiar half-sunken grocery carts shining in the moonlight.

I wolfed down some leftover dinner, then looked for the phone to call Cherie, eager to begin another week of giddy chats. But the phone, usually on the living room desk, was missing. I followed the long cord, past the couch, through the "dining area" (which is what small apartments had in lieu of a dining room) down the hallway, until it disappeared under my mom's door.

Not good.

I hesitated before asking through the door, "Are you going to be on the phone very long, Mom?"

"I don't know, why do you need to know that?" came the muffled reply.

That meant she was going to be a while. She was probably talking to Jim. She might be five more minutes, or another hour.

I didn't get to call Cherie that night nor the next two nights. Then my calls were answered by her mother advising me that, "Cherie is busy with homework this evening." When I saw her at school that week I couldn't get a word with her; she stayed in the middle of her gaggle of girlfriends, moving down the hallway like a large multicellular organism of popularity. When she did look my way, it was with a detached smile.

On Friday morning her best friend, Paula, who sat next to me in English class, had enough. My constant questions, imploring her to tell me why Cherie suddenly wasn't giving me the time of day, must have made Paula take pity on me. She pulled me aside after class. "Cherie's dad doesn't want her hanging out with you because your parents are divorced. They think you're a bad influence."

My face turned so red so fast that a passing school nurse might've suspected anaphylactic shock. I did a one-eighty and staggered down the hall. At fourteen, I already had a hunch that I was damaged goods, but now I knew that the rest of the world held that opinion as well.

I left school though it was only mid-morning, sneaking out a side door. I careened down Bigger Road, past the suburban split-levels, traipsing toward home. It was unusual to see a teenager during school hours walking down the street, and a few housewives watched as I passed their manicured lawns. But then, I thought it was unusual to see mothers at home in the middle of the day, so I peered at them too.

My mom, my sister, and I lived in the only apartment complex in a neighborhood of upscale houses. I had always been slightly ashamed of this and now felt justified. Most of the residents were divorced dads or single moms and their kids. Chapel Hill Apartments was an enclave of the Incomplete.

Later that day, after school let out, I went back and wheeled the Trojan Horse from the history exhibit and out to the parking lot. I hauled it up the hill behind the gym, poured gasoline all over it, which I had siphoned from a car because that's what children of divorced parents who aren't good enough do. I struck a match and sent it burning down the hill where it crashed near the football field. Two months of loving craftsmanship shattered, and then burned for an hour, a funeral pyre to the death of my Almost-Love.

That week, I started smoking cigarettes. Some teenagers begin smoking because of peer pressure. Some start because they think it's cool. I lit up because I knew they were bad for you and I wanted to slowly kill myself. Robert F. Kennedy was also shot later that week, and I was glad. He was good-looking and popular like Trace Trusler. Maybe Sirhan Sirhan shot him because some girl's dad had said about him, "I think he's a bad influence—I heard he lives in some apartment complex."

I hadn't checked my traps in four days—unforgivable, because if you've caught anything, you need to get to it before other predators do, or before it starts to rot. But the incidents of the last couple of days had left me almost catatonic. Finally I trudged along the now familiar creek back into the solitude of the forest. Of the eight traps I'd set, the first two were empty, further depressing me. But trap number three had been sprung and though it was empty, I cautiously held out hope for the others.

At trap four, under a foot of water, was my first muskrat, bobbing along the creek bottom, leg securely held in the trap.

Wow. I was a trapper! See, I could do something right!

I removed the carcass, re-set the trap, and continued on. In trap number five, another catch, a beauty. Wedged under a log in the stream, I got him out and re-set the trap. *Wait till I showed Dave!* I continued on through the woods with the two specimens slung over my back and shortly discovered how heavy dead, waterlogged muskrats were. No wonder trappers had pack mules.

When I got to the site of trap number six, it was gone, nowhere to be seen. *Poachers?* The stake that held the trap in place was still embedded in the creek bottom but was leaning way over almost parallel with the waters' surface. There had definitely been activity here. I studied the bank at the creek's edge for clues. No broken twigs, no droppings, no footprints.

Baffled, I lit a cigarette and was debating whether to give up trying to find the missing trap when I heard a faint rustling to my left. I peered into the foliage. Not five feet in front of me, under a bush was a small, dark shape. I got down on my knees. A muskrat! Oddly though, it wasn't moving—it just sat there, kind of crouched. Was it dead? I couldn't tell. I extended my rifle barrel and lifted the greenery.

That's when it hissed at me. *Muskrats don't hiss.* I saw my trap sitting next to the muskrat, its rear leg caught in the metal teeth. And then four things happened quickly.

First, I remembered two crucial trapping rules: Always set your trap in water deep enough to drown the muskrat quickly, and check your traps daily.

Second, I realized the muskrat had managed to crawl out of the creek and had been chewing off his leg to get out of the trap, and had almost succeeded except for a thin piece of tendon that still secured him.

Third, I now understood why he'd hissed: he'd gone insane.

Fourth, he lunged at my face. In one maddened leap, the muskrat covered the short distance between us, landing on the front of my shirt, snapping that last bit of tendon that had held him in the trap.

I screamed. I screamed as only a fourteen-year-old petrified adolescent can scream—high pitched, and seemingly forever. The animal clung to my denim shirt, snapping up at my face, and in my panic, breaking every firearms safety rule, I smacked at the animal with the barrel of my loaded rifle. I spun around and around, screaming and flailing, the maddened, three-legged muskrat inches from my chin, snapping its horrible teeth.

I don't know what finally dislodged him or how long it took, but the beast finally lost his grip, falling to the ground and scurrying toward the creek, disappearing as I ran the opposite way—blindly through the woods, back toward home. Eventually out of breath, I sat down on a log, shaking. I realized that I had left my rifle, two dead muskrats, and a string of traps behind. But these items were no longer important since I was no longer a trapper.

That night, I sat in my bedroom smoking cigarettes and listening to WING, the AM radio station that every teen in Dayton tuned in to. The DJ was taking song dedication requests from all the love-struck kids in a twenty-mile radius. "Next up is 'Spooky' by the Classics IV and goes out to Teri from Greg, who says, 'I love you so much.'" Every song played was matched up to a pair of lovers.

I sat there in the dark, hating myself. Not only was I so afraid of Ricky Dunning's bullying that I had given up my paper route, I also had to run home every day after school because two other guys had decided it was fun to smack me around. I thought about my missing dad and wanted to hate him for not being around to teach me how to fight, how to stand up for myself. But for whatever reason I couldn't hate him. But I could hate myself. And hate myself even more for not being able to call Cherie and for burning my Trojan Horse and most of all for being frightened off by a small mammal that I had managed to maim and torture. I was grateful that next week school would be out for the year.

The radio DJ interrupted my thoughts.

"Next, a dedication by Trace who sends his everlasting love to Cherie with a song of the same name—here's Robert John singing, 'Everlasting Love.'"

CHAPTER 5

Manhood by the Numbers

P recarious was my state at age fifteen. Life was full of *Goofus and Gallant* moments. I was approaching forks in the road, numerous forks, every one dictating to some degree what kind of man I'd eventually become. At fifteen I didn't see these decisions for what they were—they were simply hasty choices made in hormonally-charged moments, or peer-pressured exhortations that sent me down paths I hardly understood.

I wasn't crying out for direction, I was simply a teen with minimal oversight from a working mother, no oversight from a father, and mostly fending for myself in the *one pill makes you larger and one pill makes you small* era of 1969. But this was not to say that I was feral. I did have a framework, certain *influences*. These were men that I held up as ideals. Beginning with my grandfather, then Marty. But two major influences were men I knew only from the big screen.

John Wayne loomed so large that our TV set could barely contain him. His movies—morality plays, in effect—were portrayals of what American men were "supposed to be." Wayne's characters taught me that men were responsible and loyal. They stood up for what they believed in, and stood up for the weak. And John Wayne got it all across with a plainspoken, uncomplicated worldview. Though he appeared macho, he wasn't. Wayne always played a man of few words who backed those words up when he had to. He could take a punch and didn't cry, which impressed the hell out of me. It felt like he was talking directly to me—his fatherly advice sometimes even started with, "Well, son . . ." He taught that actions had consequences. "Because no matter where people go, there's the law."

But if John Wayne taught me what it was to be a man, then Rex Harrison showed me what it was to be a gentleman. He possessed all of the traits that the Duke lacked: wit, manners, and culture. Rex Harrison had a handful of films compared to Wayne, but he was no less influential in matters of style and genteel behavior. Though typically midwestern, I was still my mother's son, and she was very much British, so my affinity for all things English saw Rex Harrison as the consummate gentleman—though admittedly, David Niven ran a close second. Harrison's characters were always comedic and often elitist to an exaggerated degree. He had a put-upon demeanor and did not suffer fools gladly. While John Wayne dismissed his foes with a six-gun, Rex Harrison used six sharp words. His masculinity had nothing to do with physical prowess or ready-to-use intimidation, but rather with his absolute confidence, his assuredness, and the responsibility that came with being a man of privilege.

Somehow, my grandfather and these two film icons lived side by side within me, and I became the convoluted product of them—populist and elitist, worldly, yet hopelessly provincial, secular but wishing I Believed. For a time, I vaguely figured that I would simply *become* the best iteration of these three ideals—worldly, kind, respected, tough, charming. That's what growing up meant. Of course, as my teenage years progressed and I became completely enamored with, then totally immersed in the counterculture of the late '60s, I slipped further and further into delinquency that was the antithesis of these childhood ideals. I ran with the hippie crowd that roamed downtown Dayton—older working-class dudes with an Appalachian streak. Not your typical San Francisco hippies, but *Reservoir Dogs* hippies who might flash a peace sign or a gun or both. Anti-war, anti-authority, it was pretty much anti-everything except drug ingestion. Quickly I began making choices—or perhaps simply choosing *not* to choose—that began to irreparably shape my future. Most of these were bad, and almost all of them I hardly understood, but there was one man that turned out to be a lifesaver—one who would impact me in a huge way just before I began the downward spiral in Dayton—an unexpected fourth in my pantheon of masculine role models.

The previous summer when I was fourteen, my mother insisted that I get a part-time job. Since my foray into trapping had ended traumatically, I took the first position I could get, which was at the apartment complex where we lived, and involved landscaping and other grunt work in the maintenance department. My boss was George Nagengast, a Hungarian who, as a teenager in WWII, had seen his parents killed by the Germans after his village was occupied. At sixteen, he was put in a prison camp. He escaped, joined the Hungarian Resistance, was captured by the Nazis, and had a prominent scar on his cheek from his time with them. He survived the war, came to the US, and was now the maintenance manager for all nine buildings that made up Chapel Hill Apartments.

My first day of work, I was heaping mulch around the shrubbery of buildings I and II. It was a sunny day in June and after a brutal forty-five minutes of work that had me sweating profusely, I went into the laundry room of the closest building to cool off. I was standing in front of a mirror messing with my hair, trying to get my bangs to fall just right over my eyes like the lead singer in Paul Revere & The Raiders when Mr. Nagengast came in.

"Mr. Romeo! How you gonna get girlfren' when you pale from having no sun, no muscles from not working, and no money from no job?"

"I'm sorry, Mr. Nagengast."

I went back out and mulched for the rest of the day, embarrassed that he'd caught me primping in front of a mirror. On my fifth day of work, I was sweeping the parking lot, pushing a steadily-growing mound of gravel with my push broom toward a trash can fifty yards away. The pile of gravel was getting so big in the front of my broom that it was causing the broom shaft to flex under all the weight and making any further forward progress almost impossible. I should have stopped, walked over and brought the trash can back, shoveled the gravel in, and continued. But a suburban teenager, too lazy to stop and retrieve the can and too rebellious to admit that he was working far harder by pushing the huge pile, will continue to push the expensive commercial broom until it snaps. Which is what happened. Mr. Nagengast came by and only had to glance at the pile of gravel and the broom handle to know what transpired. "Hastingks, you must learn to respek your tools," he said. "One day maybe your life depend on having a tool dat someone not have broken."

Both times, I was surprised that he hadn't yelled at me. I deserved to be yelled at. But instead, for a year he taught me how to work hard and do a job right the first time. Even if my life didn't always stay on track, he instilled in me a lifelong work ethic that gave me a sense of worth. And I owe him everything for that.

CHAPTER 6

Traffic Patterns

The specialized knowledge that I've amassed over my lifetime is impressive and I like sharing it with others when the opportunity arises, even if I sometimes have to force the opportunity to arise. This is one of those times. Almost all of my knowledge of wall-to-wall carpeting was gleaned over the course of one year when I was employed as a carpeting salesman. I learned two things about wall-to-wall carpeting: first, it's a versatile option as a floor covering solution that, as my mother points out, "covers a multitude of sins." Second, by observing the wear and tear that carpeting undergoes, one can form a basic philosophy of life.

Wall-to-wall carpeting wears along the routes that people take as they routinely pass through rooms. In the carpet business these worn, discolored areas are referred to as *traffic patterns*. Usually they're seen coming in from an outside door, or in the area in front of the couch. This results in matting and excessive soiling, and worst of all, it *breaks down the supportive padding underneath*. Fortunately these problems can be mostly remedied by periodically moving your furniture into a new arrangement, thus changing your path through the room. Unfortunately that seldom happens given people's reluctance to ever embark on new paths.

In the spring of 1972 I turned eighteen and I had some big decisions to make. A few months earlier, I'd sat terrified in Atlanta's Fulton County jail on charges of "possession with intent to distribute" a bunch of psychedelics, and faced a possible federal charge of identity theft because I had used a stolen draft card as an ID. Luckily the "drugs" in my possession were actually capsules of vitamin D. I had run out of the real thing and bought the vitamins because they looked like the mescaline and, yes, I was ripping people off, but I needed to make some money to get back home to Ohio from Florida. After six weeks in that county jail, the drug analysis came back and the police investigator informed me that it was Vitamin D in the capsules, which, of course, I already knew. I was seventeen—an adult, by law in Georgia—though a minor in Ohio, and that discrepancy caused them to drop the charges and send me home.

Back in Kettering, I wondered what I was going to do with my life. One thing was certain, I would not be dealing drugs again. That time in jail left a lifelong impact. There would be a few times over the years where I would consider some illegal moneymaking caper, only to remember my time in the Fulton County jail, which snapped me right out of any thought of the illicit act, and instead started me dreaming of all the legal ways to fuck people out of their money that our great nation was built on.

At eighteen, if I was going to make my debut in the job market, I would have to cut off my hair, which came down to the middle of my back. I sat in a barber chair watching what had been my identity fall in big, fluffy mounds on the floor. It was not a haircut—it was an amputation.

I was living back at my mom's in an uneasy truce. She rented a townhome apartment at "Georgetown of Kettering" that was supposed to be reminiscent of a 1776-era American Colonial town, and had a historic old town layout except for the Olympic-sized swimming pool in the center of the complex. It had fake Tudor-style beams and stucco exteriors and faux iron hitching posts for tying up your horses, and all the signage said things like "Ye Swimming Pool" and "Ye Olde Rental Office" in early American script. If you were high on hashish, as I often was, you might actually fantasize that you were in the late 1700s, until you walked across the asphalt parking lot with its neatly striped parking spaces, to get in your car to drive to Taco Bell, which was a quarter mile away. And then, once you were inside the Taco Bell, for just a brief moment, you thought you were in an old pueblo in 1825 Mexico.

I spent most of my days at my hippie-chick girlfriend's house, where she lived with her parents, and my nights in my bedroom smoking readily available hash, because all the guys were bringing it back from Vietnam, and reading H. P. Lovecraft's gothic horror stories, praying that my mom didn't smell the smoke wafting under the bedroom door. Every morning, I made two cups of Taster's Choice freeze-dried coffee and then read the Help Wanted pages in the *Dayton Journal Herald*. Most of the same ads appeared daily. The companies had permanent ads running because they were such lame jobs, most of them being either straight-commissioned sales jobs, or for manager trainees for Ponderosa, a new, fast growing franchise. "Howdy pardner! Looking for a secure future in steakhouse management?"

For a month, I pored over job listings, looking for something that was respectable, something that I could squint and imagine myself doing, but finding nothing. My sense of guilt was enough to propel me from bed most mornings. Dropping out of high school the year prior was bad enough, but being arrested for drug dealing and my mom spending her hard-earned money to help get me out of it was horrible. So one morning I finally settled on an ad that I had seen a few times: "Write your own paycheck! Our sales professionals work 4 days a week and take vacations every 3 months! Call Les at Custom Carpet today!"

This had "self-determination" written all over it. And I could be a "professional." That was important to me. I wanted to be legitimate, whatever that was. I also liked that Custom Carpets was close—in the same strip center with the creek running behind it where I'd once been a trapper. I called and was surprised that Les himself answered the phone. And even more surprised that he had time to see me that day—as busy as he surely must be.

Les's office was carpeted with a thick plush. The wall behind his desk was carpeted up to the ceiling with commercial carpet in a Fall Leaf pattern.

Even the surface of his desk was carpeted, with just the center cut out so he could have a hard writing surface. It was a silver-blue polyester-blend that changed colors if you changed the direction of the carpet's pile with your hand.

"Carpet," he said. "That's what we're about. Carpet. Not tile, not linoleum. They're your enemy. Do you know why, Drew? Because when people put down tile or linoleum, what are they not doing?"

"I don't know," I ventured.

"They're not installing carpeting. And if they're not carpeting, then we—you and I, Drew—have dropped the ball, failed them. Do you understand that?"

"I guess so. But what if we didn't know that someone was getting tile for their floor?"

Les snapped at me, "It's our goddam job to know—there's never an excuse to not sell carpet. The simple fact, Drew, is that everyone needs carpet. Sometimes they don't even know they need it. You, Drew, enlighten them to that need and then get them to act on it."

This was revelatory. A basic tenet in sales theory and, as I would later realize, pretty much the basis for all dealings with the American public, from advertising to politics. And yes, even love. The simple assumption that people often needed things that they themselves didn't even know they needed. And that I was the person that could enlighten them to that need. This was heavy. I was learning the secrets of men and of business.

Les was inspiring. I liked that he said my name so much when he spoke to me. Like I was important. Like I was the only Drew in the world that mattered. He told me that I needed a suit. It had to be navy blue—"people trust navy blue." Then he shook my hand. I think it was the first time I had shaken hands with someone as an adult. "Welcome aboard, Drew. We're going to make a salesman out of you!"

The next day I stood in front of my bedroom mirror studying myself in my new suit. This was the first suit I'd ever owned, and it both intrigued and repelled me. It represented everything that my lifestyle was not. Suits were worn by the Man. They were Corporate. All the men with short, cropped hair that poured in and out of the downtown office buildings wore them. The one I was wearing, the pant legs tapering straight down to my shoes, made my feet look really big. I was used to bell-bottoms or jeans that at least flared out so only the front part of my shoe was visible. Looking in the mirror with my short hair in this two-piece suit, I hardly recognized myself.

I could hear my younger sister in the hallway outside my bedroom and looked over to make sure the door was locked because I wasn't ready to be seen like this. I felt like one of those guys that puts on women's clothes who gets a guilty thrill from the taboo. Because there was also something kind of exciting about my suit. I felt like a man, not an eighteen-year-old. It felt like armor.

Into my head came a lyric from the new album by Traffic, one of my favorite rock groups: "And the man in the suit has just bought a new car from the profit he's made on your dreams." Steve Winwood, railing against the corporate music industry guys for capitalizing on his creativity. But this time as I heard the lyric, I thought to myself, "I'd like a new car—hell, who doesn't want a new car?"

I went downstairs, and Karen stared at me. She didn't know what to think. My mom, who always found the one thing that you didn't do properly, simply said, "You cannot wear a brown belt with navy. You need a black belt."

My first day at Custom Carpet, Les gave me my schedule. "For the first four weeks, you'll be in training. You'll stay in-store and learn how to calculate yardage for jobs, the lay of the carpet, and all about padding types." Les then spent the next three hours giving me a crash course in salesmanship. What makes people buy, how to overcome objections, how to qualify a customer to see if they're bona fide. Methods of "upselling."

He took me to lunch and gave me four books on motivation and inspirational salespeople. One was the classic *Think and Grow Rich* by Napoleon Hill. Another, a brief tale about a guy who had lost both arms in a threshing machine but didn't let it get him down and proceeded to sell water filters door to door by ringing the doorbell with a stick he held in his mouth. After lunch, Les presented me with a leather-like, vinyl binder embossed with "Custom Carpets, 8 locations for your convenience!" and a twenty-five-foot tape measure—"The only tool you'll need," he said. Inside the binder was a pad of graph paper to draw room layouts.

I was stoked. Custom Carpets was my future. This was how I would make my fortune. I didn't need to risk jail by dealing drugs when I could make big money legitimately! I would be the Horatio Alger of floor coverings. Damn the laminates! Screw parquet! My record sales would have the mills running overtime, spewing out shags and plushes of every hue.

Later that week I met the other two salesmen. They worked off of leads and only came into the office sporadically. Both were middle-aged men and both were from Beckley, West Virginia, as was Les. These guys were sales pros—straight commission dudes, who had sold everything at one time or another. Vacuum cleaners, encyclopedias, bibles, all peddled door-to-door. They were an Appalachian good ol' boys sales network. They told corny jokes and shared sales tricks, like ways to compute the customer's carpet yardage to ensure that you made the biggest commission, which always involved fucking the customer over somehow, someway.

But I would not get to go out on customer appointments just yet. I had dues to pay. I spent my entire first month alone in the store. Anyone who came in, I was to help them, but if they wanted a carpet estimate, I had to turn it over to one of the pros. When someone came in, a little bell rang over the door, kicking me, Pavlovian-like, into Sales Mode. One day a housewife entered, armed with paint chips and color swatches.

"Good day. What have you got in mauve," she asked.

"I'd be happy to show you what we have! My name is Drew and you are—?"

"Mrs. Hamilton."

"Okay, Mrs. Hamilton, let's step over this way."

Our showroom was made up of thirty sloping displays of carpet samples in an array of color gradations. They were arranged by plushes and shags, sculptured polyester blends and Berber weaves. As we wound through the displays, I pulled samples. She'd lean back to examine them and ask me to calculate a rough cost by reading off the room dimensions from her notepad.

"Okay, we'll also need to look at padding so I can figure that up too," I said.

She seemed irked at that added expense. I wasn't surprised. I was told most people never thought about the padding.

"We have four types, jute fiber, rubber, and what we recommend, the DuPont Omalon 3 foam padding," I told her, guiding her to the padding area. Les had built what could best be described as a six-by-six-foot dance floor of padding samples for customers to walk around on.

"Which one is the cheapest," Mrs. Hamilton wanted to know.

I took a breath. "Mrs. Hamilton, 'cheapest' is not how you should look at this." And then, suddenly, I was stuck. I knew there was something I had been trained to say, but standing in front of my first customer, I had forgotten all of it except that first line. Padding was the backbone and highest commission dollars of any carpet sale, and we were supposed to stress its importance. Its density—and what else? All I could think of was my newly formed theory of what carpet represented, as conceived by an eighteen-year-old who'd spent countless hours in a carpet showroom with too much time to think. What I wanted to tell her, was this:

"Mrs. Hamilton, if you think about it, we all begin our lives like a new roll of carpet. And there's no limit to what and how far we can cover. Imagine. If you start to unroll a roll of carpet, it will just keep going until it's stopped by something, meaning we're only limited by the walls we choose to erect. You see? We all start out as new carpet, Mrs. Hamilton, you and I. Fresh, untrodden.

"Then slowly, our clean-carpet lives are dirtied. Maybe from the spills of inexperience. Stains of disappointment, regret. Others leave their indelible footprints on us. So we end up with these traffic patterns, these soiled paths. That's inevitable. Our carpet begins to fray, our fibers degrade.

"But the key is the padding underneath. That's where the resiliency is. The ability to spring back after being stepped on. If you don't have a good foundation, well, you can have the prettiest carpet in the world, but will it hold up in the long run?"

I would have then paused for a moment, looked at her, and said, "I think the ability to bounce back is important, don't you, Mrs. Hamilton? And that's why I think the Omalon 3 by DuPont is the best choice here."

But instead, perhaps because I suspected Les didn't have much patience for the poetic analogies of carpet, or maybe simply because I was afraid that showing vulnerability and sensitivity were not manly attributes, I panicked and muttered, "Uh, this one is the cheapest."

We both stood there for a second. She seemed disappointed, like she had expected more from me. In the back of my mind I could hear my mother accusing me of "frittering away your time on things that aren't going to get you anywhere."

About six weeks after I'd started, I was standing in the carpet showroom and looked up to see a familiar vehicle in the parking lot. A Chevy van was parked in the front row closest to the store, with three of my long-haired friends sitting in the front seat staring at me in my cheap suit like they were at the drive-in movies. When they saw that I'd seen them, they immediately started pointing at me and laughing. Then they started holding their long hair up, making scissors-cutting motions and this made them howl even more. I looked straight at them and tried to laugh along but I didn't look very believable, so I just shrugged. They were smoking a joint and Sonny, in the driver's seat, rolled down his window, stuck out his arm and offered the joint toward me. I laughed and shook my head, then they laughed too, but I knew they must have thought I'd flipped out. I'd heard the rumors, "What the fuck happened to Hastings—did he get hold of some bad acid or something?" Then they drove off in a cloud of marijuana exhaust.

Wall-to-wall carpeting comes in rolls that are either twelve or fifteen feet wide. And the pieces that are left over from an installation are called remnants. A remnant shares the DNA of its origins because all carpet comes from a specific dye lot at the mill. That dye lot is unique and there are subtle but noticeable variations of color from lot to lot, and so you have to order more than enough carpet from the original roll to cover the job. The leftover remnants become orphans, unwanted offspring of the Parent Roll.

Our remnants were rolled up and stacked against the wall to be sold. There was hardly any commission paid on them, yet I was always trying to sell them. But because they were such unique sizes, their usability was limited. Who buys a seven-by-twenty-two piece? There were no rooms that small and no hallways that wide. I felt like one of those remnants. An odd-shaped scrap looking for the right scenario.

Ultimately, I didn't make my fortune in floor coverings. I lasted less than eighteen months at Custom Carpets. I learned a lot about sales theory and salesmen, but ultimately, I had more faith in people than to try to convince them that they needed something that they didn't want and sometimes couldn't afford. Don't get me wrong—I could be as dishonest as the next guy, but there were more honorable ways to do it.

CHAPTER 7

Hap's Irish Pub

My hand was pressed flat against the dartboard, my fingers spread so far apart it made the tendons rise up on the back of my hand like piano wire, and another tournament dart landed deftly between my index and middle finger. The onlookers cheered and a couple of the chicks gasped. I tried to look nonchalant as I made my way through the throng to get back behind the bar.

"You're fuckin' crazy, Hastings," one guy said.

Guys who were bullied when they were teens and called "chicken" for being afraid to fight, will occasionally go into a mental place that is best described as Crazy Mode. I'm no psychologist but it's probably a behavior aimed at getting respect from others while simultaneously showing little respect for yourself, the theory being that, *If I don't care about damaging myself why would I give a shit what you might do to me?*

Back when I was a skinny hippie of seventeen, I'd asked a huge fat biker dude at a party how he got all those two-inch long burn scars on his forearm. He pushed his forearm up tightly against mine and I could see that the scars matched up with where our forearms came together. Then he took a lit cigarette and dropped it between our arms, the ember touching each of us equally. "First one to pull his arm away loses. You gonna play?"

Since the inference was "Are you a chicken or a man?" and a crowd was gathering around the couch, did I have a choice? For the first few seconds, your arm hair and the sheen of perspiration keeps the bulk of the red-hot ember at bay, but then it gets bad. I found it easier if I locked eyes with this guy, focusing on his dull stupidity. Then, he suddenly leaned over and blew a long breath on the cigarette making it glow brightly and people around me groaned. You could smell our burnt flesh and then the pop and snap of fat burning. He was lucky, he had a big cushion of fat under his skin—my slender arms went straight from epidermis to muscle. "You're fuckin' crazy, Hastings," I heard from somewhere. I lasted two minutes before I pulled away—a respectable time, I was told—and I can still vaguely see the scar almost fifty years later.

The dartboard incident took place at Hap's Irish Pub. I was twenty-two and trying to put myself through college at the University of Cincinnati. An older friend of mine, Pat Loney, was a nightly patron and told me they needed a bartender. Hap's, on the east side of Cincinnati, was a neighborhood tavern populated by locals, and a lot of them were right-off-the-boat Irish, mostly from the south around County Kerry and Cork. They all worked in the trades—roofers, carpenters—and every night they came in and drank. Fathers and sons, brothers with brothers, they sat at the long, worn bar and got shitfaced. I was the only one working there at night, pouring shots and sliding Bass ales down the length of the bar.

The Irish didn't care much for me because the bar's owner had a name-plate made that announced, "Your bartender on duty is: W. Drew Hastings." He made me hang it behind the bar at the beginning of my shift.

"It gives the place some class," he said.

"Class" was not a concept you wanted to rub the Irish's faces in. I felt having my Anglophilic name up there just reminded the patrons of the English that they despised in a very active way—considering that a man in a trench coat, supposedly a bagman for the IRA, came in monthly and picked up an envelope stuffed with cash. This was 1976, after all, and the English and Irish were killing each other weekly. But at Hap's, it was all about drinking—shots of Irish whiskey with a Guinness chaser. And

65

the Irish patrons didn't tip, those cheap, drunken, mick motherfuckers. Instead, they often told me a joke, which might have had some value if I could understand them. But their thick Irish brogues were rendered even more unintelligible the drunker they got.

"Ay, barrkipper. Eyye've gut a fookin' jewk fer ye. Dis lil' leprecawn ees sittin' on de 'illside und 'e says to duh udder leprecawn, 'Wuncha go inta town an' get us a wee bit o' the Dardenshlacht'n.' Well, affer a whalle, duh littel un' cooms bock an' saays, 'I cunnan't fahnd duh stoof!' An deh furrst leprecawn sez, 'Well ye cunn't hav deh one widdout deh udder, cun yee!?'"

Then they would howl with laughter. Hap's had a jukebox that played most of the evening. It had hundreds of obscure Irish ballads and dirges that the Irish all sang along to. The song titles read like sixteenth century Welsh.

One evening, a girl came up to the bar, pulled out a recent copy of *Cincinnati Magazine*, and opened it up to a glossy photo shoot of the area's upscale hair salons, featuring me as the male model in the pictures. "Look, our bartender is famous!" she cooed, passing the magazine down the bar. "Oh, don't you look handsome!" said one woman. "Well, wouldja look at that!" said another. Then the Irish came over from where they were shooting darts. "'E looks lyyke a fookin poof," said the O'Reardon father. "A bit faggoty, you arsk me," said one of the O'Reardon sons. I bent down behind the bar like I was looking for something as my face flushed red.

"Aah, don't let those guys bug you. Pour yourself a drink—I'm buyin'," said a woman at the bar who was a regular. I poured myself a big shot of Jameson and downed it before I even thanked her. A few minutes later I was out of bar glasses so I came out from behind the bar to pick up empties from the tables. One of the O'Reardons was standing at the throw line, focused, holding a dart in front of his face, ready to throw. These guys were all very good darters and their standing was a serious matter of pride. The guy getting ready to throw was considered the best among them.

"You've been lining up that shot for so long I think you forgot what number you're aiming for," I heard myself say before I could think.

The guy lowered his dart and looked at me, unsure which was worse— my audacity at interrupting his shot, or my questioning his ability. That's when I put my hand up against the dartboard. Funny thing about Crazy Mode is that you don't plan to go in it you just find yourself there. "Let's see if you're good enough to throw them between my fingers." Though he might've been tempted to put one in the back of my hand, no self-respecting Irishman was going to *not* show how good a darter he was. I didn't look at him because I didn't want anything rattling him. I just looked at my hand, then saw a flash and the dart was between my fingers. I wanted to quit while I was ahead but I kept my hand there. "One more," I said. I wanted this to come off as a test of courage not a flash of momentary insanity. His second dart landed next to the first, and the Irish and I were good after that.

I was looking to quit Hap's. I was sick of listening to the jukebox blare its crackly versions of "The Galway Shawl" and "The Rose of Tralee," and the night before I'd had a scary incident with a big drunk guy. I'd served him before—he was the current boyfriend of the daughter of the owner. He'd been standing at the bar across from me, drunk-ish, staring at me in that way that drunk people do where it seems like maybe they're not staring at you at all, but simply staring drunkenly into space and you just happen to be in front of them. Until he said, "I don't like your fuckin' face."

That's scary, because there's no negotiating with *I don't like your fuckin' face.* He doesn't want your watch or your money, it not like you even *said* anything that you can maybe tell him that he misheard you. He just doesn't like your *being.*

"I don't care for it either, at times," I said. But I knew that wouldn't placate him, and that's when he reached across the bar and lifted me up by my tie onto my tiptoes. "Always wear a clip-on, Drew," Gordon the owner had said, when he hired me. "If somebody grabs you, it pulls right off." But real men wear real ties, not some *attempt* at a tie.

A dude has to be really strong to reach across a three-foot-wide bar and lift someone up by the tie. He was 6'5" and burly. I was also 6'5" but built like David Bowie in his Ziggy Stardust days. I got loose from his grip and he spent a long five minutes lunging at me across the bar like a grizzly trying to swipe at passing salmon in a stream. Then the police came and carted him off. But I knew he'd be back, so when the guy sitting at the bar said to me the next day, "Do you want a job making two hundred dollars a day—all you gotta do is load some trucks," I said "Fuckin-a," because that's what we say in Ohio when we're all in.

CHAPTER 8

Homo Truck

E ric, the gay prostitute who I'd caught turning tricks in the back of
my delivery truck was balking at the deal I was offering him. I'd
done a fair amount of wheeling and dealing in my twenty-four years,
but quoting a price for him to use my freight truck for sexual activity that
might approach a market rate was beyond me. It was turning out I knew
a lot less about "trucking" than I'd presumed.

After Jimmy made me an offer at Hap's to come work for him loading
trucks, he arranged to pick me up at 7 a.m. the next morning and drive
to some downtown warehouse. When I got in the truck, I noticed that
he had a baseball bat in the front seat, and I assumed he played ball after
work. When we drove up to the front gate at the warehouse, a line of
angry-looking men were standing across the road blocking us, but instead
of stopping, Jimmy suddenly sped up, scattering "Teamsters" as he called
them, and driving on to the warehouse.

"What the hell man, why didn't you stop? I think we were supposed
to stop."

"Because we're scabs—our job is to load the trucks that these guys won't load."

Turns out that the Teamsters Local 100 was on strike and the companies that owned the freight stored in this strikebound warehouse had hired Jimmy to get it out. We were able to load the freight onto our truck—it was the leaving that proved tricky. As we went passed the gate, a brick came smashing into the windshield on Jimmy's side. He had to slow way down to be able to see, and the Teamsters pulled him from the driver's seat. At that point, I leaped from the passenger side and, using the muscle memory bullies in my teen years had instilled, easily outran them. Jimmy, who the Teamsters beat up pretty badly, never had a chance to use his bat, though he did get to use his health insurance, because he was in the hospital for three days.

A week or so later, Jimmy's wife called. "I don't want him to be in the warehousing business anymore," she said, and made me an offer I couldn't refuse, namely, to take over the lease on a small warehouse that Jimmy had with all his existing warehouse customers, plus he sold me his truck on installment. Overnight, I found myself in the warehouse business, which I never intended but was psyched about being in business—any business—for myself.

A year went by. I was slowly building and learning. How many cartons of promotional coffee mugs can be safely stored on a pallet? (Sixty.) How many of those pallets can you stack on top of each other before the entire load crumples to the ground, sending shattered "Simon Leis for County Prosecutor" mugs across the floor? (Three.) How many days' notice do I need before the state OSHA inspector makes a surprise visit to look for workplace safety violations? (Two.) How many violations will I typically be in violation of? (Twenty-two.)

The only thing really keeping me financially solvent at the time was the discovery that year that tampons were causing something called Toxic Shock Syndrome in women. The tampon manufacturer, a local conglomerate, had contracted with me and I was lucky enough to be the warehouse used for storing thousands of cartons of recalled tampons. Eventually, the manufacturer had them all removed from my place to be destroyed but the rumor was that they instead shipped them down to South

America—Columbia, to be exact—where the FDA had no jurisdiction, which was fine with me because the Colombians had been shipping tons of cocaine up here—screwing up our country—so I figured that sending a couple million bad tampons down there might just serve them right.

And now I was standing in an alley with a homosexual named Eric, trying to cut a deal for him to use my truck as a makeshift motel room. And this entire scenario had only come about because every morning the week before, when I opened the rear door of the truck to load for deliveries, I'd find cigarette butts, empty pint bottles, and occasionally a beer can. I'd assumed it was hobos coming up from the B&O train yard three blocks south for a night of drinking, smoking, and playing harmonica. But when I came by late at night to catch them, what did I find instead? Eric and two other guys in various states of undress. What I mostly remember was a young man leaping from the back of my truck and running down the alley wearing one shoe, holding the other in his hand, and yelling, "Ow, ow, ow," with every other step through the debris-littered alley.

When I turned around to face the only guy who remained, he just lit a cigarette and sat down on the liftgate. Over the next ten minutes, he told me very matter-of-factly that he was a hustler who mostly plied his trade at the gay bar down at the end of the alley on Plum Street, a place called the Badlands. It was a huge two story gay nightclub that I was familiar with because, when the straight nightclubs closed, we sometimes took our dates over there since the place was open until 3 a.m. and you could buy amyl nitrite poppers from the bartender. Eric had been busted a few times for having sex in this alley already, so he got the idea of just opening up the rear freight door to my truck.

I got him to run some numbers by me, which started my wheels turning. He was turning tricks five to ten times a night, making decent money and not having to look over his shoulder for the cops. I had to respect him—he was self-employed and seemed to have a knack for problem solving. So when he suggested paying me for use of the truck, my eyes lit up. We'd agreed on seventy-five bucks a week and I was pleased as punch because that money was all going to the bottom line—I had no fuel expense with this guy. This went along for about four months until he just quit showing up. I knew that the scenario was too good to last.

But I had bigger problems: I was chronically undercapitalized. Even as the warehouse business was getting bigger I always seemed to be robbing Peter to pay Paul. And after the novelty of owning my first company wore off, it became nothing but a mundane operation, dealing with mundane people. Pushing a pallet loaded with twenty-five hundred pounds of cat litter in the pouring rain down a loading dock, I thought, "I'm not sure this is how one gets rich." I had a knack for being in the wrong place at the right time, it seemed.

CHAPTER 9

Paper Tiger

"White collar crime is at an all-time high—theft of corporate data is costing American businesses millions every year! It's eleven o'clock. Do you know where your payroll records are?"

Administrative assistants were gathering around me as I spoke, looks of concern spreading across their faces. Emotion is a powerful marketing tool. To sell people on a document shredding service, like the one I'd just started, you create demand by instilling fear and mistrust. You exploit paranoia.

"Right now, someone is going through your dumpster looking for accounting records! Right now, an unscrupulous employee is digging through your wastebasket! Right now, I can put a stop to that."

I'd found my calling. I was really in my element at the Cincinnati Business Expo. Manning my ten-by-ten-foot rented booth strategically located next to Kodak Corporation and across from Kelly Temporary Services, I was a carnival barker on the Midway of American Business, evangelist to the corporate faithful.

They thrust their business cards into my hand.

"Do you have a brochure?"

"Can you come to our office this week?"

When the Business Expo ended three days later, I had sixty-six clients and another hundred very interested companies. What these clients didn't know is that I had no shredding business. I only had a glossy brochure and my spiel. But in my opinion, 1984 was the beginning of the Golden Age of confidential document shredding, a brand new service industry in the US, born of three converging factors: the Oliver North Iran-Contra scandal, the laissez-faire business climate under Ronald Reagan, and the enactment of the Federal Records Retention Act, or Fedra, as we called it in the business.

Once again, I found myself in an undertaking that I had no intention of pursuing. Just six months prior I'd been in the local trucking and warehouse business—putting on a suit in the morning to go find storage customers, changing into jeans after lunch to unload semis with a forklift till dark, then going into my dingy office and juggling bills. My hands were always so filthy I had to use goopy industrial hand soap, and my hair smelled like propane fumes. A sales rep would come by every month trying to sell me OSHA-approved fluorescent tape to outline the unsafe, dangerous areas on the warehouse floor, but I couldn't afford frivolous safety measures. One day he told me about one of his customers who had started a business that shredded old records and files for law firms and CPAs.

"Hell, all he has is a warehouse, a truck, and a shredder, and he's getting rich!" Since I still had a rented warehouse and a truck, all I needed was one of these shredders. Hence my hasty gamble at the Business Expo. After showing my fistful of new customer contracts to my mom and convincing her to finance a $6,000 shredder, I was in business. I'd skidded into this opportunity and, as always, whenever I found myself embarking on a career I'd never planned to be in, I gave it 110 percent. I was three months shy of thirty, had no wife, no kid, not even a cat to hold me back from my destiny.

People have no idea how much paper American businesses needed to shred in the '80s. Credit applications, internal memos, legal files, medical records, insurance claims, accounting data, mammograms, and misprinted coupons. The list goes on and on and eventually, even the list gets shredded. From go, business was booming. This should have been a piece of cake. What's there to it? Shredding paper is a *destructive act*! You throw it in—it comes out in a pile. It doesn't even matter if the paper is upside down, full of paper clips, or is soaking wet. In fact, the only way that you can fuck up shredding confidential documents is to *not* shred them.

My business model for this shredding business was simple—something called Lowball. Whatever the competition charged, I'd go cheaper. I learned this model from my years with the Jews, and it was a philosophy that dovetailed nicely with my low self-esteem. Nobody does it for less than me.

But when I really drill down and try to pinpoint where my problems in this venture began, I'd have to say it was Day One. My three employees shredded thirteen boxes of files out of a hundred and ten received on our loading dock that day. On Day Two, they shredded just fourteen boxes out of ninety-eight received. Days Three, Four, and Five had the same horrifying ratios. Every day, more than two thousand pounds of un-shredded files were backing up.

"Sounds like you're going to need a bigger shredder, Mr. Hastings," the salesman who sold me the Shredmaster 200, told me.

"Great. How much bigger?"

"Your shredder will do two hundred pounds a day under optimal conditions, but your conditions seem to be less than optimal. Based on the volume of business you're doing, you need to step up to the Data Destroyer Ultima base unit."

"Base unit?"

"Yeah. You have to shred two thousand pounds a day minimum. To accomplish that, you need a high-speed conveyor system to feed the files into the shredder, then you need a baler on the other end to gather and contain the shredded paper."

"A baler? Like for baling hay?"

"Exactly. Then you'll have a real primo system."

"How much will this system cost?"

I could hear him punching numbers into a calculator for so long it sounded like he was writing computer code.

"Twenty-two thousand six hundred fifty dollars. That price is based on you giving us back the Shredmaster 200 on trade-in."

"Holy fuck."

"Understandable, but remember this is a *good* problem to have! It means you're doing big business!"

Before I hung up I asked what kind of system my competitor was using.

"Oh, he doesn't use shredders at all. He has a custom incinerator."

My angst over figuring out how to come up with twenty-two grand was immediately displaced by this news of my competitor. It turned out that he had an EPA-exempted incinerator. He had a contract with the county to dispose of roadkill. I marveled. Tossing dead Yorkies and possums in with confidential records and burning them all at once—making money on both ends! Some guys had all the luck. I'd heard what he was charging per pound to dispose of records and just assumed he was shredding them, so I undercut him. His cost was next to nothing and now I was locked into impossible contract rates with my customers.

At the end of my first month in business, I had 45,000 pounds of un-shredded files backed up in my warehouse. And I'd already been paid to shred it.

Twenty-two grand. Lesser men facing that figure would've crumbled. But from my notebook of long-collected quotes came "Whatever the mind can conceive, and will believe, it can achieve." And what I conceived was this: just keep selling the service and picking up boxes. I needed to keep up the billing so I could have the money for the bigger system. The only problem was I had to guarantee that everything was shredded within twenty-four hours of pickup and I had to sign a "Certificate of Destruction" immediately and mail it out with their bill. I had to! I was just delaying the shredding of their confidential documents by a little bit.

Daily, I'd go into the warehouse to watch my two employees attempt to keep up. One guy took a stack of papers from a box, fanned them out on the conveyor belt like a card dealer does with a new deck. The paper moved toward the shredder blades where it disappeared then dropped onto the floor in long shredded strips like pasta. The second guy pushed the pile with a broom into a monstrously large mountain of fluffy, highly combustible shredded paper. Every two minutes or so, the shredder made a loud buzz, like when a game show contestant gives a wrong answer. The buzz told you that there was a paper jam that needed clearing. It all resembled a Laurel and Hardy sketch produced by the federal Occupational Safety and Health Administration.

I read that the big St. Patrick's Day parade was coming up and I contacted the float committee, offering them free shredded paper for constructing their floats. They picked up two tons which barely dented the pile. Two weeks later I stood along Fifth Street with the crowds and watched the parade. I waved at the Hap's Irish Pub float as it went by. It was windy and I started noticing clumps of shredded paper blowing down the street like big tumbleweeds of corporate data in still-readable chunks.

I continued making sales calls. "We transport your company's files to our high security facility and shred them within twenty-four hours. Guaranteed!" At the end of my third month in business, I had almost four thousand boxes of un-shredded stuff backed up—about fifty tons.

At the time, it just seemed like problem solving to me. If I could just apply a creative fix, I'd be home free. Some other person in this predicament might've cut their losses, gone back to their clients and said, "I screwed up badly. I'm sorry, I cannot shred these documents for you at ten cents a pound. I have to charge more." But I couldn't bring myself to do that. I couldn't face the humiliation of clients leaving me to go to my competitor. And I could hear my mom's voice echoing their derision.

I went to the bank to get money for a bigger shredder, making sure that I removed my earring and tamed down my Duran Duran hair. The loan officer turned me down saying, "We'd like to see a three-year track record of the business."

"So would I," I told him.

After five months in business, I had almost one hundred tons of unshredded files. That was a lot of confidential information to be sitting on. For every box of records I shredded, nine more would get stacked in the bowels of the warehouse. Hospital X-rays, accounting records, credit card lists. Making matters worse was that the paper I was actually shredding created this huge cloud at the back of the shredder.

One morning, I walked into the warehouse to see two of my workers standing over an open manhole in the floor. "We were just checking out this manhole," they said. I peered down into it. Ten feet below was a fast-moving stream of water. Part of the city's sewer system, probably.

"Roll the shredder over here and put the output flue over the hole," I told them. I turned the shredder on and paper fell down the hole, carried away by the water.

"I think we solved part of our problem," I informed them and headed back into the office. At this point I didn't have the luxury of Best Business Practices. I was trying to survive. Every day I sat with a pile of official-looking Certificates of Destruction, signing my name at the bottom, assuring each client that I'd shredded their corporate secrets. The sheer number I had to sign gave me writer's cramp. Ninety percent of the certificates I signed were fraudulent. *But this was not fraud—I simply needed to buy a little time, surely you can see that?*

I always seemed to find myself working hard instead of smart. I almost had enough for that big shredding system. Just needed to keep selling the service. "The integrity of your data is never compromised—all material is destroyed within twenty-four hours, guaranteed!"

Three months after discovering the sewer solution, we pulled the shredder from the manhole and put the lid back because there was a report on the local news about a city sewer lift station three blocks from my warehouse shutting down because its filters were getting clogged up. "Investigators were searching for clues to its cause . . ."

I looked around the warehouse. One hundred twenty tons. There were psychiatric patient files. Child custody depositions. Files from a woman's clinic. Toxicity reports from some chemical company. If I could somehow just get rid of all of it at once and start over . . .

That fall, the Shredmaster 200 burned out. Overloaded, the poor thing never stood a chance. It ran nonstop until its little heart gave out. But I still had to keep it in place just for show—in case a client were to pop in un-announced. Wouldn't look good to have the city's largest shredding company and no shredder. My attorney said that if I didn't actually *have* a shredder in the place and I got found out, I could be charged with fraud. At

CHAPTER 10

Mic

As my settlement over the shredding business was wrapping up, the phone rang. I lifted my forehead from the desktop. It was a large Chicago outfit that was in the same business as me. The gist of it went something like this:

"Mr. Hastings, we're looking to get into the Cincinnati market and wondered if you might be interested in selling?"

The tears of gratitude that streamed down my face would have weakened my negotiating position in a face-to-face meeting, so I silently thanked God that this was a phone call.

"Why yes, this might be an opportune time for both of us," I said.

The only condition was that I stay with the company, which meant I now had a highly-paid job with perks, and even the almost-flashy title of Division President. I spent the first month of this new arrangement in the glow of accomplishment—*I built this business from scratch and sold it at a profit!* My mom had been quite proud. She never said so, but her lack of any negative comments was all the evidence I needed. The next three months had me relishing my new large-ish, disposable income. A month after that

I was grumbling about the new internal forms that Chicago wanted my employees to use and the weekly report I was required to file. Quickly I realized that the records storage and document shredding industry is exactly as boring as it sounds. It was exciting before because it had been my own.

One day I got a call from Chicago. "Drew, great news!" my new corporate boss said. "We just acquired a small mom-and-pop operation in Gaithersburg, outside of Washington, DC, and the board of directors would love to have you go over there and oversee the transition."

That sounded as exciting as watching grass grow and was also rather inconvenient. I was playing polo at the Cincinnati Polo Club with my newfound bi-weekly salary, and dating a hot stockbroker. I couldn't *move*.

"Um, Larry, right now is not a good time for me to uproot myself and maybe you could let the board know. But I'm honored—flattered—that they thought of me."

"Drew, the nice thing about being an entrepreneur is that you are your own boss. But unfortunately that isn't what you are anymore."

The first morning that I walked into the Gaithersburg operation, I called all twenty-six employees together for a meeting to welcome them into the new Chicago corporate family and hand out policy manuals. A middle-aged man sitting in the back of the room spoke up.

"Uh, we've operated for eighteen years without any policy manuals, why the need now?"

"And who are you?" I fumbled. "What's your name?"

"I'm Bill. I was the owner here until you guys bought my wife and me out. I was the face of this business—who everyone dealt with."

I gathered myself. "I'm sorry for not recognizing you, Bill. I understand the personal aspect but uh, now, this uh, corporate logo, the big blue pyramid here on the cover of your manual, should be considered the face of the company. And, uh, you shouldn't take this personally Bill, because it's really just about uniformity."

I excused myself and went outside for a cigarette. Fuck me. I couldn't believe I'd said that to him back there without laughing. Or retching. And before I had even finished my cigarette, I understood. I hadn't been talking to Bill—I was talking to *myself*—the guy who had been seduced by exotic trinkets like health insurance, a 401K, and a company car.

At the end of that week I made the long drive back to Cincinnati and thought about trade-offs. What did I want and what was I willing to live with in exchange for getting what I wanted? I'd learned something about how life worked and something about who I was and wasn't. I was ever so slightly more equipped going forward and thus more confident, which in turn gave me the patience to bide my time and stick with this soulless job in godforsaken Gaithersburg. I ended up driving the eight hours to Cincinnati almost every weekend to see my girlfriend and my horses, then eight hours back.

Finally, one of those weekends back in Cincinnati in late 1987, I ran into an old friend.

"You're making five hundred dollars a week *doing comedy?*" I asked, incredulous.

"Yeah, clubs, they're opening all over—I can give you some names, contacts." He and I had been part of a group that performed standup comedy for fun back in '81 through '82 at a hole-in-the-wall college bar. I'd loved it and seemed to have a knack for it from the get-go. As a kid, I'd been fascinated by comedians on television, but never had it occurred to me that standup comedy might be a profession. High school guidance counselors didn't discuss "standup comedian" as a career path, and in fact, my frequent comedic antics at school were seen as a behavioral problem. But when my friend pulled out a newspaper and showed me an ad for a club he was playing, it became real. I had to squint to see his name in the lineup but there it was. *He was making a name for himself doing standup comedy and getting paid for it.* That was all I needed. I called Chicago.

"Larry, I quit," I said.

"But we have such big plans for you!" Larry said.

"I know," I answered.

Like every other venture, standup comedy seemed to come out of nowhere, looming in my windshield as I hit the gas. But standup comedy clicked—a business *and* an artform. I was getting paid for my sense of humor, and could remain self-employed. It was tailor-made for my anti-authority streak. There were few rules. I could wear an earring onstage. I could wear a suit and bowling shoes. The only important questions were: Could the audience relate? And if so, did it make them laugh?

My immersion was quick and total. I took any gig I could get. Within two years I was working five nights a week, fifty weeks a year, crisscrossing the Midwest, honing material in every suburban comedy club, dive bar, and strip center pop-up that had a marquee, or what passed for one. I took comedy seriously. I kept my mind sharp and was quick on my feet. I had to be—a comedy audience was a great, restless animal. Expectant. Waiting to pounce at the first sign of weakness.

As time went on, I cautiously came to believe that this *was* my calling, my vehicle for getting Drew Hastings known to the world. I worked hard, writing constantly and pestering bookers. I became more confident. My material became more personal. But the downside of life on the road inevitably crept in. I'd been used to twelve hour days and now I worked an hour a night with the remaining twenty-three free to chain smoke and overthink. I didn't recall being eccentric before I embarked on a standup career, but too much time alone examining the self in an effort to mine humor from one's psyche, year after year, was a good recipe for neuroses. I became irritatingly self-centered. Everything tended to be in service of The Act. I became more disconnected from friends, family, and the "normal" rhythms of life. Returning to Cincinnati after six weeks on the road, I found myself standing in front of friends' refrigerators looking at pictures of kids and family events wondering, *What is this strange world that these people live in?*

But the road was seductive, rewarding my short attention span and need for immediate gratification—truly promiscuous work. Introduce myself to a new audience, seduce via humor, say goodnight after an hour, and leave town. Over and over and over, and my fixation on the ultimate payoff of fame and fortune outweighed any disintegration of my character or loss of friendships. Those first five years, moving from town to town, I became estranged from everyone I knew except fellow comics. I liked the simple business plan of standup: start as an opening act, proceed to feature act, then ultimately, become a headliner. Keep my nose to the grindstone and rise. That was the only structure I had and that's what I clung to—that it would all pay off one day. And suddenly, that day got a lot closer.

In my fifth year on the road, Drake Sather, the headliner that I was opening for in Omaha said, "Jesus Christ, Hastings you're a walking sitcom—you *have* to move to LA. They will love you."

"Sounds like a plan," I said. Odd how a random person in a random town on a random day can be part of The Plan. Drake, already a rising standup star, was someone I respected, but the most relevant part of the plan was that someone believed in me and believed that I was ready for the big time. I slept on the floor of the apartment where Drake and his nineteen-year-old Australian girlfriend Marnie lived. Those were fun, innocent times, and often at the expense of Marnie's naïveté.

"Oh, look, do you guys know that girl in the alley across the street? She's waving at us!" Marnie would say, pointing to a girl standing in the shadows.

"She's called a *prostitute*, Marnie." And we would howl.

Drake was my biggest cheerleader when I arrived in LA in '92, introducing me to his comic friends, who were all well on their way to success: David Spade, Jack Black, Janeane Garafalo, Judd Apatow. He got me in at Hollywood Improv and the Laugh Factory where I could perform sets a few times a week. He hooked me up with his manager, an influential guy named Jimmy Miller, who got me a sitcom development deal for my own show with NBC. They threw a huge pile of money at Drake and me, and I began writing a pilot script in '93. My sitcom was heavily favored to get picked up because not only did I have the most powerful consortium of Jews and Gentiles assembled to represent me, but the only other sitcom that NBC was even looking at was seen as risky—an ensemble comedy, and word on the street was that the cast was all pretty faces with no comedy backgrounds. The pilot that we'd written was good. *Taking Stock* was a workplace sitcom that took place at a financial TV news channel, based on the then-fledgling CNBC.

I was in a good place and in a holding pattern for the entire summer, waiting until the network picked the show up for the fall schedule. I took the summer and headed for the Guatemalan jungle to explore Mayan archaeological ruins, taking care not to scratch up my face for a planned network photo shoot when I returned.

Fall rolled around and it was "sitcom announcement day." I sat in my apartment whitening the teeth in my unscratched face. "You have nothing to worry about, Hastings," my people assured me. I had a reputation as a smart, edgy standup. I was getting movie scripts delivered to my door to audition for, and lots of industry folks were falling all over me. My phone rang.

"Hello?"

"Oh, Drew, I'm so sorry!" said the female voice on the other end. She said this in a way that sounded like she'd heard my dog had been hit by a car. Except that I didn't have a dog. The voice was my manager's assistant.

"Julie, what's up? What is there to be sorry about on a beautiful sunny day like this?"

"NBC didn't pick your show up. They went for the ensemble sitcom."

I remember mumbling, "Okay, thanks," and started to hang up the phone. Before I hung up I asked, "What was the name of that other show?"

"It's called *Friends.*"

My mom called. "So, how did it go?"

"They didn't pick my show up," I said.

"What does that mean, then?"

"Well, it means that I was discovered, now I've been undiscovered, and I will try to figure out how to be re-discovered."

I had tried all along to maintain an "I'll believe it when I see it" attitude, but still it left me disoriented. "Everyone has a plan until they get punched in the face," goes the quote. I felt like I'd let Drake down. I should have networked more, schmoozed more, somehow tried harder. I had just turned forty, not young by Hollywood standards.

I started taking long walks, mostly as one of my never-ending attempts to quit smoking. One afternoon I found myself among the tourists on the Hollywood Walk of Fame. Twenty-seven hundred prominent bronze stars dotted the sidewalk as far as one could see. A couple was looking down at a star and shaking their heads. "I've never heard of him," said the woman. "Me neither," said the man. I looked down. It was Rudolph Valentino's star.

How had they never heard of Rudolph Valentino? He was the biggest star *in the world* in his day! When he died, more than a hundred thousand people went to his funeral—women committed suicide when they heard the news.

I walked down the boulevard, watching people point excitedly when they saw a star they recognized and shrugging their shoulders at others. For the first time, I questioned my long-held fixation with getting Drew Hastings seared into America's collective memory and began seeing it for what it had been: a confused kid's way to make sense of his world. I was embarrassed for myself, a man in his forties having "a-ha" moments that most people probably experienced in their twenties. And I'd been forced to admit that I wasn't so sure I'd even wanted my own television show that badly—I didn't even watch TV.

Early in my career, a comedian had advised me, "In this business, you only have two things: your integrity, and the power to say 'no' to something." When Drake and I had been writing our pilot, the network often came back with notes—"It needs bigger laughs." "Drop most of the financial terms, no one knows them." In other words, dumb it down. Drake seemed fine with these. "The name of the game is to get the show on the air," he said. *Yeah, but at what cost?* I'd say silently to myself. I'd limited my successes over the years numerous times for asking that question. Drake disappointed me in not asking it. He was well-known as an edgy "alternative" comic, respected about town, but he saw no problem putting his name on what I thought was becoming a mediocre script. I had my integrity, I had the power to say no, and out here both were tested at every turn.

You can't be "re-discovered" in Hollywood until you've disappeared for a while. I went back out on the road, flying back and forth from the Midwest, writing, performing, and feeling like I had regained some control over my life.

The next four or five years in LA was a series of lesser representations. One agent always spoke to me from within a cloud of marijuana smoke that obscured his head. Then came a manager who wore a suit that had drawstring pants. On his feet he wore sandals and sported a toe ring. I survived by doing road gigs and trying to stay relevant in the Hollywood showcase clubs. My growing cynicism showed onstage. Political correctness had been taking hold throughout the '90s and I wasn't buying it. Profane was fine as long as it could be sufficiently sanitized to be sandwiched between Subaru commercials, but my social commentaries on "the Disneyfication of homosexuality" wasn't going over with the Industry crowd, no matter how funny. I cussed too much and my politics was hurting me—I didn't get that doing anti-Clinton material was bad for business, and the suspicion that my stuff smacked of conservatism was getting me crossed off audition lists. Fellow comics passed me in the hall, smacking me on the back, "Great set. Ballsy stuff, Hastings!" But they weren't the ones with the power to hire and fire.

I wanted to explore themes, larger ideas onstage, but standup was limited in that regard—it was as short-form as it gets. I saw a small film, *Slingblade*, and discovered that it had started out as a twenty-minute, one-person show created by Billy Bob Thornton. Fascinated by this new performance mode—well, new to me anyway—I started on one.

I put up *Yard Sale* at the Tamarind Theatre in Hollywood in '97. A simple idea—a guy having a yard sale instructs the audience in the art of sales and underhanded ways to take people's money. A classic rogue's tale with themes of immediate gratification and consequences, it was well received. The following year came two more one-person storytelling shows that, though compelling and hilarious, lacked an overall theme.

This format clicked with me and my standup dates on the road supported my time off to write and produce these theater pieces. In 1999, I wrote a new show, *The Business of Living*, about a low-level motivational speaker touting the effectiveness of his successes. One dimensional and unreflective, Jack Freeman was truly a tragic figure. The show, directed by Bob Odenkirk, a well-respected writer/actor, went over well. So well that comedic actor Jason Alexander, of *Seinfeld* fame, came to the show three nights in a row, giving me hope that he might want to produce it for television. Just four months later he had a new series on the air about a motivational speaker—thankfully cancelled after five episodes because it was such a dismal, watered-down copy.

But in spite of my new-found excitement writing and producing these shows, I was despondent. I had a history of failed romantic relationships and wasted too much time on vices. I'd smoked for so long that it seemed my life was measured incrementally by the time between each cigarette. Worst of all was the realization that *The Business of Living* had been so easy to write, and effortless to perform, because the failed success guru, Jack Freeman, *seemed to be me.* As Jack liked to say, "I've been in nine relationships in just the last two years—let me show you how to achieve those kinds of numbers in *your* life!" I'd come to Hollywood to get my own sitcom, had come within an inch of having it. But in life's game of *Chutes and Ladders* I had slid down a very long chute. Though my small writing projects were the ladder to gain some height once more, I was not sure I had it in me to make that long climb again.

CHAPTER 11

And Then—A Most Peculiar Event

My final four years in Hollywood are fuzzy. Sketchy. I remember snippets of misery, and not many of mirth. It wasn't that my life was devoid of fun, friends, or monetary reward, but up until this point these things were the sole occupiers of my mind. It was only in the late 1990s that I became demonstrably self-aware—a newfound capacity to *reflect*. I felt as if I'd been the third guy from the left on that famous chart of the Evolution of Man most of my life and then suddenly I'd jumped three spaces with all the psychic pain that a growth spurt like that might inflict. The day-to-day timeline of events eludes me. Did I do that comedy tour in England in 2000 or 2003? I know that both my mom and my sister came to visit during this time but I don't recall it at all. If anything it's selective memory. Like when you think back on a stormy relationship and seem to remember the bad things about that partner, not the parts where you gazed into their eyes and swooned. In my case, my career and life seemed to be converging in an inevitable train wreck.

"Fuck! What is wrong with me?? I quit for two weeks and yesterday I slipped—had just one cigarette and—now today I've already smoked eight!! Have to quit. Can feel myself slowly dying."

This is my journal entry from April 6, 2000. I flip back through my journal and read the entries about my efforts to quit smoking; it disgusts me.

"Thirty days today and no cigarettes! No going back now!" Followed by, "Started back. Thoroughly depressed. Going to try acupuncture next month." The same small successes and big failures follow one after another for six years. That's how long I'd been trying to quit smoking. My angst was constant. *How long since I've had one? I'll let myself have one at seven, not before. Okay, it's been six days since I quit! That's 120 cigs I've not smoked!*

I hated myself. The sheer energy expended over trying not to smoke. I'd smoked since that day I lit my Trojan Horse on fire in junior high, and didn't give it much thought until my late thirties when I started getting short of breath and finding frequent burn holes in my stuff. I didn't try to quit until I got to LA. And now, every cigarette I smoked seemed like a personal failure. For most smokers, the early 2000s was probably the easiest time to quit. The anti-smoking movement that had started in the early '90s in California was in full, Inquisition-like swing. But this infringement on my rights only made me more defiant and now I found myself smoking out of spite, on top of my addiction. It was just one of the converging lines that was leading to a reckoning.

By the early 2000s, Drake and I had drifted apart. We no longer had standup in common because he hadn't performed onstage for a few years. He'd been writing for television shows, then running them. He had movie scripts in the mix, bought a huge house. His successes kept him busy and I'd felt like I'd let him down by not taking advantage of introductions he'd made. Not being ambitious enough—a cardinal sin in LA. The chasm between his successes and my failure was awkward, at least for me, and I spent more time talking to his wife, Marnie, than him.

I was becoming less enamored with Hollywood every year. To me, the system, particularly in network television, rewarded mediocrity. It's why you saw the same interchangeable people year after year. *Failing upward.* The rules were simple: show up on time, say your lines, don't make waves. Thus, all sitcoms were different, and yet the same. It was glorified factory work. Long, bored hours in a dressing room, my makeup drying like a cheap facial mask, until being called to the set. Walk through a faux front door, step in a pile of fake dogshit, look down at my shoe, then up at the camera shaking my fist, yelling, "Oooh, that damn dog!"

"And cut! Thank you Mr. Hastings, you can go back to your room until we call for you again."

My standup comedy—blunt, to the point—had brought me to a town where those attributes were not only not of value, but a hindrance. Adhering to even a basic code of ethics was difficult when the moral fabric of Hollywood was made of spandex, infinitely stretchable. As I'd once been told, I only had two things in this business: my integrity, and the power to say no. Not impossible to live up to, but this town was making my life very hard.

In late 2000, I was cast in a sitcom pilot for NBC in a small supporting role that was designed for the moments of big laughter in those familiar rhythms that taped sitcoms produce. The project starred Tiffany Amber Thiessen, already a celebrity, and yet a completely normal one, which made her even more attractive. A standup acquaintance of mine was cast as the co-star, and I was cast as the comic relief. A problem ensued when my appearances in scenes started getting more laughter than the co-star's and the producers were worried that I had a presence onscreen which he lacked. There were hurried meetings with network execs. The co-star was being groomed to be the Next Big Thing but this supporting guy was outshining him—what do we do? Solution: increase the co-star's time on camera and cut most of the funny lines from this upstart. The result being an unfunny sitcom that didn't get picked up, the co-star faded into obscurity, and the supporting actor went into a deep depression over the lunacy of a system that often disregarded talent in favor of politics.

Though I knew you couldn't take these scenarios personally, I did. I was used to a Midwest ethic where outworking the guy next to you was almost viewed as sport or at least with pride, and that attitude ultimately paid off in terms of success. I hated myself for feeding my tendency to avoid life. Smoking pot, spending too much time online. The internet was still young and online dating debuted. Promiscuity at the speed of dial-up. Of course, I was perfectly capable of more acceptable outlets. I played chess six nights a week, three hours a night, for a year in an all-night diner with my friend Marty. Then video games came about. Nights playing in my darkened apartment. So fixated that if I had no ashtray handy, I'd simply stand my finished butts on end so that by night's end they formed a Stonehenge in miniature, a small monument to my depression-induced laziness.

Yet, somehow, I was still accomplishing. Maintaining a semblance of a work ethic. A few hours a day writing my next one-person show, though my jaded outlook was on full display when I performed my late night standup spots down at the Improv on Melrose. I was morose, my every exhale sounding like a sigh. I had never *assumed* that coming to LA would bring me fame and fortune, though it had seemed like I was supposed to end up here—that there was a destiny-like feel about it. But increasingly it now felt like someone, something, had decided that I was no one special. Like I was being punished for something I'd done or not done.

As early as my twenties, I'd always been lucky. Inordinately lucky. As my best friend often marveled, "Hastings you have a horseshoe up your ass." In a given situation, all things being equal, things usually went my way. Others noticed it, regularly shaking their heads in amazement. "Hastings pulled it off again." "How did Drew manage to get out of that one?"

But then it changed. Had it started when my sitcom deal went south in '94? Or maybe in '95 when it seemed certain that I'd locked up that role in *Jerry Maguire* until Tom Cruise's people nixed me for being too tall? But maybe that was just business—I couldn't think clearly. There were constant auditions; you were picked or you weren't. I got in my head that not only was my luck changing, but that Life had decided to average itself out against my lucky past, and was now going to increase my unfavorable outcomes in a Great Leveling.

I withdrew even more. Playing *Tomb Raider* for twelve hours at a stretch. I played poker in the LA card rooms. I started having pitiable crying jags that came out of nowhere and went on for a year. I ate bowls of Grape-Nuts without sugar or raisins. Eating it quickly before the milk had time to soften it, the Grape-Nuts hard, cutting into my mouth like gravel.

I woke up one Tuesday morning profoundly sad. It was in 2002 I think, but I don't know what month or season, only that it was a Tuesday. I was scared in a way I'd never experienced. If there is a rock-bottom, that's where I was sitting. Distraught, trying to hold back tears, I remembered a large Episcopal church two blocks away on Hollywood Boulevard. I'm not sure why I thought of it. I'd never been there nor had I ever been to any church in LA. But it suddenly seemed like the place to be and I threw on some clothes. Even though it was so close, I drove. I was not at all sure I could walk there without sobbing in public.

There was a large parking lot in the rear of the church and I parked right in the middle of the lot because there were no other cars there at 8 a.m. I jumped out of the car and walked fast to the church doors, holding back a flood of tears. I pulled on the door but it was locked. I tried a side door but it was locked as well. There was a separate building, a rectory, and I banged on its door. A few seconds later it opened and a minister stood there.

"Can I help you?"

I wasn't sure what I wanted, but I blurted out, "Can you unlock the church for me I just want to go in there and sit maybe for a little while."

He hesitated for a moment.

"Okay. There's no one in there right now, though."

"That's all right," I managed.

I went inside and sat in a pew and my ass had barely touched the seat when I erupted in tears. I sat there crying and wiping snot on my shirtsleeve and immediately felt sheepish. I was uncertain how to pray. How to explain myself, to ask for help. And so I blubbered and I could hear the echoes of my words off the high ceilings. I was lost. Didn't know what I was doing with my life other than a lot of destructive things to myself. Those were the things I talked about and I remember thinking that everything I was saying out loud seemed so stereotypical. But then, wasn't it precisely at that point of desperation that people finally do rush into a church?

It's not easy for me to type *I needed to be saved.* It sounds so un-intellectual, so churchy. But that was exactly what I needed—saving. Whether it was salvation from myself, from circumstances, or from Satan, I didn't care. I was desperate.

Forty-five minutes later, I said not very convincingly but out loud, "Okay, I guess I feel a little bit better now." I didn't actually feel better—but at least I wasn't in the panicked, desperate state in which I'd arrived. I left the church and walked out to the parking lot to my car. Another car was now parked next to me, which immediately struck me as odd because it was a big parking lot and these were the only two cars there. I hadn't even parked in a spot close to the church. It was like when you're using a urinal and someone comes in and uses the one right next to you when there're ten other empties.

As I crossed the lot, I leaned over to see if anyone was sitting in the car, but it was unoccupied. When I was just six feet away I noticed the car's license plate. "ILoveDrew." I know, it seems hokey. Roll-your-eyes-give-me-a-fuckin'-break hokey. But that's what it said. My first response was a dull, surprised, "Well, that's weird." I looked around like it must be a joke, as if a hidden camera crew might pop out and say, "Gotcha!" But no. There was no one else around. Just "ILoveDrew."

From the time that I saw the plate to when I got in my car was only about a minute. I was exhausted, worn out. My reaction to the plate never rose above a tired curiosity. I just slowly shook my head back and forth muttering, "What are the fucking odds of this happening?" I drove back to my apartment and thought about the episode again but still could not get my head around it.

I cannot recall what make of car was parked next to me that day. I think it was a shade of blue. And I cannot recall if they were California plates, though I think they were. After that day, I put the incident out of my mind. Once or twice in the next couple of years it came back to me and I still had the same thought, *That was the weirdest fucking coincidence*, and then I'd drop it. I didn't think about it again for a long time.

CHAPTER 12

The Garden

I never intended to start gardening. It was my therapist's idea. I never intended to start seeing a therapist either but I happened to have health insurance in 2003 and discovered that mental health services were a covered condition. In Hollywood, standard rates for a therapist were about $200 an hour, so having a mere $10 co-pay seemed like a no-brainer. I liked going to these appointments. I wasn't sure how many answers I was getting, but it was a godsend to talk to someone about this stuff rather than twirling in second-guessing circles with myself.

In about the third or fourth session, she asked me about my daily routine.

"Um, twice a week I perform standup sets at the Improv. And once or twice a week I go to auditions for television commercials."

"Good, good." She was good at that soothing tone. "What else?"

"That's it. I don't leave my apartment for much else."

She concluded that I just needed to get out more. "You, Drew, need to socialize! We need to get you back to that person you used to be. Where's *that* Drew, the one that you described last week as being vivacious, charismatic, and the life of the party? I know he's still in there!" She pointed at my chest as if to indicate this was where chakras and other intangible traits resided. She continued, "Maybe a tennis club or possibly the Sierra Club?" I suggested joining a militia. She chuckled at that but then scribbled a remark in her notes.

A few days later I sat in my overstuffed chair, chain smoking, gazing out the window. At some point I noticed the sign across the street above a medieval-looking wooden door that was embedded in a row of tall hedges. "Wattles Gardens, a private gardening association. Members only."

The Wattles Garden was a huge private garden complex at the corner of Hollywood Boulevard and Curson Avenue. The original Wattles mansion and grounds stretched an entire city block, surrounded by a ten-foot-high iron fence and dense hedges to prevent anyone from seeing inside. I had seen that sign a hundred times, but for some reason on this day it suddenly had some resonance.

"A garden club. That might be just weird enough to be interesting," I thought. It would get me out of the house and was only across the street. Depression likes convenience. I also liked the "Members Only" aspect. It sounded upscale, exclusive yet vaguely sweaty. I pictured hot women casually leaning on rakes, flirting with me. After another cigarette, I decided to head over there after changing into linen pants. On the way out the door I picked out a walking stick—the one with the brass duck head. Perfect for strolling the grounds of private gardens and pointing at various things.

The garden entrance was closed and this afforded a good occasion to use the brass duck head to rap on the door. A minute or so later, the door was opened by an old man dressed in dark work clothes and holding pruning shears.

"Yas?" he said looking me up and down.

"Hi. I'm here to—to apply for membership in your garden club."

The old man hesitated then said, "Ah, yas, you vant to get plot?"

"Plot? I'm not sure what you mean." I realized he must be the gardener, the caretaker who probably lived on the grounds. He motioned me inside.

"Plot. You are here for garten plot?"

I had hoped that he'd direct me somewhere where maybe I would be given a flute of champagne and a tour.

"Sorry not to introduce, my name ist Zima. I am ze Gartenmaster here. I am ze one to approve pipple for plot."

It suddenly occurred to me that maybe I had romanticized the Wattles Garden Association, just as I'd done fourteen hundred other times in my life. Zima showed me the almost two hundred garden plots laid out in a huge sprawling grid. Like a big, sunny, leafy AIDS quilt. He gave me a newsletter, told me to explore, then left pushing a wheelbarrow.

Back in my apartment an hour later, I looked over the list of rules and the newsletter. I had imagined a garden society peopled with the leisure class, something out of a Merchant Ivory film, but Wattles was simply a community garden—so *communal*. Zima gave me a choice of two available plots and I picked the one that looked the least like a shallow grave. He had also given me a key to the front gate. Not what I'd hoped for but maybe it would make me get out of the house. "I'm a gardener, kitty!" But my cat seemed unimpressed.

The next few days were spent exploring the garden grounds. All the plots were ten-by-ten feet, and each had a defined perimeter; some were bordered by poles, some by wire, others had little fences. These gardeners were a territorial bunch. But I saw the appeal—the plots gave one a sense of control of one's life, even if it was just ten feet square. It was *manageable*. I marveled at what these people were able to accomplish with their plots—neat rows of bright green vegetables. Color everywhere—purple eggplants and squash. But mostly I saw red. Strawberries were the crop of choice it seemed. Almost every plot made room for strawberries.

My third day in the garden I spotted Zima over by the faucets. He took me to the community tool shed and issued me a shovel and hoe. I pulled out the completed application I'd been carrying around in my back pocket for the last three days and handed it to him. Zima looked it over and pointed at where I listed my occupation.

"Ah, you are comeediennn? You make laughter, yes?"

"Yes," I answered.

"I remember laughter," Zima said, his clear gray eyes giving away nothing.

He's Russian, I decided. We started down a pathway as he answered my questions about how to prep my plot. As we strolled the grounds he walked with his hands clasped behind his back like all old European men.

Though he was casual and seemed at peace, Zima also seemed like a man with secrets. Later, when I was breaking up the hard soil in my plot, I considered the possibility that Zima was a retired ethnic cleanser. It seemed logical that after committing wartime atrocities you'd flee to America and putter around in a garden in your golden years. That's probably what I'd do. He seemed nice enough now though, and I began the backbreaking work of soil preparation.

It took me two weeks to get my plot ready to plant. A jungle of weeds had to be cleared, then I had to break up the soil, which was hard and grayish and sterile. Nothing like the midwestern dirt I'd grown up with. I took breaks often, soaked with sweat, and went to the central faucets for water. I usually took a few minutes to walk around the garden paths. One day I saw two people tending their gardens. One was an old Russian woman in a babushka on her knees picking strawberries. The other woman was an American hippie type, fifty-ish, who was talking to herself as she raked. Two-thirds of the gardeners here were Russian. Not the cool, fashionable Russians that graced the runways of Milan or the courts at Wimbledon. These were ancient Russians straight from the shtetls, most with weathered faces that bore the years of Soviet scarcity and long winters. They gave the garden a kind of Renaissance Faire quality—an eastern European theme park with a socialist labor camp flavor. It made sense that the Russians had found the Wattles Garden. Like me, they were probably looking for an escape from the warped reality of Hollywood. We had that in common at least.

I played poker in a weekly game made up of an assortment of comedian friends. A month after joining the Wattles I brought it up.

"I joined a garden club, took up gardening," I said, throwing chips in the pile to call a bet.

There was a pause as if they were waiting for a punchline. To them, I might just as well have said, "I'm going to shave my head and suck cock in the alley to make extra money."

"You're serious?" Jack asked.

"Yeah. I just thought it would be something different. And I've been in a funk," I added, thinking that might end the discussion.

They all chimed in, basically that I was crazy.

"Drew, you're in Hollywood—*in show biz*. If you're down or in a funk, you take drugs. That's the go-to here. You abuse drugs or drink. You don't *garden*."

"But I already do drugs," I say. This gets a laugh. These guys all see me as kind of a "Mr. Rat Pack." A type-A guy who wouldn't have "depression" in his vocabulary. They apparently missed my cry for help. I changed subjects and we continued the game.

The garden became a habit. I spent a couple of hours a day there, five days a week, if for nothing else than to water my strawberries. One tended to forget that LA was a desert. The only thing keeping the city green was the constant watering by the thousands and thousands of sprinklers that sprung to life in off-hours, and it was no different in our garden except that we were the sprinklers, a manual task that connected us to our plants. The fact that I even had that awareness about interconnectedness—of my relationship to the plants—was new. Maybe I was operating on another level, or maybe I'd just never had a reason to think about garden plants before.

There were a lot of days that I just came to sit and think and not be in Hollywood. Behind the giant hedges that lined the east and west sides, and the thick grove of avocado trees that bordered Hollywood Boulevard, an oasis kept the sound of constant traffic muffled down to a distant roar. I stood out there. I was the only male that looked like I should be at work somewhere. Almost everyone else was an elderly Russian or one of the American women that struck me as Hollywood wives—former actresses that gave it up to marry wealthy producers. It made me feel guilty all over again. *Why am I digging in the dirt with a stick when I should be sending out scripts or out meeting people that can help my career?* I wondered. And as if to rub salt in my wound, an old Russian woman looked over at me and smiled, looking like a *National Geographic* cover titled, "Ukraine— Breadbasket to Europe!"

And yet, somehow I was having successes again. Regularly. It had started when I landed an appearance on *The Tonight Show* a year prior. I'd even gotten a standing ovation, though I hadn't thought my set was particularly ovation-worthy. Then I was hired to do voiceover work for a short-lived NBC animated series. Six months after that, my friend Bob Odenkirk cast me in a movie. A few months later I got a part in another pilot for CBS. I could've seen these events as a sign that I was being rediscovered, that my Hollywood career was back on the upswing. I was appreciative, but saw these events as too little, too late in what had been the arc of my ascendancy in Hollywood. My development deal had been my pivotal moment. I was leery that the extent of my success in Hollywood from here on out would consist of getting just enough opportunities that I existed only on the outer fringes of fame.

My insurance company notified me that I only had one covered session left with my therapist. I wasn't sure how helpful therapy had been anyway. I'd had a few revelations with her but I didn't recall having been improved by them so weren't they just wasted epiphanies? Anyway, the garden seemed to provide a degree of centeredness to my life and a quiet place to reflect, which I seemed to be getting the hang of.

"I'm so pleased that you've stayed with the gardening, Drew,"

"Funny, I don't think of it as a garden, it's more like a tiny piece of real estate I own. I'm a real estate developer and I'm developing it—improving the property—the strawberries are incidental, a bonus. Here's a sample of what I'm capable of."

Then I handed her a plastic grocery bag half full of mostly stunted strawberries.

CHAPTER 13

The D-Word

I had just finished doing five nights of shows in Cincinnati and was driving the three hours east to St. Clairsville. This was where my dad lived, it turned out.

This visit had come about because my father had three kids from his second marriage and they had come to one of my standup shows a while back, no doubt curious about their half-brother. The oldest, Drew Hastings—the one who'd "replaced" me all those years ago—was there. Cordial enough, but it wasn't like we exchanged phone numbers. Another sister, Laura, had also been there, and the youngest, Jennifer, had stayed in contact with me, and she'd recently called to say that my father was now living alone since their mother had recently divorced him and moved away. She gave me his phone number. I'd been told that he had never contacted me because he wanted to maintain the peace in his household—apparently his wife could be a rather jealous woman.

When I'd called, he'd seemed somewhat confused:

"Uh, Hi. Uh ... Dad? It's uh, Drew. Your son, you know ... your *other* son."

Fuck. That didn't sound like I'd planned.

"Drew?" A long pause. "Well, hello!"

I still wasn't sure he knew exactly which Drew he was talking to, so I added, "It's Drew—*Pam's son.*"

"Yes, I was baffled for a minute there. I'm glad you called."

I cut to the chase. "Listen, I just finished doing some shows over in Cincinnati and I was thinking maybe I would come over there and see you before I fly back to LA."

"That would be great. I'd love to see you."

He sounded stiff or like he was trying too hard. He was probably just as weirded out as I was.

St. Clairsville, Ohio, was just a couple miles from where both my father and grandfather had been born, and a stone's throw from Martins Ferry. Turned out he'd been living just three hours away from me most of the time I was growing up, knowledge I was glad I'd been spared. I found the house on Cindy Drive, knocked on the door, and my first words when he answered were, "Hey." Like you might say when you can't remember someone's name or if you passed someone on the sidewalk.

"Hey there yourself!" he replied, and we gave each other an awkward hug. He smelled exactly like my long-dead grandfather.

"Come on in—I made some coffee, you drink coffee?"

"Of course. I'm a huge coffee drinker!" My overly perky answer sounded like, "Here's one of the many little facts about me that I need to bring you up to speed on!"

He still looked like the man I remembered, only older. Tall, maybe 6'3", dark hair, black-framed glasses. He looked like an older version of me. But different. He was thicker—he had more Welsh-Scots-Irish in him and I was thinner, thanks to my mom's slender genes.

"So, how was your drive over?" he asked as we sat down at his kitchen table.

"Good, good. I came out on I-70. Not much traffic."

We made small talk. We both came off as guarded but we weren't, really—just unsure how to proceed. If he was anything like me, he wasn't prone to emotional drama. He asked about my mom and sister, but maintained a certain distance in his questions, a tentativeness, as if he was acutely aware that he had no real right to ask, let alone get any answers. He asked me about my standup comedy and did I make a good living at that. I said that I did but not as much as most people assumed. We relaxed a little and I listened as he described his financial situation.

"Now, anybody that tells you that Social Security is worthless is full of beans! I don't know if you know this, but every year that you keep living, your payments go up—anywhere from thirty to fifty bucks a month—that's your cost of living increase. Now, I'm getting about thirteen hundred a month in Social Security, then you add on to that my pension from the steel mill—about four hundred a month, and my VA benefits, and I've got a decent little package going. And this doesn't even include the three days a week I work over in the call center at the telemarketing company. Hell, I make another twelve thousand a year there—and Social Security can't touch that money—it's pure gravy. So all in all, I'm doing pretty good!"

Intrigued, not so much by what he was saying, but the way he talked, there was something folksy in his manner—maybe it was some of the words he used, but he also had a certain command of language, an authoritative delivery. He reminded me of Professor Harold Hill from *The Music Man*. My dad sounded like a lecturer at a small town library. I hadn't grown up with him but we spoke much the same way, our cadence was almost identical. I was simply an urbanized version of him.

Most of all, I was surprised not to encounter any of the emotions I thought might overwhelm me. Maybe if I'd been a teenager reunited after a ten-year absence, I'd have flung my arms around him, sobbing into his chest. But I was a year shy of fifty, and the simple equation of time plus melancholy had long ago replaced most of my sense of loss with what seemed like a wistful curiosity. I had no interest in confronting him, no interest in accusations. I really just wanted to sit with him, next to the man I had come from. And maybe I hoped that by sitting across from him I might get some understanding or something like closure, but mostly, learn something about myself.

We had more coffee and talked about our obvious similarities—our height, hair, black framed glasses. I noticed we both smoked Marlboro

Lights. Later, it came up how much he was into history and archaeology—both my favorite subjects—and we talked regional history for a while. His anti-government views came out, which happened to align almost perfectly with my own. We seemed to share the same mannerisms as well. I wanted all these similarities to be meaningful—evidence that there was a blueprint for my existence. But was I reading too much into it? A lot of people smoked Marlboro Lights and I wasn't the only guy who had fringe views of government.

He wanted me to stay at his house for the night. "I have a roll-out bed I can make up." But that was too cozy and too fast. I told him I was going to stay down the road at the Ramada. He asked me to come back in the morning for breakfast, then he'd drive me around to see some local sights.

I checked into the motel, went to bed, and my mind raced for a while. He had been so bigger-than-life to me all these years, had such an effect on me by his absence, and now he just seemed entirely *human*. He was just an old guy living in a house in a small town who had been too afraid—either of his decisions, or his wife—to ever contact me. My awe and apprehension of him dissolved into something resembling empathy.

I checked out of the motel and got back to my dad's place about ten, where he had eggs and bacon waiting under a layer of paper towels to keep them warm, which didn't work but did manage to wick some of the grease out. After breakfast, he drove us up to the old National Road, the first road that traversed America. It was long gone but he showed me where there was still a stretch of stone pavers where the highway had predated Route 40, which in turn had predated Interstate 70. Both of us were excited by this bit of history. Then we wound through the hills of Belmont County until we got to Mt. Holly Cemetery.

"This is where your grandparents are buried," he said, assuming that I hadn't been here before. The tone in his voice sounded like it was another historical gem that I had not seen.

"Oh, I've been here to visit five or six times," I said, which seemed to surprise him. What I didn't say was that most of those times I'd been horribly depressed, would start out talking to my grandparents and invariably end up in tears, which I only ever let myself do around people that were already dead.

As we sat there, my dad said, "You know, my parents and I did not get along a lot of the time." That was jarring. The thought that my grandparents weren't loved unconditionally would never have occurred to me. "Your grandad could be very demanding, and Grandma had a real mean streak." That bordered on blasphemy as far as I was concerned, but for whatever reason he felt the need to get it out. I didn't really want to hear it but I also sensed that he was trying to convey that we're all victims of our parents, one way or another.

We drove on, my dad pointing out various landmarks until we pulled into Weeks Cemetery in the town of Bridgeport. He showed me the weathered headstone for William Andrew Hastings, my great-great-grandfather. If my grandfather had brought me here as a child, I didn't remember, but I was humbled at seeing this distant ancestor's name now. He had fought in two separate tours of the Civil War and had a corroded Grand Army of the Republic marker next to his grave. As we sat looking out over the hillside falling away from us, my dad reached into his jacket and pulled out an envelope.

"I want to give you something," he said, suddenly somewhat solemn. He pulled out some folded papers and handed them to me. "It's a cemetery plot," he said. "Right next to the plot I'm to be buried in."

I looked over at him to see if I heard right, and if so, was he kidding with me, but no, he looked rather pleased with himself. "It's a grave? A gravesite—in this cemetery?" I said, trying to mask my disbelief with an appreciative tone.

"Yes. It's just something that I want to do."

I forced myself not to laugh and looked over to see if he was smiling or if there was any hint of irony. *A free grave. That's what my father is giving me.* After a forty-year absence, what does he offer up? Advice? Explanations? A trust fund? No. He presents me with the Gift of Interment. The comedic voice in my head says, *Is this when he finally wants us to spend some quality time together?*

That's when I finally laughed out loud and blurted out, "Whew, well that worry is gone—at least I know where I'll be!" I tried to make it sound like a friendly, appreciative joke. I looked down at the papers and they were in fact official-looking cemetery documents. He took them back from me, and said, "I'll hang on to these with my vital papers, but know that I have them for when the time comes."

"Thank you. That's really nice of you." I wanted to say, "Thank you, Dad," but I couldn't get myself to say the D-word. We sat there a bit longer then headed back to the car. While he went over to a restroom, I turned around, looked back at the gravesites on the hillside, and said out loud, where only the dead could hear me, "Well, it looks like I'm in the real estate business. Maybe my headstone should read, *Coming soon: Another Drew Hastings Development!*" I could hardly wait to break ground . . .

It wasn't until I was back in my LA garden pulling weeds two weeks later that I realized the true sense of what I'd lost when my father was no longer my father. When I re-ran the scene where my dad offered to cook dinner the day we got back from the cemetery, the many facets of the void that he'd left came into focus.

"Are you hungry?" he asked. "I was going to make us some breakfast for supper—I eat breakfast at night a lot of times. You like corn mush and bacon?"

"Sure that sounds great," I replied and immediately thought to myself, *See that? I love corn mush—how weird is it that he eats it too?* Then I remembered something and said to my father, "Didn't Grandad like to make fried mush too?"

"Yes, he sure did. Made it all the time, and actually I think he told me that his dad used to make it too."

At the time, I didn't see the significance of four generations of Hastings men having a habit of eating fried corn mush. But now, I realized it wasn't just a weird coincidence—*it was a tradition.* I got my taste for it from my grandfather, just as my father had. And my grandfather had gotten it from his father. It had been a tradition in my family, albeit a very small one, which my dad's exit when I was a kid had almost severed me from. Whatever my great-great-grandfather had passed on to my great-grandfather, and whatever my great-grandfather had instilled in my grandfather, and whatever my grandfather had, in turn, shared with my father had vaporized when he left. What is tradition but the behavior, habits, customs, and yes, corn mush recipes that get passed down through a family?

That second night, when he was cooking corn mush over the stove, he mentioned that he had a second job, working part-time as a Wal-Mart greeter. Of all the different things that I imagined my father might be up to, *Wal-Mart greeter* was not on the list. But then, neither was Jehovah's Witness and he had been one of those for a decade. In a conversation with my mom, telling her of my visit, she'd told me that my father had been a longtime student of Eastern philosophies and that when he and my mother split, he'd moved to NYC on his Harley-Davidson to get involved in the new pro-Castro movement.

One of the few recurring facts I'd been told about my father was that he was very intelligent, maybe even an intellectual. He had varied and esoteric interests, was a voracious reader. My mother said that he often seemed directionless, "a lost soul" in her words. But what if he wasn't quite as my mother described him? Just as my mom didn't really know me and saw many of my behaviors as shortcomings, maybe she never really knew my father either. Perhaps like me, he just got bored easily, or maybe he'd never wanted to have children in the first place.

As my dad drove me around that morning, he pointed out where the men of our family had lived and died. "Albert Hastings, your great-grandfather, was a cigar roller and worked at that most of his life, and the first William Hastings, your great-great-grandfather, worked in the coal mines in the area." In fact, many of the Hastings men had worked in either the coal or steel plants around Martins Ferry. None of my ancestors seemed to have been accomplished businessmen, go-getters, or leaders of any note. In fact, I had come from a long line of regular Joes.

Ultimately, my father was just that, another man. But a man that I could now see in front of me and not through the fuzzy squint of some childhood memory or idealization. The original Drew Hastings that this Drew Hastings sprang from. And though we shared names and certain proclivities, we were very different. Or were we? I had an uneasy sense that maybe we weren't as different as I would've liked us to have been.

CHAPTER 14

Over and Out

When I returned home from the road after seeing my father there was a message on my answering machine.

"Hello, this is Ida from the garden. It was reported that the borders around your plot require attention. Clearly defined borders must be maintained at all times. Regular cutback of plantings will prevent encroachment into neighboring plots. Thank you." Jesus, these Russians took the place seriously. Understandable, I guess. The history of Europe was all about cut up parcels of land, tenuous borders that needed constant policing. No wonder the garden looked Balkanized.

I went over to the garden the next day and Miss Ida had been right—my garden had gone to shit. Someone had poached most of the strawberries that had ripened while I was gone and weeds were everywhere, looting nutrients and water from my plot, and now arcing over into the adjacent gardens. I sat down on my metal folding chair and halfheartedly picked whatever weeds were within my immediate reach. The garden had lost some of its appeal—I liked the task-oriented nature of gardening, but I was restless. I was just not enamored with pursuing sitcoms and commercial auditions any longer. I had entertained the notion of leaving LA but it felt like giving up. Plus there was a definite cachet to being a national comedian based in LA. Standup was my first love and I wanted to protect my good reputation.

I pulled a few more weeds, just enough to reduce the imperialistic threat they posed to my neighbors, and went for a walk around the grounds. In the next section where the plots got better sunlight, I stopped to talk to a handsome woman, about fifty-five, who was wearing an Al Stewart *Year of the Cat Tour* T-shirt. She had about fifteen coffee cans scattered around her garden and all had a sprig or spray of something growing from them.

"I'm developing a homeopathic remedy that reverses the onset of menopause," she informed me.

"Exciting times in the garden," I confirmed.

As she made small talk, I tried to picture her in front of an FDA panel, making her case for the approval of her herbs. I tried very hard to picture this but I could not.

"I'm Laura, by the way," she said.

"As in Nyro."

"Yes," she smiled, pleased at the reference I made. I headed back to the apartment because I was out of cigarettes.

The last half of 2003 was marked by a suspiciously large number of positive events, thankfully most were not Hollywood-related, but instead, standup opportunities—and better yet, far away. My new manager got me into the prestigious Montreal Comedy Festival. Two months later, a fall comedy tour in England. Finally, I flew back to the Midwest to do a few club dates and was scheduled to be on *The BOB & TOM Show*, a nationally syndicated morning radio show, very Midwest-centric, and a four-hour format, conducive to my anecdotal—some might say long-winded—style. I'd been on before but this time I really clicked with the hosts and started making regular appearances whenever I was playing the Heartland.

The rest of the year was a blur of hamster wheel neurotic activity periodically interrupted by actual living:

Think about cigarettes. Smoke cigarettes. Feel horribly guilty about not being able to quit. Am I running out of cigarettes? Think about my writing. Write new material for one-person show. Edit. Feel horribly guilty about not networking and trying to get my material noticed. Why bother? Am I running out of creativity? Pot. Porn. Video games. Think about pot. Smoke pot. Feel horribly guilty that I still smoke pot. Am I running out of pot? Watch porn. Feel horribly guilty about wasting time on this crap and about how my grandparents would be so disappointed in me. Am I running out of any decency I once had? Play video games all night. Feel horribly guilty about the time I was wasting that could be put into *anything* more productive. Loneliness. Lovelessness. Feel guilty about what my days and nights consist of and why any woman in her right mind would enter my life. Is it any wonder I talk out loud to my cat? And if my cat could talk, what would he say back to me?

I also usually had five or six auditions for television commercials every week—just enough to force me to shave every day and shower two or three times weekly. If I thought that film and sitcom actors were a daffy, self-absorbed bunch, they paled in comparison to commercial actors— viciously competitive, their persona "type" always cranked up to a Max Headroom-level.

The very last commercial audition I ever went on I was asked to show up in a business suit, so I assumed it was for some upscale brand. But no, this audition was for another product, though we weren't told what it was. Along with three other guys in their forties I was brought into the audition office where the casting agent, a feminine man prone to flamboyancy, gave us instructions. We were to be dogs in this audition. He pointed at each of us, assigning a breed. I was a Great Pyrenees. Then he gave us an emotion: we were all overjoyed about what was in front of us, though we didn't know what that product was, but whatever it was, we wanted it. As he put his finger on the start button of the video camera, he instructed, "Okay, get down on all fours and face me!" Within a second the three other dogs were on their hands and knees and I was still standing because I'd hesitated. I was not crazy about getting my Hugo Boss suit all wrinkled.

"Great Pyrenees—down!" he ordered. I carefully dropped to the carpet.

"Okay. So, all four of you dogs, look over toward that box. You want what's inside, you're begging for it. Think of it as the best treat a dog could possibly get! First, I want you to wag your tails! Wag! That's it! Come on,

shake your butts! You really want what's in that box! Faster, Boston terrier!—Great Pyrenees you need to wag much harder!"

I looked over at the other men. Their eyes were riveted on the casting
guy watching his cues. All of them were shamelessly wagging their "tails."

"Excellent—good, good. Now I want you to get up on your knees, put
your paws up in front of you like you're begging! Begging for the best treat
in the whole world!"

He was getting worked up—a falsetto-voiced kindergarten teacher
jacked up on amphetamines who was becoming exponentially gayer by
the minute. He turned on a cassette recorder, which began blaring a tinny
Tchaikovsky's 1812 Overture, and Mr. Extremely Nelly paced quickly
back and forth in front of us clapping his hands in glee as I halfheartedly
acted like I was begging. I was starting to sweat and my glasses were sliding down my nose.

"That's it, beg for it! Get your paws up higher in front of you. C'mon
poodle, I know you know how poodles beg! Great Pyrenees—this isn't an
aloof cat commercial! You're an excited *dog*—let's go!"

Clapping, clapping, clapping. His eyes danced with excitement as he
pointed at the poodle, then the terrier, then the bichon.

"Now *whimper*. You *really* want that box over there. Whimper for
it—that's it!"

I stood up just as he was telling them to "roll over." He looked at me.

"What are you *doiiing*, Great Pyr—" He stopped and walked over to
the sign-in sheet to see what my name was but I was already out the door.
As I was walking out the other three men were happily rolling over and
over in their suits like they were on a freshly mown lawn.

I lit a cigarette in the car. Fuck I was pissed. How I'd demeaned myself.
After a while, I quit beating myself up over my lack of integrity when I
decided maybe I'd only had a *lapse* of integrity—that maybe I'd kept it by
walking out. Though my walking out was a huge no-no that would quickly
get around to the other agencies. It didn't matter. I thought about those
three men up there. I couldn't compete with the lengths they'd go to book
a national commercial. I went back to the apartment and spent a justified
eight hour stretch playing video games and smoking pot.

My trips over to the garden were becoming less about gardening and more about just trying to break the cycle of dysfunction that made up my life in my apartment. At least I was trading my indoor depression for a sunnier, healthier-feeling, outdoor one.

Then, starting in January of 2004 attendance at my shows suddenly doubled. I actually had sold out shows. Offers for gigs started coming fast, due to *The BOB & TOM Show* appearances. Apparently, I'd found my audience. And then, sometime in late January, I opened the letter from the Social Security Administration that contained irrefutable proof of my haphazard existence. I made my chart, and then spent a long day in the garden just thinking, sitting in my folding chair surrounded by all the weeds I'd grown. I thought back about my visit with my father, him telling me how his Social Security income *was a decent little package* and that *he had it pretty good*, and I shuddered.

In February, a woman I'd met six months earlier in Cincinnati moved in with me. Why I allowed this I couldn't explain. She was quirky and smart and she told me she'd been shot in the head by a former boyfriend which was why she was so quirky. I then found out that she was lying, had never been shot in the head, and had told me this in an effort to explain away her quirkiness which I had now come to realize was somewhere past quirky. At that point, I was scared of her, felt sorry for her, and still I let her talk her way into living with me. This was, for me, a new low in judgement calls. Though she did make me laugh regularly.

In March, the day after my fiftieth birthday, I got a phone call telling me that Drake Sather had killed himself, shot himself in the head. I sat in shock and great sadness for a long time and by day's end was angry at Drake for leaving behind an uncomprehending wife and four kids. The funeral was a large turnout of friends—well-known comedians and writers—and it was the first and only time I ever saw a group of comics together with no laughter being generated. Though we'd not been as close in recent years, I knew Drake loved his wife, was crazy about his kids. I was shell-shocked. Rattled, big time.

Drake had been known as a hip, smart, edgy standup and writer. Respected by his peers. But success in Hollywood has its costs. Drake wrote for some great shows, for numerous Oscars hosts. Got rich. I'd heard he'd had a well-known screenplay stolen. He moved up to being a sitcom showrunner—the top position. Near the time of his death, I think he was living in New York and commuting back and forth to LA. He was laid back and an avowed family guy—being on the other side of the country for long stretches would probably not have helped his already depressive personality.

But it was the show he was running at the end that was a telltale sign to me. He'd just finished a re-make of a 1960s' sitcom, *Mister Ed*, about a talking horse. To me, even more improbable than the idea of a talking horse was the idea of Drake Sather being within a thousand miles of that project. I think he found himself on all fours, paws outstretched, begging for treats and couldn't see a way out of the room. My twelve years in Hollywood began with Drake Sather and ended with him. The time had come to get out of here.

I sat in my garden looking around at the half-finished undertaking. A few areas of my plot were thriving but most of it was just a tangled mess. Exactly how my mind must look, I thought, my perennial qualities buried under the unchecked growth of my vices. My therapist had once suggested that I consider taking the anti-depressant Paxil. It occurred to me now that she was simply recommending a good herbicide. But I'd once spent a few months on anti-depressants—"Multiple applications may be required for desired results"—and found they didn't get to the root cause, they just killed everything in sight.

I wanted to leave Los Angeles but I needed to convince myself that I was not giving up. That required that I not just leave, but that I also have a goal in going somewhere else. As much as I liked Cincinnati, I wasn't about to move back there. That would have felt too much like throwing in the towel and going home. Furthermore, my girlfriend was from Cincinnati and if I moved back there, she'd inevitably follow, which I did not want. But I felt responsible for her and wasn't about to leave her in LA on her own. We'd had some great times and I had feelings for her, but ultimately I felt like her caretaker, and I had me to worry about. I was in a creative slump. I was in a life slump. I'd always been an urban guy, lived in Cincinnati, New

York City, San Francisco. What was the antithesis of my persona? Where was that place? Wait—*rural*—I'd never experienced rural. I started looking online at anything rural. Idaho—too rural. Missouri—too Missouri. Kentucky—more like it. But at heart, I was an Ohioan.

The more I looked online at cabins on hilltops, weathered bungalows at the end of overgrown lanes, and promises of owner financing, all nestled among southern Ohio hardwoods, the more excited I got. Soon I realized that I wasn't quitting anything, or severely altering my familiar path—that arc of success I'd long subscribed to. This as-yet-unknown destination was going to be Ground Zero for my new arc. My level of excitement at this new prospect was only equaled by my nail-biting apprehensiveness. The only person I'd ever heard of moving to the wilds of southern Ohio was Jorma Kaukonen of Jefferson Airplane who'd always struck me as the poster boy for LSD burnout, and who now gave guitar workshops from his remote cabin. How was I going to swing this? I was making a decent income at standup but my savings were nil and my credit score was a lofty six.

The side benefit to this was that Dana was not rural. She read *Cosmo*, *Vogue*, and liked to go out and consume. "I can't possibly live under these conditions," I imagined her saying. Perfect.

In April I was having a yard sale and the phone rang. The Wattles Garden lady once again calling to remind me that, "an orderly garden is a fruitful garden."

"I could not agree more," I told her. "I will be moving to greener pastures, so to speak, and will be vacating my plot, but I thank you for all that the garden has provided me." That afternoon I turned in my key to Zima and took a final look at my plot, which now seemed so little and scraggly next to the lush, colorful plots all around. My garden had become untended. I had let my life get really small over the last few years, ten-feet-by-ten-feet, to be exact. But that was going to change. From my notebook of collected quotes, one jumped out: "Quitting while you're ahead is not the same as quitting." And I *was* ahead. My standup career, which had always been what I most valued, was intact and on the rise, and I'd become far more self-aware, though painfully so. Maybe I'd just had to hit some kind of rock bottom like alcoholics did—an acceptance that the Assumed Success I'd always presumed was not going to look like I'd thought.

Fort Hollywood. That's how I had always thought of the town—no different than a military base, manned by an all-volunteer army of fresh-faced recruits. Like the other enlistees, I had awaited my orders to get shipped out to a TV studio or a film location, or showcase stage. But like all military bases, ninety percent of your time was spent just waiting. You perform drills to maintain your readiness in case you're called to the front lines. I kept my humor honed to a razor's edge, made sure my teeth were whitened to perfection, and kept—or tried to keep—both my clothes and face, wrinkle-free.

Some of my fellow comedians enlisted, reported to Ft. Hollywood, and got washed out after Basic. Some became career soldiers, rising through the ranks. Others did a tour of duty and were discharged. Me? Other than a few close friends, I never told anyone I was leaving; I just went AWOL.

PART II

Ruralization

CHAPTER 15

Transition

U ntil August 2004, I had never been to Hillsboro, Ohio, and, in fact, had just barely heard of it. If you live in Cincinnati, you're only familiar with Hillsboro because it's one of those distant towns that you always see on the local TV weatherman's map as he scrawls overnight lows, "in the outlying areas, temperatures will drop into the teens."

That's Hillsboro—*an outlying area*—and precisely what I'd been seeking when, in June of 2004, I towed both a U-Haul and my girlfriend in my '76 Eldorado to the I-275 outer beltway that surrounds Cincinnati, put all of my belongings in a self-storage place with bright orange roll up doors, and then began driving the back roads of southern Ohio looking for somewhere to call home. For two months, my girlfriend and I stayed in motels and campsites from Gallipolis to Ripley, Logan, and McConnelsville, trying to find somewhere that clicked. The tension finally broke in a remote cabin that, thankfully, was reminiscent of every teen horror movie. "I cannot continue to live under these conditions," she told me, and so I dropped her off at her mother's house near Dayton. I felt like a cad for engineering our breakup, but it had turned out that she was ready to move on from me also. I thought about this as I sat looking over the breakfast menu in a diner in uptown Hillsboro.

"Can I borrow your newspaper?" I asked the old man sitting on the stool next to me.

"Yep."

When I pulled into Hillsboro the day before, I hadn't considered it as a place to reside. I ordered breakfast and read the classifieds, casually looking over the real estate listings and stopping when I got to a small ad that said, "Farm for sale—3 BR house and two barns on 40 acres—a perfect starter farm! Immediate possession!"

"Hmm," I thought. "A *farm*." I hadn't even considered the idea of a farm, only a house out in the sticks. I barely tasted my Western omelet, lost suddenly in an idea that I couldn't stop from forming—a stock market tickertape printing a stream of justification in my head. "A farm. A farm is *rural*. In a way, it's just a house with a *really big yard*. Yeah—a *farm*—and really, isn't a farm just a *big garden*? And I have *experience* with gardens..."

"More coffee, hon?" The waitress snapped me out of it.

"Yes, thanks."

I looked again at the ad, the part that said, "perfect starter farm!"

"Yeah. Farms are so *American*—honest, hard work—I'd be a *landowner*. And a starter farm sounds *much less* punishing than a full-blown farm."

But how could I possibly swing buying a farm when just a year earlier, while in the fog of depression, convinced that my financial Armageddon was imminent, I'd dug out an *emergency only* American Express card with a $30,000 credit limit, and spent it all before AmEx got wise, stockpiling new Apple computers, designer suits, and pricey eyeglass frames, so that in my future poverty, I would not be so . . . impoverished. Unfortunately, it had been a wasted act of desperation because my fortunes had taken an unexpected upturn when I became wildly popular on *The BOB & TOM Show*, and my standup appearance rates tripled overnight. Then, just two months prior to my breakfast in a Hillsboro diner, I'd been parked in a cabin far out in the woods outside of Logan, Ohio. I needed an Ohio checking account so I went into a US Bank office in Logan.

"Hi, I'd like to open a checking account, please."

"One moment. Let me get our loan officer who handles the checking accounts."

A man walked toward me, and stuck his hand out. "I'm Bob Lewis! And you are the infamous Drew Hastings, am I right?" He was the straightest looking guy I'd seen in ages. A 1950s beatnik would have called him a *square* and he looked eerily like Michael Douglas in *Falling Down*.

"Uh. Hi Bob. Yes, I'm Drew Hastings—I guess somebody has to be," I said, using my patented, self-effacing, faux-beleaguered tone. I was getting used to being recognized, especially in the Midwest, but was still always thrown when it happened in some out of the way place like this.

I filled out the checking account forms, nodding my head and half listening as Bob told me how funny he thought I was. He'd been to see my show more than once and he listened to me all the time on *BOB & TOM*.

"Drew Hastings! I just can't believe this. If that doesn't beat all—hey, my girlfriend will never believe this—how about I call her and you just say hi?"

"Okay, but I'll need to get going shortly."

He'd already dialed the number. "Vicki, a friend of mine wants to say hi to you." He thrust the phone at me.

"Uh, hey Vicki," I said.

Bob was sitting across from me chuckling to himself, "I can't get over this—Drew Hastings walks into *my* bank."

Bob looks at me and takes the phone back. "Vicki, that was Drew Hastings. You know, the comedian we just saw a couple months back. Yeah! He's sitting right here!"

After he hung up the phone, he asked why I was in Logan. I told him I'd been traveling around southern Ohio looking for a place to buy.

"Well, maybe I can help. I'm the loan officer here and if you can get pre-approved for a loan, it's a lot easier to get a place."

"My credit is not very good right now."

"That's okay. Tell you what, you come back tomorrow morning and I'll get some mortgage info together and a simple application!"

I didn't want to, thinking it would be futile, but he was so upbeat and insistent that I agreed to come back. As I walked out the door, I could hear him behind me, talking under his breath. "Drew Hastings. I'll be goshdarned."

The next morning I came in and Bob walked briskly toward me. "My loan office is on the second floor. Let's head on up! You want some coffee?"

"Sure, thanks."

I don't remember much about his office and other than it had wood paneling on the walls and overlooked the parking lot. What I absolutely remember was that there were three framed pictures of me on his office wall. *Three.* Bob didn't say anything at all about them and I walked over to them to get a closer look. One was a copy of my current promotional headshot, but the other two weren't pictures of me I'd even seen before. They were grainy pics like he'd found them on a Google image search and printed them off on the office computer. I tried appearing nonchalant as if I was used to seeing framed montages of me on the walls of bank offices.

As we sat down, Bob motioned toward the pictures and simply said, "So whattaya think?"

I glanced over at the shrine. "I'm glad you like my stuff, Bob," I managed to say.

"So Drew. I'm going to cut to the chase. You're right, your credit is not what we would call desirable. Not at all. *But.*" Bob leaned in toward me so that his next words would sound italicized. "*All of our mortgage loans go before a loan committee for approval.* But I've been here for a few years and my seniority gives me a little bit of leeway."

I wasn't sure what he was getting at.

"I'm allowed to make one real estate loan without it getting official bank approval. I can go outside of the normal channels. One loan that I can approve *on my own.* It's like a 'Get Out of Jail Free' card."

"Really?" I said. I tried to sound impressed, earnestly hopeful, but with those pictures on the wall, his pitch came off as just too weird to be taken seriously. Actually, anything that Bob Lewis said at this point seemed a little suspect.

"Really. And you can take that to the bank!" He laughed at his own joke, leaning back in his chair, beaming. Bob took his business card out of the desk, and on the back of it, carefully wrote, "get out of jail free," and handed me the card. "I'm serious. Go out and find the property you want. When you do, call me, and we'll make this happen."

Now, almost two months later, sitting in my car in Hillsboro, I dug out that stupid card from my wallet. I imagined calling the number and Bob Lewis answering and yelling, "Suckerrr!" For a moment I pictured Marty standing in the distance, football in hand. I almost pitched the card out the window but in a testament to my Midwest optimism, I dialed his number. Bob answered, we exchanged a few pleasantries, then I told him I'd found a place. "Do you remember the 'get out of jail free' card you gave me?" I asked cautiously.

"Of course I do! Fax me over the purchase contract you made on the farm."

And sonofabitch, if Bob Lewis didn't come through like some visiting angel. Less than a month later I closed on the farm and moved in.

My farm is a modest three bedroom, single story ranch home of 1,350 square feet, which is pretty small for a house, but that's because farmers tend to put their money in their land, not in their house. The family that lived here in the 1970s and '80s raised three kids here. That's 270 square feet per family member, which is slightly larger than a standard shopping mall parking space. The only time I've ever lived in something anywhere near that size, I was attached to an umbilical cord. In 2004, when I bought the farm, I lived here alone with my cat, providing us each with 675 square feet—plenty of room to get on each other's nerves. He's now dead and resides in a shoebox in a hole in the ground that's just under two square feet.

The farmland itself is another story. It was huge by my standards—forty acres, with a large two-story barn, far bigger than the house. But modern farming is all about economies of scale, and forty acres was just enough scale to insure I would not turn a profit unless I contracted to grow crops for a cartel. Not to be deterred, I started thinking about what I wanted my farm to produce. I had jumped into this with all the enthusiasm I have for anything I undertake. I've never let the fact that I know next to nothing about something deter me. I simply read up on it, ask a lot of questions of people who actually *do* the thing, and hope my brains and optimism will carry the day. I was fifty years old, had lived in cities all my life, and only visited a farm twice as a kid with my grandparents. One morning at a farm equipment auction, I was picking an old farmer's brain about equipment and livestock—and his fingers. He was missing two of them and I asked, "How did you lose those fingers? I'm really new at all this and I don't want to lose my fingers."

He didn't take offense, and told me that he'd reached into a hay baler to clear a jam. "I shouldn't have done it, but I was in a hurry."

He was not the only farmer with missing digits. I also asked two old guys why they limped, and if that was related to their farming. It was. Farming, I learned was dangerous work, some of the most dangerous according to government statistics.

"I'm not sure what I want to raise out on my place," I said to the farmer with eight fingers.

"Young man, farming is really just all about corn," he said. "What you need to ask yourself is, 'How do I want to get my corn to market? Do I want my corn to be in the shape of a pig, or in the shape of a cow, or do I want to just grow corn itself?'"

That seemed very profound to me; I was talking to the Yoda of agriculture. I was sure that his was inside information I'd been given and now had an advantage over most farmers, until I learned that every farm kid over ten years old in the Future Farmers of America already knew that. At one point, I called the county extension agent. He was essentially a farm consultant who worked for the county, assisting farmers. He came over and I asked him what was most likely the best use for my farm, given the lay of the land and its soil. He asked me about my background, and my lack of experience. After a while I said, "So, what do you think I should plant?"

He replied, "I'd think about planting a 'For Sale' sign in the front yard."

Undeterred, I finally decided livestock was the way to go and cattle was my livestock of choice simply because everyone else around was raising them. Now I just needed to learn about cattle. And a bit about rural living, too.

One day I was pestering a farmer about how to set up a cattle chute. "How about I stop out at your place in the morning after breakfast?" he said.

"Fine! Come on by."

124

Sound asleep, I was awakened by a loud banging on my door in the middle of the night. I struggled to find my lounging pajamas, pushed my sleep mask up onto my forehead, and stumbled to the front door.

It was the farmer. He looked me up and down and said, "Are you sick? If so, I can come back."

"What? No, I'm not sick—what time is it anyway?"

"Just after six-thirty."

At least three other times, farmers who came by in the morning asked if I was under the weather. I got irked by their comments until it dawned on me that, in their mind, anyone living on a farm who wasn't up and dressed by 6:30 *must* be ill. After that, I started telling people to stop by after lunch.

I would come out of my barn and look up to see a car slow down and snap a picture of me. This happened regularly. "What's he doing with that shovel—oh, look he's digging with it—get a picture!" Like they think I should have an assistant for that kind of thing. There were still people out here naïve enough to think fame equaled wealth, and I was probably the most notable name that had resided here in decades. One morning in the fall of '04, hunched over a studio mic, Tom, of *BOB & TOM*, asked, "So where exactly did you buy this farm?"

"Hillsboro, Ohio," I replied. And just like that, I put Hillsboro on the map, so to speak, and myself as its unlikely celebrity. Sometimes people stopped to take a selfie with me and always they were listeners of the show.

I became a regular on *BOB & TOM* and their portrayal of me as "a metrosexual with a little too much fashion sense for a straight man" was popular with listeners, and my off-the-wall, conservative opinions resonated with Midwest audiences. But it was when I'd announced in their studio in late '04, "Oh, by the way, I moved out of LA and bought a farm in Ohio," that Tom Griswold jumped on it, seeing the comedic possibilities. My audience grew substantially and over the next five years and I gained an entirely new fan base that I would never have figured on. Farmers.

Toward the end of 2004 I was trying to figure out what one had to do to "winterize" a farm, if there was such a thing. I stood in my yard watching the heating oil guy with a cigarette hanging out of his mouth fill the heating oil tank for my home. I'd just stacked twenty bags of fertilizer in the garage and realized that my home was basically a bomb on a foundation. My yard had a mole problem and there were raised paths under the grass going every which way and it made my yard look like it had varicose veins. What a strange new world I'd staked out.

About a year later, I was standing in my driveway and my only neighbor within a half mile was screaming at me. He was pacing back and forth in his yard, though *yard* was a stretch—it was more of a clearing with a double-wide trailer. There were three cars lined up end to end out front that seemed to serve as a privacy fence, and all of this was no more than seventy yards directly across the road from me. His wife stood in the doorway like a ringside boxing manager, egging him on as he got more and more belligerent. His name was Shawn—not to be mistaken for the other Shawn that lived a half mile down the road. This Shawn across the road was pissed.

Two days before, I had put up a big sodium light on a pole out by the barn. At night it was pitch black and you couldn't see your hand in front of your face unless there was a good moon out. Shawn didn't like the light and had shimmied up a tree, reached over and spray painted the entire light cover black.

"Are you fucking kidding me?" I said to him the next day. "You come on to my property, climb a tree, and cover my light because *you* don't *like* it?"

"We like it dark up here on the hill at night," Shawn said.

It escalated. I don't remember what I said but whatever it was they must have been *fighting* words because he started coming toward me.

"I will kick your fuckin' ass," he said. Shawn was in his mid-twenties—half my age—lean and wiry, which was easy to see since he had peeled his shirt off as he came toward me.

As I stood there smoking a cigarette, only one thought went through my head: "How ironic—just when I'm ready to stand up for myself in a fight, forty years of smoking makes me gasp just climbing a flight of stairs."

Shawn was now in the road, still screaming, and about thirty feet from me. In my head I heard, "If he gets me down on the ground, I'm finished." Then I took the cigarette out of my mouth and flicked it away toward the yard. I saw the cigarette, turning end over end, arcing through the air, and as I watched it, I said to myself, very matter-of-factly, "That was my last cigarette. I am going to get my lungs back and I am going to kick that hillbilly's ass."

And at that very moment, Shawn stopped. Maybe he saw whatever was in my eyes or maybe he just stopped because he knew that once he set foot on my property, he was the one at fault from the sheriff's standpoint. He turned around, still cursing under his breath, and went back to his trailer.

I never had another cigarette. I never had withdrawals, I never even *thought* about cigarettes after that day

That first two years was a whirlwind of learning curves during the week and touring on the road doing my standup on weekends. I was always busy, but had no real friends in Hillsboro, which at that point was just a place where I drove to get groceries. The first time it hit me that my life had taken a turn for the *much better*, I was onstage. I've had more than one revelation about myself or my place in the world while on a standup stage. My style has always been to explore a topic aloud, mostly through improvisation, while using the audience as a sounding board for the material's humor, but more importantly for its honesty. Discussing my transition from LA to a farm, I'd observed, "In Hollywood I spent five years in therapy and it turned out all I ever needed to do was *chores*."

I'd been so engrossed in learning about farming specifics and rural life in general that I hadn't stopped to consider the change to my mental state since moving. My cynicism was waning ever so slightly, my optimism was cautiously re-emerging, and my long, life-sucking depression had disappeared. How could it *not*? Out here in the country people *waved* at you as you drove by. Housewives left eggs in a box by the road—you could stop and take out a dozen for $1.50 on the honor system. When someone came out and repaired your tractor they billed you when they got around to it, which was often months down the road. Other than the meth labs, it was like being dropped into a Norman Rockwell painting.

In spring of 2006 I was sweating like a pig trying to dig two unbelievably stubborn, overgrown yew bushes out of the ground in the front yard. Like every project on the farm, I attacked it like I was still thirty, trying to cut the roots with my shovel with such force that I thought I might break the arch in my foot. Then a horn honked and I turned to see my father pull into the driveway in a Dodge van.

"Hey there," I said.

"I can't tell who's winning that battle, you or the bush!"

It was a little jarring, maybe even a little irksome to hear him being so buddy-buddy, but I was still glad to see him. He'd called the day before and said he wanted to come over and check out my new place. It had been close to two years since that first time I'd gone to visit him in Barnesville. We went inside, I showed him around, made some coffee, and we made what most people would say was small talk except it wasn't small because I still hung onto his every sentence trying to get an idea of who I was.

"Now did you know that in the early 1800s, a lot of people mixed their coffee with chicory bark? There was a reason for this . . ."

After a while he said, "Let's go out and tackle those bushes," and we did. He took my shovel and poked at the hole that I'd dug all around the bush.

"These roots are deep. I think we're going to kill ourselves trying to get that out with just a shovel. I have something in the van that might work." He came back with a "come-along," a small winch-type thing, and wrapped one end of the thick cable around the root ball and gave me the other end.

"Pull your truck up here and attach that to the bumper. The truck might just pull it out." I hooked it to my truck and he talked me through it: "Give it some gas. Okay, ease up. Okay, now slowly creep forward." It took a few tries but then the bush popped out of the ground. We did the same to the other one.

"Wow. I've tried three different times this week to get those out and you come along and they're out in thirty minutes!"

"That's what happens when two great minds get together."

Was he just parroting a cliché or did he actually mean to say that? My thought was interrupted by the phone ringing in the house.

"I'll be right back."

It was my current girlfriend. She asked what I was up to.

"Remember those bushes I've been trying to get rid of in the front yard? My dad came over to see me and we figured out a way to get them pulled out." I paused. "That's the first time my dad and I have ever done anything together."

I barely finished the sentence before bursting into tears. A son shouldn't have to utter that sentence at age fifty-two. I tried to tell her that. I wanted her to know I wasn't just being a psycho crybaby, that this was momentous but I was crying too hard and only managed "I'll call you later," and hung up.

Later that day we went into uptown Hillsboro to the diner and ran into someone I knew. When I opened my mouth, I said, "Hi Buck, this is my dad. He came out to visit." They chatted but all I could think was how alien it sounded to say "my dad." Not just alien, it sounded taboo—my experience had never allowed for it. I felt like I'd appropriated the word *dad* from a culture I'd never belonged to. Over the course of my life I'd probably said *nigger* more times than I'd ever uttered *dad*. A telling and sad commentary that the one word, for me, had far less baggage attached than the other.

My dad stayed the night and in the morning we had breakfast and he left. We promised to see each other again soon. I went back inside and, because the exhaust fan over the stove wasn't working, the house smelled like corn mush for the rest of the day.

I started up a small cow/calf operation, meaning I owned cows that I would impregnate with the help of a borrowed bull. Then I'd tend to my cows until the calves were born, which is almost the same gestation period as a human. The calves stayed on the farm until they were old enough to wean and put some weight on, at which point they were sold. It was essentially bovine sex trafficking.

Though I wasn't really making money raising cattle, it still felt good to make the land productive and make myself productive as well. Where the farm *had* been productive in a very odd way, was through my standup. The material wrote itself. Whether it was my pitiful lack of tools, my ignorance of livestock, or simply the rural environs as in:

"It's scary out on my farm—did you know that at night a possum walking through a cornfield sounds exactly like three men with an ax?"

I spent my days figuring out farm life and my weekends on stage discussing the same. I was trying to figure out how to tighten a barbed wire fence and Hollywood was but a distant memory when, in the summer of '07, my manager called for the first time in ages. "I got you a deal for your own comedy special," he said.

"What? Why now?"

"You're welcome."

For seven years, I'd tried to land a special of my own when I lived out there and now, when I'd done my best to forget the place, they were coming around.

"I also got you a hundred thousand dollar performance fee. You'll have to come to LA for a couple of months to do practice sets and then shoot the special in September."

"I can't. I have calves being born in September and I need to be here when that happens," I told him, aware of how odd that sounded. I reminded him that my biggest fan base was in the Midwest so it made sense to shoot it out here. I'd only have to be away from the farm for a couple days that way. My manager got the suits at Comedy Central to relent and we filmed *Irked and Miffed* in Toledo that Fall.

The special aired the following spring on a Friday—at one in the morning. It was bad enough when Hollywood jerks you around face-to-face, but to get screwed over from two thousand miles away was, well, not surprising at all. A few days later my manager phoned again to tell me I was number one in the over-forty demographic.

"That's good!" I said.

"Yeah, except Comedy Central said that they don't want to appeal to the over-forty crowd. They want to skew to a younger audience. You did really good numbers, Drew—I don't know why they buried it."

They aired it twice more at 3 a.m. I later learned that *Irked and Miffed* was one of the highest rated specials among some of the biggest names in standup, but somewhere, someone didn't want me to get any more fame than I had. I should have been irked, maybe miffed, and definitely cynical.

But those things had disappeared. I was on a farm with a view that went for miles, I was making $200K a year, and lived in a friendly, small town.

For decades, all I'd wanted was my own comedy special, but when it came around, I realized that the most consequential change in my new life actually took place on the day I saw a teenager lighting up a cigarette at a local gas station. I knew his parents and I said, "Do your mom and dad know you smoke?" The kid tossed the cigarette and pedaled off on his bike and I laughed at how hokey I'd sounded. And I understood for the first time what the concept of "community" meant. The interaction with the kid had been me giving a shit about someone that I had no connection to—other than by way of our shared locale, our *community*. I'd *cared*—a concept that I was mostly unfamiliar with. I'd lived my entire adult life in the anonymity of cities: New York, San Francisco, Cincinnati, Los Angeles. Cities foster anonymity. If your neighbor in the apartment upstairs was clomping around it might as well be a large rat scurrying about. If someone died in my apartment building the news was, "Did you hear that the old lady who lived on the third floor died?"

Not in Hillsboro. Death was personal. When Mrs. Wilkin died, you knew who she was—she had a daughter, you'd met her grandkids. *It suddenly seemed to matter.* Hillsboro showed me those connections between people. I knew Mr. Walton from the stockyards, his son owned the tire shop uptown. I talked to the bagboy at Kroger and found out he's Mr. Walton's grandson. And now I was connected to these people. I felt like I belonged to something.

When you exit the Cincinnati/Northern Kentucky International Airport, it's only a mile until you reach I-275, the freeway that goes around Cincinnati. When you reach the onramps, you have but one decision to make—turn right, taking 275 East, toward Cincinnati and beyond to Hillsboro, or turn left toward Lawrenceburg, Indiana. Ninety percent of drivers will turn right toward the city, the suburbs, and families. Ten percent will turn left where there's only one destination—the Hollywood casino.

On any given Sunday from 2006 through 2009, after a weekend of mostly sold out shows on *The BOB & TOM Comedy Tour*, I'd exit the plane on Sunday afternoons and skip to the parking garage with cash and checks totaling five or six grand. This went on week after week, all year long excluding summers, for four years. More money than I'd ever made in my life, and almost entirely disposable income because my only fixed expenses were an $850 monthly mortgage payment on the farm, cat food, and hay.

That first year, ten times out of ten, I turned left on 275 and was in the casino within twenty minutes. I would invariably drive home around dawn on Monday morning, passing by farmers already long awake, and sometimes out of sheer guilt I'd take time to feed the cattle before I fell into bed.

I did the same thing the second year.

The third year, as I walked through the terminal to the parking garage I started having The Conversation in my head, the one that you have when trying to talk sense into yourself to refrain from imminently doing something that you know you shouldn't—like gambling or meeting up with a married person—but you already know which voice is going to lose the argument. But you have The Conversation with yourself anyway because at least then it seems like you *really tried.*

By the fourth year, I was hating myself for losing fifteen hundred dollars every weekend and frittering away my success and otherwise wonderful life, but justifying it because, *Why not? I'm going home to an empty house and there's no one that I'm leaving all my stuff to.* I had a problem.

One Monday morning, I was driving through uptown Hillsboro and saw that a real estate auction was happening at the old armory building uptown. I had meant to attend it but because I'd been at the casino the night before, I'd forgotten about it. I pulled over and asked the auctioneer if I could have a bidder's number. "Well, there's only you and this gentleman," he said, referring to an older man in bib overalls. I liked the armory, a solid two-story brick structure uptown, but I didn't know what it was worth or how high I should bid. I reached into my pocket. I had exactly $3,200 on me, what was left of my $6,000 from Hollywood the night before. The auctioneer had said that 10 percent was due today and the balance in thirty days. "Okay," I said to myself, "I'll bid up to thirty-two thousand. I know it's worth at least that much. If I get it, great. If not, I'll just deposit my money in the bank and go get some breakfast."

If you know anything about small town auctions, bidders are cheapskates and, as a result, slow. The auctioneer started the bidding at five thousand, in one thousand increments, and it took fifteen minutes to get to ten thousand because every time I would up the bid, the other guy would stare at the ground and kick the dirt for seven minutes. After we got to twenty thousand, I thought he might speed up, but no, he took his sweet time and finally said, "twenty-one." I immediately said "Twenty-two!" almost before he finished getting his bid out of his mouth. He looked at me almost dumbfounded. As if to say, "You're losing your advantage, you're showing how much you want this."

And, as if to maintain the time-honored rhythm of the auction, he kicked at the dirt for four minutes, looked up and said, "Twenty-two thousand, two hundred."

"Twenty-four!" I said immediately, trying to be polite and not show my exasperation.

He sped up a little bit and when we finally got to $28,000, I couldn't take it anymore. "Thirty!"

Both the other bidder and the auctioneer looked at each other, then at me.

"But sir, the bid is only at twenty-eight thousand," said the auctioneer.

"Yeah, I know. But I'm starving and need to get some food in me."

The other bidder looked at the auctioneer as if to say, "Can he do that?"

But instead, he took a minute, and said, "Thirty thousand and one hundred." Looking at me as if to say, "You didn't scare me none. I'm still here."

Before he could finish his look at me, I retorted with "Thirty-two thousand!"

He looked at me disgustedly. "He can have it."

I gave the auctioneer my $3,200, got a closing date, and went to breakfast. I ate my eggs, immensely proud of myself. *I just bought my first commercial building.* What mattered though was that it got my casino visits under control. I had thirty days to come up with twenty-nine grand. And another twenty thousand for repairs. That freaked me out enough that I turned right onto I-275 as I left the airport and went straight home every weekend for the next six months and by 2009 my gambling was under control.

Early on we're taught to know our strengths but it's later in life that we figure out that it's often more valuable to know our weaknesses. The real estate ads were doing their damnedest to find buyers in the recession of '08, and if a vacant building could have low self-esteem, these headlines confirmed it. Empty storefronts greeted most visitors when they drove through uptown Hillsboro, and I was shocked at how cheaply properties were selling for. I had a longtime interest in real estate but it was out of my reach until now. I began buying mostly vacant commercial buildings, partially for investment and partially because they were my "Enforced Savings Plan" that kept me off the craps tables.

"He's a savior and a godsend for pumping much-needed investment money into uptown Hillsboro!" the locals said.

"He's a goddamn fool is what he is," the locals said.

Either way, in the span of three years I found myself becoming the largest property owner uptown. A former bank building. An empty opera house. A feed mill. The old municipal offices. I was crazy busy. I was doing shows in Philadelphia, Rockford, and Champaign, Illinois, and four separate shows in Indiana. If it wasn't standup, it was real estate development. I'd bought all those buildings and now needed to renovate them. And if it wasn't real estate related, it was about cattle. Grand Rapids, Wilmington, Toledo, Burlington, Iowa, Wabash, Illinois. Leave on Friday, come home Sunday. Feed cattle. Deal with building contractors.

Suddenly I had major investments to protect. I thought about that day just a few years before—the lowest point of my life—when I'd wandered, sobbing, into that church in LA. I still had no idea what that day was about, but somehow so much of *me* had returned—no, it was a *better me*, a more evolved me. My luck, my creativity, I had energy to burn and whatever this community thing was. Feeling settled for once? Belonging? Acceptance?

Regardless, these became the best years of my middle-aged life, raising cattle during the week, weekends on the road doing shows, and investing my paychecks in Hillsboro real estate. And in the process I negotiated a peace treaty with my vices. This was my new life and I wasn't planning on disrupting any of that. Why would I?

CHAPTER 16

A Convergence of Sorts

Almost everyone who goes into politics does so because they planned to. They *want* to be in politics. Maybe they're involved early on as an activist, or as a party organizer. They plot. They build. Maybe they start out as a city councilman, then a county commissioner, then state rep, maybe a run for state senator. They figure out how they might make the jump to congressman. These people always have an eye toward the next post. In fact, the only people I can think of that are in politics that didn't plan to be there are those widows that you occasionally read about, whose husbands were senators or congressmen that suddenly dropped dead, and their political parties ask the spouses to fill out what's left of the guys' terms. But no one died and made me mayor. Yet again, a completely unexpected turn appeared in the road, and I just gunned it.

In June 2010, an old friend from Cincinnati, now a producer for Rocky Mountain PBS, flew in to talk to me about a project.

"Drew, I want to do a reality show about you and the farm."

"Hmm." Skeptical.

"It'll have kind of a *Green Acres* feel, and to round it out we'll cut to some of your standup and follow your dealings uptown with the historic building projects."

"The idea of a reality show is as appealing as a bone marrow transplant."

"I want this to feel like documentary, not reality TV. You have a lot of visibility in Hillsboro, we want to capture that too—the fish out of water aspect. Let's shoot a pilot, see how it looks."

I trusted John's sensibility. "Okay, what can it hurt?"

Meanwhile, after two years of cajoling, I'd finally gotten my best friend of twenty-five years, Bob Lambert, to move to Hillsboro after he'd been laid off from working at an assisted living center out west. It was great having him around and I'd been showing him the town. One day he and I were walking up Main Street. Uptown Hillsboro was a sad affair. Four tattoo parlors, three used clothing consignment shops, two check cashing stores.

"Jesus, who the hell runs this place?" I said, waving my hand across the landscape, disgustedly. "I could do better than this."

"So why don't you?" said Bob.

In November, John came back to shoot footage for the pilot. Bob staked out locations around town and I'd show up, walking into a scene trying to keep it as natural and as improvisational as one can in the middle of a small town. One scene was in a diner. Locals were all seated on counter stools and in booths in that perfectly natural tableau that you see in every folksy Iowa caucus clip. The crew sat me on a stool and after a few observational snippets about Hillsboro's woes, someone piped up: "Drew, everyone around here seems to know you. Heck, why don't you run for mayor?"

I laughed. "That'll be the day."

"And cut!" said the director. Someone had prompted that guy to ask the question. And yet, weeks before, I'd talked to a couple of people very discreetly about the idea of running for mayor. But there is no such thing as discreetly talking about anything in a small town. It's like a murder conspiracy—someone always talks.

It was while I was in the bank making a deposit, making small talk with the bank teller, a middle-aged woman who knew me from my frequent visits.

"I'm kicking around the idea of running for mayor," I said. "What do you think? Would you maybe vote for me if I did?"

"Heck, it doesn't matter to me if you're gay or straight, you'd have my vote," she said, counting out my cash.

Gay or straight? I thought. *Why did she say that? Did she think I was gay?* It was probably my hair. I've always made a statement with my hair. At that time, it was colored with spiky highlights and cut in a kind of David Bowie meets Rod Stewart look. But I just looked like an aging rocker, not an aging homosexual. Granted, I was in a rural Appalachian town and wearing tight black corduroy jeans and a black turtleneck.

"You have a farm south of town, don't you?" she asked.

"Yes. I have a cow/calf operation in Newmarket. My girlfriend helps me a lot. She's a huge help—my girlfriend that is." Why was I trying to convince her of my heterosexuality? I already had her vote.

"This whole town is run by a bunch of good ol' boys. Has been for years," she offered as I was leaving.

I went down to Holtfield Station, the truck stop/convenience store/sandwich shop/coffeehouse that was down on the south end of town for some lunch, thinking about whether this mayoral thing was actually something I wanted to do. I stared at my coffee, debating the pros and cons, when I was interrupted by a voice behind me.

"Hear you're runnin' for mayor."

"What?" I said, turning around. The only person I'd even mentioned it to was the bank teller, barely an hour ago.

"Word around town is that you're going to run. It's about time we got someone who actually wants to try to do something around here," the thirty-something guy said as he kept walking to the deli counter. "Good luck!"

"Uh, thanks," I managed, still dumbstruck. A minute or so later, the same guy came walking past me and I heard myself blurt, "So, what do you think the biggest problem is, in Hillsboro?"

Without hesitating, he said, "Goddamn fire department—you need to do something about that overpaid fire department."

As he was walking out the door, I yelled after him, "I'm going to do something about that!" And just like that, I committed myself to public service. From that day on, it all felt a little out of my control.

It would be convenient to tell the story of my unlikely path to the mayor's desk by pushing the narrative of my Awakening—where a unique outsider jolts Hillsboro into a renaissance, infecting citizens with optimism and community involvement. In my twenty years of touring small cities in the Heartland, I'd seen firsthand the slow disintegration of most towns and the vibrancy of the few that had re-invented themselves, and it would be easy to pretend that that I, by using my visibility, could effect these changes in our town.

All that was true, but initially—before I was swept up in the possibilities of great things—I was propelled by less noble considerations: survival. A rivulet of self-doubt ran under or through my big aspirations. By late 2010, my standup career was stalling. The *BOB & TOM* tours had all but ended, and the political correctness that infected everything was becoming a pandemic of intolerance. But more troubling was that I hadn't written new material in almost three years. The seduction of the big theater tours where fans just wanted to hear their favorite bits made any urgency to create anything new melt away. I was headed toward becoming a comedic jukebox living on dated routines, and I was never going to let that happen.

I was also getting somewhat bored. I'd been on the road for a quarter century. I saw the mayor's office as my new creative endeavor and it was all fresh and brimming with possibility. The thought of staying close to home was appealing, even though home was part of the problem. I didn't really have a home, I had a house. At fifty-seven, I was no longer a single man—I was long past eligible bachelor status. I was a middle-aged man living by himself on a farm feeding his cattle and cat without much sense of purpose. What could go wrong there? Dabbling in opioids, in the company of strumpets and Jezebels, all against the backdrop of casinos? Because that's the direction my car was hydroplaning. And when I looked at this path and asked, "Why?" the answer usually came back, "Why not?"

I was backsliding. So maybe this mayoral thing wasn't just about me trying to turn around a city—this was equally about a city helping to turn around me.

And if I needed any more incentive for a change, the week of Christmas 2010, the front page of the local *Times Gazette* blared "A Holiday Hit," a story about a local candle maker who'd just created a "mancandle," named after me and called the "Drew la-la." Marketed as a candle "that smells like there's a man around the house . . . the Drew la-la is in a class all its own." "Beautiful. Just fucking beautiful," I said to myself. "This, Drew, is the rest of your life here if you don't do something more meaningful."

I asked those closest to me about the idea of running.

"What in God's name are you thinking?" said my mom.

"Why the hell would you want to be in politics? You don't need that bullshit," said one longtime friend.

"Interesting that you'd want to derail a perfectly great comedy career," my friend Tom Griswold said.

"We're going to part ways now," my manager said.

What was entailed in a mayor's job anyway? What experience did someone need? What did it pay? What were the hours? I didn't know anything about elected offices. It turned out that the bar is so low that any idiot can hold public office, as I was soon to prove. Turns out that no experience for any public office, including the mayor, was needed. There was actually little that was required of a mayor—most of the work of the city was done by others. Yes, there were decisions to be made, but overall, you made your own schedule. There were no set hours, and in fact, the mayor's office for the City of Hillsboro was considered part-time. All of this was completely alien to my sense of how to run a business. Part-time?

Hillsboro's mayor's office for much of the last twenty years had been run by Democrats. I knew the current mayor, Dick Zink. A lifelong Democrat, he had followed the traditional route to the office by being on city council, then becoming council president, and finally mayor. I'd met with him two or three times, usually to ask about zoning or some development question. Whenever I walked in, he was sitting behind his desk with his hands folded in front of him like he was getting ready to say grace before a meal. His desktop usually had little on it except for a pen. The bar seemed pretty low indeed.

The pay for being the mayor was $25,000 a year and I tried to compute that. The only correlation I had was comparing it to a standup gig. The mayor's gig was the equivalent to seven shows. I didn't even know how it would affect my comedy career. At the time, I was still doing shows three weekends a month plus a couple of mid-week corporate shows. Would I have to cut back?

And yet, this mayor thing was intriguing. When people said, "Why would you want to go into politics?" I scoffed. I wasn't going into politics, this was just me taking a mayoral job. It was my return to the business world—governing a small city was no different than running a medium-sized company, right? This was simply a "turnaround situation." A bloated corporation, fraught with waste and poor morale that had lost its competitive edge and needed a new CEO to get the ship righted. And to begin this job I simply had to win a pesky election.

But the 85 percent of the time that I was clear-eyed and lucid, living my day-to-day life in my adopted hometown, I started seeing a bigger picture. *I could make a difference here.* This was a surreal concept for me. Not even when I'd been taking psychedelics in the '70s did notions like this ever materialize. The idea of doing something for a cause bigger than me was, well, ludicrous. What possible cause could be bigger than me?

And yet, I was intrigued. And the more I dwelled on it, the more I was convinced it was the right thing to do. The idea that I might be able to make Hillsboro a model for midwestern-small-town-revitalization was compelling. And if we could do it here, perhaps it could be replicated in other small towns that suffered the same problems. Sure, it was a beyond-bold plan, but then, I was never known for doing things half-assed.

Yes, I needed to do something more with my life, and yes, I wanted to do something new. My car could have hydroplaned in a different direction. Had I run across a box of cassette tapes at a yard sale called, "Make money by learning how to be an auctioneer in just thirty days!" I might've dived into that scenario instead. Timing is everything. But I also wondered if maybe I could even do this mayoral thing well.

If I spy a political bumper sticker, I sometimes pull up alongside just so I can see what the asshole looks like who would vote for that candidate. That's as far as I'd go out of my way to get politically involved. Part drug-using Republican, part Polite Anarchist, I'd always been anti-authority, but was also anti-government in a big way. If I was in a tame discussion about the rising costs of my monthly cable bill, I'd still find a way to bring up what the feds did to Randy and Vicky Weaver up on Ruby Ridge. Through the '90s and early 2000s, I became, like many Americans, infected with the politics of anger watching a deteriorating Heartland while performing to an increasingly cynical Midwest.

There was a distinct change in the zeitgeist of the Midwest. People resented the intrusion of the culture wars and forced mandates that seemed to be popping up everywhere, particularly in the workplace. As I played town after town in the Rustbelt Midwest, I was pissed—and sad for my part of the country. Peoria. Terre Haute. Richmond, Indiana. Dayton. Lima. Toledo. Decatur. South Bend. Ft. Wayne. Davenport. Keokuk. Dubuque. Cedar Rapids.

By the time I decided to run for mayor, I had a hard-boiled sense of what needed to happen. People were upset that far-off agencies like the EPA were mandating unaffordable improvements, drug houses seemed to operate mere blocks from the police station, and I wanted to find a way to curtail the exodus of young people leaving town by finding reasons for them to start families here. How I was going to accomplish all that, I had no idea yet.

It was the politics of right-wing anger merged with a plan for economic development. I was exactly the disenfranchised citizen that would one day usher in Donald Trump. And although I saw Hillsboro as a small town that simply needed new revenue sources, a balanced budget, and a cleanup plan, on a grander scale I didn't see Hillsboro as a distinct city—I viewed it as a tiny piece of America. Though it wasn't obvious to most voters, I wasn't running for mayor of Hillsboro. To me, Hillsboro was every beat-down town in the Midwest and I saw Hillsboro as a template for revitalization that, if successful, could be replicated all over the state of Ohio. Therefore, my campaign resembled a state race rather than a local campaign. The confluence of events made this a small town mayoral race like no other. But it would catch up to me later.

"So how the hell do I actually do this?" I asked, pouring our coffees.

Bob Lambert had grown up in Middletown, Ohio—just down the street from J. D. Vance who would go on to write *Hillbilly Elegy*. Hillsboro, like Vance's Middletown, was steeped in Appalachian culture. Bob's father had been a city council member in Middletown so Bob knew something of small city politics.

"First thing you need to do is establish residency. Your farm is six miles from town. According to the Ohio Revised Code, you must have your residence in the city limits."

That should be easy, I told him. My mom had purchased a small cottage the previous year as a place to stay when she came up to visit, three or four times a year. I could claim that house on West Street as my residence.

"Okay, so how do I prove my residency?"

"Just get the utility bills in your name for that address and go to the Board of Elections and change your residence from the farm to the house in town."

"Piece of cake."

"Then, you need a campaign manager. You want to find someone who's respected in town, who knows a lot of people. They make sure your yard signs are getting placed, and they organize fundraising for your campaign."

We made a list of local Republicans—business and community leaders that would be credible. I rubbed my hands together, "This is exciting! Aren't you glad I got you to move here!"

"Oh yes, this small town with no future and no Chinese takeout is much nicer than sunny Southern California."

I knew he was glad to be back in Ohio though. We'd been best friends for a long time and I'd missed his dry sense of humor. It felt good to be busy with something meaningful and he was on board with all of it.

Three days later, I met up with Bob again.

"Of the eight people on our list for campaign manager, six were very polite about turning me down," I told him.

"And the other two?" Bob asked.

"They also turned me down and weren't polite about it at all,"

Disappointed about being snubbed by the Who's Who of Hillsboro—retired bankers, current bankers, realtors, and assorted business owners, all I could think was, *What was there not to like?* I was a very likeable guy. I had good ideas.

I was reading up on how elections are held when Bob came over. "I think I found a campaign manager," he said. "Michelle Truitt worked on the state rep's campaign and he got elected. She's a huge fan of yours, so maybe she would manage the campaign."

Hmm. Michelle seemed so small town—not like the savvy, ready-with-a-quip campaign managers you saw in TV soundbites. I was also concerned because she was a huge fan of mine. I had learned something about fans—if they get to know you as a person, sometimes they aren't fans anymore.

"I'd love to!" Michelle squealed.

I asked her a lot of questions about local elections—about visibility and marketing and town halls. I asked her if email was the most effective way to get the word out of my mayoral run.

"Oooh. I don't have email," Michelle confided.

"You mean you need to set up a new email account?"

"No, I mean I've never had email. I don't even know how to use it."

"What? How do you deal with things online, like purchases, stuff like that?"

"I don't have the internet—I've been meaning to get it, though." She sensed what she thought was my disappointment but was actually my incredulity. "Campaigning is not rocket science. We just get yard signs and you have to go door-to-door a lot. Anyway, a lot of older people don't have email or go on the internet much, so you need to visit them face-to-face."

I recalled my campaign "announcement" at the bank. Maybe she was right.

"All right, you're hired!" I said, not really knowing how we were going to make this work.

"Oh, you don't have to pay me," she said quickly.

"That was just a figure of speech," I said. It seemed like we were off to a good start.

On a freezing February morning in 2011, Michelle and I went down to the Board of Elections to file my candidacy for the mayoral primary. This election was already shaping up to be something the likes of which Hillsboro had never seen simply because there was going to be a Republican primary. Traditionally, the Republicans met, chose their ordained candidate, and everyone else got out of the way. Not this time. Not one, but two other Republicans filed to run against me in a primary. They assumed I had no chance. One was a young audio/video technician whose only political experience was videotaping city council meetings. The other was a city council member who was a military veteran and was only known because he was always somewhere on active duty.

One would think that, with my celebrity status and the *Times Gazette* covering me on every slow news day (i.e., almost every day), this would be an easy choice for citizens.

"Drew because you moved here from LA, most people think you're from there, which is not good," Michelle said.

"I grew up less than fifty miles from here!"

"Well that's what is being spread around town by the other two candidates and by people that don't like you."

"Who doesn't like me, for Christ's sake?"

"Uh, people that think 'for Christ's sake' is blasphemous, for one. Then a lot of folks think you're rich. You look different with your crazy hair. But mostly, you're not from here."

"Fuck. I'm not rich—I've bought some battered buildings uptown and have a small farm."

"That's another thing—people think you cuss too much. And around here, if you've been on *The Tonight Show* and have released CDs and lived in Hollywood, you can't convince some of them that you aren't rich—but you are still really popular with most people."

Just growing up here gave the other guys an edge even if they had no real solutions for Hillsboro. They were campaigning to neighbors they'd known all their lives. In my mind, I was campaigning to fellow Americans who were as frustrated as I was about out of control government—and our local fire department was the example I used.

My fellow candidates went knocking on familiar doors:

"Hi, Mrs. Wilson!"

"Oh, Hi Terry! I haven't seen you since I taught you in my third grade class."

"That's right! I'm running for mayor now."

"Would you like to come in for some pie?"

When I went to the same house:

"Hi, Mrs. Wilson, my name's Drew Hastings and I . . ."

"Oh, I know who you are."

"Is that good or bad?"

"Depends what comes out of your mouth next."

"It smells like you just baked a pie!"

"I haven't baked anything."

More than once I'd spill my guts about what I saw as the big problems Hillsboro faced, then I'd go off about how the bloated fire department was getting paid triple time, not knowing that the woman in front of me was a fireman's relative.

The negativity ramped up.

"He's not from here."

"He doesn't know anything about our problems."

"He's aloof, disconnected. And I don't like his hair."

This was all so surreal to me, but I just kept plodding along, listening to Bob, my unofficial consultant, and to my implausible, but official campaign manager, Michelle.

"Michelle, where the fuck are we going?"

"Oh! You hush now!"

"Hush now? Nobody says 'Hush now.' Are we in 1896? Why am I hushing?"

"You can't say those f-words! We're stopping in at this fish fry to meet and greet some folks."

I didn't know the first thing about how local politics worked or how the divisions of power between a city council and administration worked. I just saw a problem to be solved. I was an outsider, and that was my big advantage, at least in my mind—I was unfettered.

In political campaigns, you have a very short time to get someone's attention. Political yard signs are a good example. As I started designing mine, I had phrases like, "Making Hillsboro a better place to live!" and "The future of Hillsboro is no laughing matter," cutesy plays on my comedic background.

"Oh God no! you don't want the word 'laughing' on a campaign sign," a panicky Michelle would cry. "And you can't have these long sentences on your sign—people will never see them."

She was right. A driver doing thirty-five miles an hour past an eighteen-inch sign doesn't see much. I thought about what I was trying to convey to people. I wanted to help get this city get turned around financially, and clean up the blight.

"Hastings for Hillsboro," I blurted.

Michelle, said, "Perfect. See, you're getting it."

The primary debate was April 5 between the three Republican candidates. Not only was it rare to have a Republican primary, it was unheard of to have an actual debate in advance of one, and sponsored by the *Times Gazette*, the local daily newspaper.

I figured I would have an edge in a public debate because I was used to public speaking. I had also spent a lot of time doing my homework on Hillsboro's last twenty years and the problems that seemed to always get talked about but that no one ever seemed to change.

There was an overflow crowd of two hundred people at the community center and the crowd was peppered with supporters in blue "Drew Crew" T-shirts. Throughout the two-hour event, we discussed the fire and EMS issue, which was a top concern. When my turn came I simply said, "The people of Hillsboro have had to listen to this issue forever. We need to just flat out resolve it and move on."

Traffic congestion, a longtime gripe, was discussed, as well as the condition of streets. Potholes seemed to be everywhere due to a lack of funds and other priorities. I brought up agri-tainment, the Midwest trend of enticing suburbanites out to agricultural events. My two opponents rolled their eyes at the idea, but the audience gave me loud applause. I don't think they were enamored with agri-tourism as much as they were just excited that someone was coming up with out of the box ideas and was enthused about presenting them.

Then the topic went to uptown revitalization, which was one of the issues I was really passionate about. Three months earlier, a 1957 film of

Hillsboro's sesquicentennial had mesmerized me. The vibrant uptown shopping district, every building filled to capacity with retail and business services, and the streets thronged with people scurrying about. This was the story of every small town in the Midwest. Their downtown shopping districts, once the center of everything, had become decimated first by the shopping malls, then the Walmarts, and now by Amazon.

But that '57 film was also a focal point I used to inspire people. For those people that had never seen it, I would describe the vitality of Hillsboro, "I'm not naïve enough to think that we are going to have that Hillsboro again, but we can look at the film as inspiration to revitalize uptown to its rightful place as the center of activity." I made digital copies of the film over the coming months and gave them to people, and I uploaded it to YouTube. At the debate, I realized I hit a nerve with the fear that so many small towns were being smothered by everything from federal mandates to the decline in homeowners, the big box stores, and, very concerning to me, an insidious trend shaping small towns, the "rise of the non-profits."

At the debate's end, I felt pretty good about my showing and Michelle was all atwitter about how I came off. "You were the only one that seemed like you had a plan!" she gushed.

"Thanks, Michelle, but I was in Hollywood for a long time. This was a politics version of an audition and I've done a lot of those—this isn't in the bag yet."

The following months were filled with "Meet the Candidate" events at the Senior Center. VFW fish fries. Then standup dates—Traverse City, Michigan, and Columbus, Indiana. Back for more door-to-door until May 3, primary voting day. Bob Lambert, Michelle, and I went to the newspaper offices to await results. I carried 64 percent of the vote. Three to one over the second place candidate. I'd been pretty confident but this elected office stuff was a whole new ballgame and I didn't take anything for granted. Now onto the general election in the fall.

Linda Vaccariello didn't know what to make of me. The executive editor for *Cincinnati Magazine*, she had come out to do a story. Journalistic cynicism oozed off her like an expensive perfume. The reality show people from

Denver were back shooting farm scenes for the pilot. They were trying to put makeup on my face while I was on the phone booking standup dates when she walked into my kitchen. She probably thought I'd engineered an elaborate PR stunt—which in an earlier time I would certainly have done. She grilled me for two days trying to make sense of my reality—a Hollywood expat, farmer, comedian, real estate magnate wannabe, and mayoral hopeful.

Linda, with photographer in tow, followed me around the farm as I speared hay bales for my cattle and talked about using agriculture to attract tourism. She had attended the earlier primary debate and I reiterated my ideas for reviving Hillsboro's economy. I was to be the keynote speaker for a Future Farmers of America conference the following week and Linda was taking it all in as I tried to juggle the life I had going on besides this election. Two radio interviews that weekend were followed by calls from a few building contractors. Then she left to get facts and figures on our unemployment and drug epidemic problems.

"Could a standup comic be the next mayor of Hillsboro?" said the cover of *Cincinnati Magazine*'s July issue. I flipped through the pages, heavy with twelve color ad layouts touting upscale shoe boutiques, discreet Botox treatments, and the unique benefits of a Montessori education. Then a huge picture of me in sunglasses chewing on a piece of hay. The opposite page blared, "NO JOKE—Comedian Drew Hastings wants to bring jobs, tourists, architectural preservation, and agri-tainment dollars to Hillsboro, Ohio. In return, he'd like to be able to order a hummus plate. Is that too much to ask?"

The headline was accurate, though all I'd said was that Hillsboro only had fast food and I'd like to see some ethnic places open. Suddenly I was the Gentrifying Colonizer. I turned the page where the article actually began and it kicked off with sixty-point font that read, DREW HASTINGS NEEDS HELP. *Fuck you, Linda Vaccariello*, I thought. I had told her that I needed an administrative assistant to help me with everything I had going on and she printed a headline making me sound like a basketcase.

There wasn't much in the article that was inaccurate or untrue. She had done a good job capturing my vision for the city and the problems inherent in the local economy. But when you looked at the whole picture she had painted, it did seem as if I faced a pretty insurmountable task. I put the article down and, for the first time, gulped.

The article closed with an incident that had occurred two months prior, where a woman I'd been dating had filed a complaint with the sheriff's office claiming that I was harassing her. Like I had time for that. She also alleged that I had confessed to her that I had a drug problem that was out of control, complete with quotes from me: "My life is not working." "I have an escape problem."

My first thought, "Wow, I can't believe I opened up to her like that!"

So maybe I did go home and escape some nights. And yes, maybe I was partial to drugs at the time. But after reading the article and seeing the problems this town faced—like so many others in the Midwest—and the uphill battle to fix any of them, I wasn't surprised anyone had an escape problem.

There is no better way for a candidate to connect with voters in a local election than stopping by their homes. Campaigning door-to-door is essentially trick-or-treating for votes. You scope out the most promising houses, ring the doorbell, and a homeowner opens their door, often feigning fright at the specter standing before them. Except that you don't frighten them with a costume, instead you scare them with descriptions of what could happen if they vote for the other guy. Then, after you get your treat—the homeowner's promise of their vote—you scamper off to the next house.

But here's a bit of sobering news. In any given small city, only about 70 percent of residents are registered voters. Of those, only about 25 percent actually vote. So you can see why each one matters. Most candidates have a system for going door to door and they stick to it. You know, much like they plan for their life. They say, "Today, I'm going down this street, around this block, and then return up the opposite side of the street so I end back at my car—that's the most productive and efficient way."

When I campaigned, I might start out with those intentions but then usually got distracted and wound up way off course. Start down a street, ring some doorbells, talk to a few voters, then see someone I know across the street and veer over there to chat. Or I might spot a vintage car I wanted to peer into. Then I'd go back across the street only to forget where I had left off because I hadn't checked them off on my list on account of having left my pen in my car.

Michelle instructed me how it's done in Hillsboro. "When you leave someone's house you'll be tempted to walk the thirty feet across their yard over to the next house. Don't do it! Instead, you have to walk down their walkway, out to the street, along the street, and up the next driveway."

"That's twice as much walking, Michelle."

"Yes, but some voters will crucify you if you take the shortcut—they look out their window to pass judgment on anything moving. They'll say, 'That man is lazy.' Or, 'Mr. Jones just planted new grass seed not two months ago and now this man has come along and ruined it by stomping all over it! I would never vote for him!'"

"For fuck's sake."

"Oh, you hush now!"

Because Hillsboro had been neglected for so long, people just wanted something done about the basics. Potholes. Trash everywhere. Street lights out. Water bills skyrocketing. And as I talked to people, two or three major issues kept coming up.

Early on, I'd asked Michelle what she thought were the biggest problems in Hillsboro.

"The fire department. Everyone is complaining about them," she said without missing a beat. It had come out recently that not only was the fire department the highest paid public employees in the city, many of them were making in excess of $100K a year in a town where the median income was about $31,000. It seemed even more outrageous to folks because it wasn't too far back that the Hillsboro Fire Department was an all-volunteer outfit that did cookouts in front of the station.

"Okay, what else?"

"The police department. People think they're cocky, and unresponsive."

It figured that public sector unions were at the heart of this. Having already taken over the big cities, they were now pushing out to rural areas that were less sophisticated and ripe for plucking. I studied these two topics for months, promising voters I'd do something. I could see that some of my loftier goals of bike paths and economic development were going to maybe simmer on a back burner.

I talked to seniors a lot. I have a soft spot for seniors because they all seem like my grandparents. They liked me too. Old people have a good bullshit meter because they've been around a long time and can tell when they're being told a bunch of crap. My bluntness usually ended with them saying, "Well, you certainly cuss a lot young man but I'll vote for you anyway."

For months it was crazy busy nonstop. Hollywood seemed like a trudge through molasses compared to efforts here. Weekdays I oversaw contractors doing historical repairs on the opera house with grant funding from the state. Then I'd make the three-hour drive to the *BOB & TOM* studios to promote appearances every week or so. Then head out of town for shows on weekends.

In July, a lunch appointment with Laura Curliss was arranged. She was the executive assistant for the mayor in Wilmington, eighteen miles to the north. Laura was an attorney, and a diehard liberal. But she seemed intrigued, maybe a little fascinated by a spiky-haired, anti-authority comedian running for mayor against a good ol' boy system, so I was perfectly willing to put political leanings aside if I could learn something from her. She brought along Sam Stratman, who offered to help me even though my mayoral effort was a big step down from the circles he'd run in. He'd been with Henry Hyde, longtime congressman from Illinois, in DC through the '90s. Sam had been on the Clinton impeachment committee, and was now a political consultant, and involved with local politics in his hometown of Wilmington. I had never known anyone with a political background, let alone someone with his credentials, but it was like people were being led to me and I wasn't about to discard any help.

Our campaign meetings were called "The Bob Evans Summits" because we'd take over a big booth, stuff ourselves on all-day breakfast menus, and strategize. Bob Evans had oversized paper placemats, perfect for scribbling campaign ideas with the crayons they provided for children, but handy for grownups too absent-minded to remember to bring pens.

If politics makes strange bedfellows, then mine were the strangest.

Michelle: "I'm going to make some persimmon pies to take to the senior center so Drew can do a meet and greet."

Sam: "We need to look at doing a targeted series of robocalls to likely primary voters."

Laura: "I'm compiling the true per-person fire coverage costs from across the state."

Me: "A guy on Facebook just called me a faggot."

Bob: "All of you are making valid points."

In late October, there was a debate with my Democratic opponent, John Levo, a longtime bank employee who had opened checking accounts for generations of locals. To the old boys, it was his turn to be mayor. He would be a "same old, same old." And that was the crux of this platform. He hadn't really run a race because I wasn't worthy of his effort. At the debate he'd said, "I don't smoke, I don't do drugs, I'm a Christian."

"Well, you're a better man than I," I said.

Frustrated at my lack of defensiveness, he tried to trap me, saying to audience, "I'd be willing to do a drug test and a background check."

"Then go do one," I replied.

I knew what he was trying to do. It was no secret that there were R-rated standup clips all over the internet of my sexual escapades and past drug use and peppered with profanity throughout, and my detractors had done their best to get it all in front of voters. Even the Associated Press had brought it up.

I was elected Mayor on November 8, 2011, with 62 percent of the vote, a landslide in political terms. Calls and emails from friends and fans poured in telling me that the news of my election was in their local paper or online across much of the country. I was surprised. I never thought of this as being of much interest beyond Cincinnati. I was wrong.

The day after the election, the phone rang. It was a 310 area code. Yes, it was literally Hollywood calling. Ross Mark, a longtime friend of mine in LA, was the talent booker for *The Tonight Show* with Jay Leno. "Jay wants you to do the show."

I was blown away but I at least had the presence of mind to immediately ask, "Do I have to do a set or can I just do the couch?" An important distinction. Comedians always did their standup set, then, if time permitted, Jay might have you on the couch for a minute or two. If I was booked to do the couch only, it was a much bigger deal. "A-list" celebrities and authors went straight to the couch.

"Yeah, the couch," Ross said. "Jay wants to talk about you becoming a mayor and you can work some material in if you want."

"Let's do it."

But before I worried about *The Tonight Show*, which was a week away, I had more pressing matters. Like, thanking people, and putting an administration together. I came out of my uptown office and an out-of-town TV reporter and her cameraman were waiting for me. After asking me for a few comments, she said, "According to your comedy specials and YouTube you've been pretty open about your past drug use, especially marijuana. Do you still use marijuana?" She thrust the mic into my face.

"Ma'am, I do everything but gargle the bongwater." That answer threw her, and she had no follow up question. The cameraman pulled his head away from the eyepiece to look at me. I think he may have laughed. At that, I walked off down the street, both proud of myself for my humorous honesty, and suddenly anxious about whether that was a mistake. *You are the mayor of a city now, Drew.*

It was the first of many reality checks. My thinking that people could and would separate my standup career from my job as the mayor was too optimistic. I'd always assumed that people have a brain and a sense of humor, or at least a sense of irony. That would be beaten out of me quickly.

Jay Leno came back to my green room before the show to chat. "So how you been, Hastings?" He was a truly good guy and always came to talk with you before the show to make sure you were okay. Once on the couch, Jay talked about me being on the show a few years prior and getting a standing ovation, then the reason I was there. "As the very unlikely mayor of a small city." Jay asked, "So, what are some of the biggest problems facing Hillsboro?"

"Small towns are rapidly losing population. So the problem is that every time a teenage girl gets pregnant, somewhere in town, a guy moves out." This got a huge laugh. I took the conversation toward the serious though, talking about issues that needed to be highlighted. I said, "That's why I'm on here, Jay. I'm promoting small town America, promoting Hillsboro." I was fortunate to be on the show with both Vince Gill and Robin Williams, which gave it big ratings. Robin had come backstage before the show to tell me he'd loved my standup special and quoted bits from it. I was honored. He stuck around after his segment on the couch next to me for my bit. He knew that it would be a help to me if he was seen laughing at my lines.

Then Jay said, "So, I understand that you actually had to run as a Republican to get elected, is that right?" I looked at him, a little taken aback. "But I am a Republican, Jay." Robin got a horrified look on his face and Jay seemed a shade flustered, but I was glad I could show America that there were guys with long hair, wearing black turtlenecks that called themselves conservatives. And Hillsboro got a lot of publicity.

I flew back to Ohio knowing that I was probably one of the few who'd ever been on *The Tonight Show* twice for two entirely different careers. Sam, Laura, and I spent the next six weeks looking at résumés and, one week before I took office, we got all of our hiring done. Sam Stratman said, "We have a government." That seemed momentous and I said to the newspaper, "It's more than simply an administration. We've put together a great team that will have a level of professionalism that Hillsboro can be very proud of. You would be hard pressed to find a better team."

The headline on December 28 said, "Fire, EMS to be discussed at special meeting. Contract expires 12/31." The outgoing mayor passed an emergency sixty-day extension to kick it down the road. At least I knew what was facing me.

CHAPTER 17

Mayor

The courtroom was packed on Inauguration Day. Like a house party that way too many people had heard about. My close friends were there, my sister Karen, Lambert, Sam, and my girlfriend at the time. She had felt I should wear a shirt and tie with my suit but I stuck with the black turtleneck.

"I want them to know that I'm not the typical Republican."

Ohio Supreme Court Justice Terrence O'Donnell came down to swear me in. A US congresswoman had come. I read a speech that was too long, too bold, and not the stuff small town mayors ever spoke about. But Hillsboro was a blueprint for something bigger.

I'm sure a lot of elected officials say, "I was humbled . . ." but it's true. It is very humbling to have complete strangers, of all age groups, believe in you and what you will do for their community. I remembered months before, driving down a street seeing one of my yard signs in someone's front yard. "Wow," I thought. "Someone believes so strongly in what I'm about that they are willing to put a sign in their yard with my name on it, for months—Jesus! I can't let these people down!" Then again, maybe half these folks only put my sign in their yard to spite their neighbors.

There are three levels of government in the US: federal, state, and local. We tend to think that it's the federal government that most affects our lives, simply because we see so much coverage of it in the news. But it's local government that has the biggest bearing on our day-to-day. As we go about our business, berating the state of things around us, what is it that impacts us? The traffic. The goddamn dogs running loose. Did you hear what they're teaching over at the school now? Why isn't the city doing something about the potholes? My property taxes just went up. All local issues.

When we walked into the city building on January 3, 2012, we had no idea what we'd find because the outgoing administration wouldn't let us have early access to the offices. I'd already been getting word that some of the employees, mostly loyal Mayor Zink staffers, weren't happy I'd won. The only people I could trust were my new administrative assistant, Deb Sansone; Rick Giroux, the new Safety Service Director I'd just hired; and Laura Curliss, my legal pit bull.

Many elected officials, when coming into office, clean house by firing anyone from the opposite party or the former administration. I only let go two people, one being the former mayor's administrative assistant. I asked Laura to fire her as soon as she had her coffee. Regime changes could be swift and brutal even in small towns—not quite African-strongman caliber, but still impressive. We then terminated the deputy law director because Laura was taking that spot.

My new office was the smallest in the entire building. It was ten feet by eleven, windowless, about the size of an al-Qaida holding cell. Other than the old desk in the middle of the room, there were two large flags on stanchions: a large American one and a state flag. They were mounted on poles so long they scraped the tiles of the eight foot dropped ceiling, making the office look even smaller. Every time I backed my chair up, I'd hit these flags. I made a note to have them moved to a more suitable place, like the lobby, but never got around to it in my eight years. I sat down and tried scooting my chair up to the desk but my knees banged against the desk drawer and wouldn't go under. When I did force my knees under, the whole desk tilted forward on two legs making me appear to be sitting at a child's desk like Tom Hanks in *Big*. I opened the drawers. There was a pen, some correspondence from 2007, and a Quill office supply catalog from 2005.

I walked around to the various departments to introduce myself to the employees I hadn't met. I chatted with the water department ladies then over to the income tax department. The three women there were cordial but guarded. I went to see the city receptionist, Ruth, who sat behind a big glass window, and then visited the auditor's office. Since the city auditor was an elected official, his employees were not under me, but reported to him. The auditor wasn't in but his two employees were. The vibe in their office was noticeably different than the rest of the building. The air seemed strained, tense. You could almost smell anxiety. The first woman I will leave nameless and refer to only as Prisoner #1. She would look toward the auditor's private office, to verify that he was gone before she answered any questions I posed. The auditor's other employee, Prisoner #2, was a chain smoker with the demeanor of someone who is used to being confronted with jumper cables and wet sponges. This auditor must be a piece of work.

Deb, Rick, and I went to lunch at Bob Evans. Rick gave me a brief assessment. "Things are a mess. Nobody made it easy to transition or figure out where we are on projects or negotiations. But don't worry Chief, I have it under control!"

I had high hopes for Rick. We had looked at tons of résumés, interviewed probably fifteen candidates, and Rick, in his interview, said all the right things. Deb and Sam were both giddy finding this gem of an applicant. He was what I called a career Safety Service Director—a hired gun who, after hearing me talk about my vision for change and a disruption, assured me with phrases like, "I'll handle that." I put a lot of faith in Rick (though I really had no choice) as I was new in this whole municipal management game and he had run five small cities in the last eight years. No red flags there.

I went in to get Deb's take on the state of affairs. "It's a train wreck—files are stacked up everywhere. Two, three feet high. You can't tell what their status is. Are they active projects, or just behind on filing? Stacks on my desk, on top of cabinets, under tables."

It sounded like fodder for Dr. Seuss:

Miles of files! And piles of files!
Piles that teetered and piles that tottered!
And piles that looked like waters uncharted!
Files stacked here and files stacked there,
It made Deb want to pull out her hair!

I snapped out of it as Deb continued. "The top of these heaps seem to be recent and age as I go deeper down into them. I've already found two checks made out to the city that were never cashed that are over three years old!" She handed me a pile of pink phone message slips. "You already have a ton of calls, mostly people wanting meetings."

I fanned through them. City council members. Business people. The police chief.

"No one from the fire department wants to get with us?" I said, half-kidding.

"They haven't reached out to me, boss," Rick said.

I wasn't surprised. The fire department was going to be our first big fight. They were the largest of the city's eight departments in both personnel and budget, eating up about a third of the city's general fund budget annually.

That night I sat on my couch surrounded by books, binders, and reports. It dawned on me that there was no way this was going to be a part-time job if I wanted to get anything accomplished. I'd been self-employed my entire life and never afraid of hard work, but the schedule of how to do this mayoring was another matter. I didn't even know when I had to go to the office. Most of the city employees started at 7 or 7:30, like Deb. I was used to standup hours, and even if I wasn't doing shows I'd always been a night owl. The second day on the job, I asked Deb, "Do you think it's okay if I don't get in until 9 or 9:30?"

She looked at me kind of funny and said, "You're the damn mayor, you can come in whenever you want."

It seemed strange that that I had no set hours—hell, if I didn't want to come in at all that day or even that week, the office would just work around it. There was minimum expectation. It was a little scary looking at it from a citizen's standpoint.

Deb came into my office on Wednesday morning. "You have a planning commission meeting Tuesday at five-thirty p.m."

"What? I'm on the planning commission? How often do they meet?"

"The third Tuesday of the month."

"So, that's . . . once a month, yes?" Trying not to sound like an idiot.

"Yes. Thursday at ten you have a Revolving Loan Fund meeting. They're one person short so you'll need to come up with someone to appoint."

"How often do they meet?"

"The third Thursday of the month. You're also the chair of that board, so you'll set the agenda and run the meeting."

"How do I set an agenda?"

"Don't worry, I do that."

"Good, I'm not someone who has agendas by nature. Damn, there's a lot of meetings I didn't really plan on. Is that it for the week, I hope."

"Yes. But Wednesday morning you have a Design Review Board meeting."

"Don't tell me, it meets the third Wednesday of every month?"

"No. They actually meet the first Wednesday of the month but this month is a special meeting."

Well, I had told myself that I needed more structure, and it was now coming non-stop. Deb informed me of all the other commissions that I didn't have to attend but still appointed people to, which sounded to me like I was making others go to meetings that I didn't want to bother with. Which is exactly what it is.

I bought a book called *Local Government in Ohio*. It laid out what Ohio government consisted of—townships, counties, villages, cities, and school districts. I knew very little about the structure of these governmental entities and the relationship of one to the other. Let me put it another way—I didn't know shit about any of it. Apparently there are two types of mayors in Ohio: a weak mayor form of government and a strong mayor form. Yes, these are formal terms. Under a weak mayor system, power is diluted and the mayor has little authority as the chief executive. A strong mayor system gives much more latitude and power in general to the mayor to govern. The city of Hillsboro has a strong mayor system which mostly

159

derives from being a statutory city (as opposed to a charter formation) and, as a statutory city, it has the right of Home Rule—meaning "local self-government," which amounts to the ability to conduct its own affairs by enacting and enforcing local laws.

The local governmental entities that interrelate are the county, the township, and the municipality—a city or village. The county sits on a large piece of land. Within it are a number of townships, then the municipality sits in one of those townships, which makes for necessary relationships between the three. When those relationships go bad, things can get very nasty. And I should also mention school districts as well. They are also a local government entity, funded by local taxes, and are run by elected officials. They are a whole different animal and more can be learned about them by listening to "Harper Valley PTA," a country song made popular a few years ago.

At the end of the book it posed the question, "Why does government exist?" The answer was that "government exists to maintain order." It makes no other promise. It exists to maintain a status quo of orderly existence, which is why government is inherently boring to almost all Americans. Government only gets your attention when something beyond mere order is at play. This is where I entered and where the uproar started.

The Ohio Revised Code, which lays out the laws in Ohio, says that the mayor is the chief law enforcement official of the city. His duties include seeing that all laws, bylaws, ordinances, and resolutions are obeyed and enforced. Contrast this with my history of non-conformity and suddenly the top law enforcement official is also the top anti-authority guy in the city. How can sparks not fly? Additionally, the mayor recommends measures to the City Council, which includes ordinances, resolutions, or policies. He keeps the council fully advised of the city's financial condition and future needs. He prepares and submits reports.

The mayor is superior to and directs the activities of the police and fire departments as well as all other departments such as water, sewer, income tax, and his administrative office. Mayors run the gamut when it comes to their aspirations or activities. Some are largely ceremonial, and do a lot of ribbon cutting, and there are more "Godfather" type mayors who do a lot of throat cutting. A well-rounded mayor should do both. And if he can use the same pair of scissors to cut both ribbons and throats, then he's making good use of taxpayer funds. Shared Services, they call it.

The proper form of salutation when addressing a mayor is to call him "Mayor," as in, "Good morning, Mayor." Or, "Mayor, go fuck yourself." I've never been comfortable with being addressed as "Mayor." I usually tell people, "Just call me Drew." Also, constituents are less likely to say "Go fuck yourself Drew" when they have to see you as a person instead of a nameless elected official.

"I'm an unlikely mayor because these are unlikely times." That's the first line of the speech I gave to the local Rotary Club my second week in office. I talked about the comprehensive City Plan I was getting ready to unveil—a proactive, bold plan for the sensible growth of Hillsboro. I talked about using my visibility as an entertainer to promote Hillsboro and attract jobs, and about making Hillsboro a destination for prospective employers. It sounded good. An ambitious and grand vision for Hillsboro.

But just a week after delivering that speech, I came upon a bad car wreck on Route 50 on the west edge of town. The car had hit and snapped a phone pole. It was upside down in a field with three people injured. There were downed power lines, moans from the car's occupants, and chaos. A few minutes later the police and fire department arrived and went about their respective tasks. *They have all of this under control,* I said to myself and I left. As I drove back through Hillsboro, I could see that the west end of town was blacked out due to the accident causing a power outage. I drove up to the center of town to survey how far the outage extended. I thought, *What if it was five degrees out and the electric company said the power would be out for three days? What would we do about the seniors with no heat, the moms with babies? What arrangements would we need to make?*

It was a sobering moment. In the end, that was my job. The smaller, mundane, but crucial day-to-day governing to make sure our city kept running, no matter what. So for all of my grand plans, government really was all about order. Simply maintaining order.

The month before I took office, the American Electric Power company (AEP) that provides electricity to Hillsboro and southern Ohio had jacked up their rates to consumers, particularly small businesses, assuming everyone would just grumble, then pay their bills, like always. Specifically, rates were rising because electric costs were being shifted from large businesses to small ones, and the increases were up to 40 percent for a lot of customers.

When I took office in January, small businesses started getting their bills and were outraged. Then schools and local governments got their bills and they were in shock as well. Complaints came into the statehouse and Governor Kasich, not seeing any political benefit to him, said he would not step in, but would instead let the Public Utilities Commission of Ohio (PUCO) handle it. The PUCO is the regulatory agency that oversees utility rates. Local businesses were calling my office, panic-stricken over these huge bills. I started reading up on the issue and saw that a number of communities in south-central Ohio were pissed and trying to organize some kind of effort to bring more attention to this. So in our city council meeting, I presented a resolution condemning the AEP's actions. This is where Sam Stratman shined. He knew the language of politics and how to voice official complaints through the political process, as in, *draft a resolution*. I had no clue how this type of thing was done. Like most people, my way of voicing a complaint was to yell at the sky, "This is bullshit!" But now, as mayor, there were actual documents and platforms to amplify my voice. After I explained its importance to council, they passed the resolution unanimously, my first official action as mayor.

This was the kind of fight I'd been itching for and it had come in my first month in office. The AEP, the mammoth electric company—nobody liked utility companies—and the PUCO, this huge regulatory entity that oversaw the electric company and helped fashion the impossible-to-understand utility bills we all received in the mail. This was Big Regulation at its worst. It was exactly how I had envisioned using the mayor's office—as a regional platform for conservative activism.

So after a ton of complaints, media coverage, and Hillsboro helping to lead the effort, the PUCO agreed to look at the AEP rate increase again, though no one expected results. They had never overturned a rate case in their entire history. Well, the PUCO agreed to throw out the AEP rate increases and make them start the process over. Longtime observers of Ohio utility regulation call the PUCO's actions "unprecedented."

A few days later, the *Times Gazette* quoted me as happily surprised about the PUCO's reversal, but insistent that the AEP issue was just one part of a three-headed monster that I saw threatening small communities, the others being new rules targeting family farms and EPA regulations that carried high price tags. But no one could say that I wasn't paying attention to the everyday, local issues in Hillsboro.

In February, I got a call in the office from a local resident.

"Is this Mayor Hastings?"

"Yes, it is. How can I help you?"

"I understand that you perform marriages, that you marry people?" she asked.

"Yes, I do. Would you like to schedule a wedding? I can put you with my assistant, who can—"

"No, I want to find out if you will do a special ceremony for me. I'd like you to marry my two dogs."

"Seriously? Your dogs?" I asked, not sure if I was being pranked.

She told me that she was, indeed, quite serious and wanted to bring her dogs in for me to perform a wedding ceremony.

"Ma'am, I will not do that. Sorry. Not only do I consider it a stunt that's demeaning to the office of mayor, I'll be damned if I'm going to stand there and say, 'Do you take this bitch to be—'"

The woman gasped. "Well, you don't have to put it like that!"

"That's how I'd put it. Thank you." I hung up. This was the first of a long line of crazy citizens that I would deal with over the coming years.

Somehow, the newspaper heard about it and the next day's headline read, "Dogs Will Have a Ruff Time Getting Married."

In late March, the AEP held a public forum to get input on their new rate plan that they wanted to submit to the PUCO for approval. Sam and Laura helped me write a statement for the hearing. I wanted to let my voice as an

163

outraged citizen come out but still come across as measured and having thought it out—visceral, yet polished. Much like my standup.

I'd been at a comedy festival in Grand Rapids a few days prior to the AEP hearing. I did a standup set, then sat down with Marc Maron to do his podcast. Afterward, I tripped over something and broke my leg, arriving back in Hillsboro hobbling around in a cast. Sam and I kept re-writing and editing the PUCO statement up to the last minute. We sped up to Columbus, barely making it in time to read my three-page statement to the AEP Board of Directors in a room packed with reporters, activists, and concerned citizens.

I got my points across my way. The influence of my counterculture past was evident when I took a phrase, "Prairie Fire," from the 1970s' radical Weather Underground political manifesto and used it in my remarks: "You have started a prairie fire." I doubt that Bill Ayers and the Weathermen ever thought their language would be co-opted by a conservative mayor.

The statewide newspapers that day all quoted from my statement and featured pictures of me on crutches addressing the forum. In the recent past, these same papers featured fluff pieces of my upcoming comedy appearances and quotes from my act.

I was immensely proud of my involvement with winning that fight. It was the first time in the long history of the PUCO that they had ever backtracked, much less reversed a decision. Of course, it wasn't all me, there were other local county officials who had gone up there with us, there were outraged citizen activists from other communities, and the media played a big role in bringing attention to the issue. But the stage was set—there were other dragons to slay. I had hit the ground running so hard that any awareness of my implausible new identity as *Mayor* was lost in the manic-ness of new. It was the end of April 2012, and I'd been in office barely a hundred days. It was a win, but there was plenty ahead, especially if I wanted to handle the issues that residents wanted, namely the fire department and the street repairs. It was going to be an education. Mine and theirs.

CHAPTER 18

Burning Down the House

One morning in the Spring of 2013, I walked across the road at my farm, opened the door to my mailbox, and found a dead cat inside. He was facing out, staring at me with his tongue lolling, and it scared the crap out of me. After I slammed the lid and involuntarily shuddered, I walked back into the house because no one should have to pull a dead animal out of a mailbox until after their second cup of coffee.

I drank my coffee, pondering who would do such a thing. Was it someone who'd bought my last CD and hated it? No, this took some effort. It was most likely a firefighter with the Hillsboro Fire Department. I finished my coffee, put on some gloves, and went back to the mailbox. I tried to pull the cat out but he had rigor mortis and I had to twist *and* pull. When I finally got him out, I went across the road and threw him into the pasture. That's one nice thing about a farm: you can just fling a dead animal over the fence and something will come along, take it away, and eat it.

Now a few other things were making sense. In the last month, I'd had two other dead animals, a cat and a possum, in my front yard about ten feet from the edge of the road. I'd thought it was odd at the time, but you don't need to watch *Forensic Files* to know that animals hit by cars don't fly ten feet off the road. There were some pissed-off firemen out there.

On my wish list of *Things I want to accomplish before I die!,* dealing with a dysfunctional fire department, their wage issues, and how they provide fire and ambulance coverage across a county would not have been even the very last thing on that list—in no possible drug or brain trauma-induced scenario could I have come up with that.

But now, not only *was* it on my list, it was Number One. The typical American has no idea how a fire department works—their makeup, staffing, or cost to taxpayers. They just want to be able to pick up a phone, dial 911, and have an ambulance get to them quickly. In the years after September 11, 2001, when firemen became the new heroes—deservedly—many fire departments took advantage of that emotional time by demanding exorbitant pay raises and expanded union rights, positioning their jobs as being as dangerous as that of a policeman.

Think about the last fire that you witnessed. It was probably on TV. Structural fires—buildings—are a rarity nowadays; you're more likely to burn alive by performing one of those *Jackass* daredevil stunts than in a house fire. That's because of huge improvements in fire safety—sprinklers, smoke detectors, and the big reduction in the number of smokers. Now, fewer than 5 percent of calls to fire departments are for fires—but the number of people that are paid to fight fires has increased more than fifty percent in recent years. Hillsboro, though technically a city, thought of itself as a small town and ran itself as such. That works for most day-to-day governance. Except there really was no day-to-day governing in Hillsboro, with a part-time law director and part-time mayor. So when contract negotiations came around and the two part-timers went up against the International Association of Fire Fighters union (IAFF)—that have huge batteries of lawyers and negotiators in Washington who spend their entire lives shaping and honing wages and contracts to their favor—towns like Hillsboro get eaten for lunch.

The year before I took office, a new firehouse had been built and promptly dubbed the "Garage Mahal" because of its obscene expense. In order to pay for their increasingly expensive department and to ensure complete dependence on them, the fire department got the city administration to expand the department's coverage area by going beyond the city limits to contract with most of Highland County. As the fire department's budget kept ballooning, the Zink administration figured out that they weren't charging nearly enough money to the county residents for fire/EMS coverage, and that the City of Hillsboro was now subsidizing the county residents while the citizens of the city were footing the bill.

The city screwed themselves yet again by signing away their management rights in the firemen's contract, which meant the fire department got to manage themselves. I would later be told that labor lawyers, teaching law students and junior lawyers, would hold up this contract as an example of *the worst-case scenario that a municipality could find itself in at the mercy of a union.* This meant there was no reining in the out-of-control costs in the department. Worse, the rates being charged to the county were so abysmally low it would be nearly impossible to get rate hikes anywhere close to the true cost of coverage. With the city and townships at an impasse, and the bloated fire department uncontrollable, I took office and inherited the entire mess.

I knew nothing about labor negotiations, knew squat about wage issues, didn't know shit about the difference between a fire department, a fire district, or a fire sale. The only two pre-conceived notions I brought along with me were that I wasn't crazy about unions and I didn't like bullies. And unfortunately for the Hillsboro Fire Department, they were both.

The same week I was sworn in as mayor, I called for a meeting to discuss the issue. The city's contract to cover the county townships expired in sixty days and we wanted a new contract at a higher rate. Later that week a fireman walking down the hall stuck his head through the open door to my office. "We can go and sit in on those meetings. We usually get involved in talks."

"No, I think we can handle this," I told him, irritated, because these guys felt like they were part of the administration. Ballsy. Rank and file firemen thinking they should sit in on and guide management meetings. No wonder the city was broke.

Another fireman walked by the office, his radio squawking like an anemic electronic duck. I went out to the hallway. I'd noticed that firemen seemed to roam the halls of the admin building all the time. "Excuse me, but why are you hanging out up here in the city building? You've been wandering around here all morning." The two firemen looked at me in disbelief and I realized then that their department had completely forgotten that they had superiors.

This war was going to be fought on two fronts: getting the county township trustees to go for a fair contract, and reining in a rogue fire department by getting concessions. My plan was simple enough: cut through all the past politics and animosity and fix this thing. There was no room for bullshit. I knew I'd have to be forceful but someone had to be if the problem was to be solved. As a wise old man once said about the fire department squabbles: "Everyone just needs to put their big boy pants on."

My first meeting representing the city was with Laura, and we sat across from the elected township trustees of Highland County in a drab, windowless room in the basement of the county administration building. The vibe from the trustees was suspicion, to put it mildly. I was simply curious. Who were these guys? Some white shirts and ties? Retired teachers? Turns out they were almost all farmers. Most in coveralls, some in plaid work shirts, and all with their arms crossed in front of them. Sitting across from these fourteen or so guys was me, in a gray flannel Hugo Boss suit and post-modern black leather slip-on shoes, and Laura, in a black business suit that had not a hint of femininity.

"Gentlemen. I'm glad we're all together here and can finally find a solution to this fire thing. This is Laura Curliss, our new deputy law director, and she's going to help us wade through this. So let's get started, shall we?"

The first thing that Mr. Cut-to-the-chase learned was that farmers never get right down to business. They start off talking about the weather, then move on to livestock. They may say a little about a neighbor who recently died. Then there's some discussion about the recent election, followed by some more talk about how the election just might affect the weather. That's usually the first hour.

I wanted to hear their side of things.

"So, gentlemen, what's your take on this situation?"

"Tell you straightaway—we don't trust the city of Hillsboro. They've lied to us over and over," said a trustee.

Grumbles of assertion echoed in the small room.

"Well, gentlemen, I don't lie. I may tell you things you don't want to hear, but I won't lie to you." The politics and animosity I'd thought I'd cut through like butter turned out to be more deep-seated than a room full of Bosnians and Serbs. The disgusted stares some of them directed at me was telling. They were pissed that they even had to deal with what they saw as some LA comedian with faggoty hair. As for Laura, most of them barely acknowledged her presence. An out of town woman lawyer whose first exchange with the trustees was to look at her watch and say, "How about we cut the chit-chat and get down to brass tacks here?" Even I winced at that one. Laura was a knowledgeable attorney but not known for her cordial social skills.

We managed to bring up the idea of forming a county-wide fire district. A few were warm to the idea but it seemed like a huge effort to make it happen. And why should they? They were getting us to provide service for next to nothing.

That first meeting was mostly about sizing each other up. We adjourned and agreed to meet regularly and hammer out an agreement.

Our next meeting, a week later, was very different. Negotiations went like this:

Me and Laura: "The city needs to get higher rates to provide service to you."

Township guys: "We agree the rate probably needs to go a little higher."

Me and Laura: "That's good. What are you guys thinking might be fair?"

Township guys: "Hmmm. Well, we're probably giving away the store but we could go up five percent."

Laura: "That's not going to happen."

Me: "I think what she meant to say is that we can be flexible but we probably need a little more than five percent, right Laura?"

Township guys: "So how much are you thinking?"

Me and Laura: "How much are *you* thinking?"

Township guys: "They say the ground should start drying up this week. Supposed to have sun startin' Friday."

Me: "I heard the temperature's supposed to get up to almost sixty-five. Which, ironically, is about the same percentage increase the city needs to get for your fire coverage."

Township guy: "That's a good one. Does that joke go over in your little comedy club skit?" Snickers all around.

They'd just made it personal and their disdain was laid bare. My face got hot and I felt that old feeling come up—like maybe I wasn't good enough. I said something lame to blow off the comment. But I wasn't that thirteen-year-old getting slapped around back in Kettering any more. That moment hardened my resolve—*I'm going to win this fight and if I can fuck you along the way, all the better.*

The third meeting went like this:

Township guys: "Well we finally got some decent weather. If it keeps up maybe the ground'll thaw enough for me to get some fence in."

Me: "Gentlemen, this is all fine and well but the clock is ticking and it's your clock, not the city's. Your contract expires in a week."

Township guys: "Well, we talked and we think we can go from five percent to maybe fifteen."

Laura: "You're not even in the ballpark."

Me: "I think she means that we're somewhat far apart but we can probably find a happy medium here. We need to get a much bigger increase this year."

Township guys: "Whew! No way. We can't go back and tell our residents about a big increase!"

Laura: "Well then, you can go back and tell them that an ambulance won't be coming when their daughter mangles her legs in a thresher."

Me: "I think what Laura means to say is that an ambulance won't be coming *if* your daughter mangles her legs in a thresher."

We finally agreed on a 25 percent increase, which we got approved in the next city council meeting. Then the township guys reneged—*we decided we want to pay less!* Back and forth, turning into middle school drama. They started turning on each other, then coming to me looking for side deals—*don't tell the other guys!* A few of the townships left us and joined the new Paint Creek Fire District up in the northern part of Highland county, a welcome relief to me.

"Drew, remember, you have that ten a.m. meeting this morning," Deb said as I came in the office.

"I'm excited! Think about it Deb—getting fiber-optic cable under the streets and creating a huge Wi-Fi zone uptown—this will be big!"

"Well, this is just the meeting for a study to assess the viability of—"

"Yeah, yeah, formalities. We'll still make it happen! This is the kind of technology that can change lives for the better. What's the eleven o'clock?"

"A family living just two blocks from here didn't want to pay a monthly water/sewer bill so they've been defecating in buckets and throwing it out their back door into the creek. So the police officer that was dispatched is coming up to give you an assessment of the situation."

"Why do we need to assess the situation? We need to rectify it."

This captured Hillsboro precisely. The hopes and promise that I held out for our town and the dismal reality that was all too big a part of it. Deb and I then spent the afternoon reading over Hillsboro building codes, which were mostly non-existent. This town was the Wild West when it came to enforcement of anything.

"You have two weddings to perform today," Deb announced.

I married my first couples in April of 2012. The standard boilerplate vows that had been used by every mayor here since 1910 were so antiquated I couldn't get myself to utter them. "Doth thou sweareth to cleave to thy bosom and forsake all others . . ." So I spent the rest of the morning updating the vows that should have been revised after WWII.

"How does this sound, Deb? 'Do you promise to be soulmates, best buddies, and have each other's backs at all times, till death do you part?'"

"Much better! You can use them this afternoon."

I read the new vows in the two ceremonies but I didn't know how much of them they actually heard, as both couples spent the entire ceremony trying to get their kids to behave.

Five months in office and little of what Sam, Laura, and I had planned was yet to transpire. The dynamic in our office was always upbeat though, but kind of a dark, cynical upbeat. It was idea driven, energized, but there was a colorless, odorless gas that seeped into our offices from the various forces that wanted me gone.

I gave a speech up in Wilmington—this was the third event they'd invited me to speak at. Why did other communities love the ideas I was putting forth but in my hometown they fought me viciously? These folks in Wilmington liked my lofty talks but it was beginning to feel a little pie in the sky. I was self-doubting. I told the audience about a recent incident.

"We have a lot of known drug houses—cars going in and out all hours. I go to our police department and give them addresses. 'We can't do anything about it,' my police chief says. 'We can't bust them because we have to have expensive, EPA mandated biohazard suits to wear on scene just to pick up the pan of meth cooking on the stove and dispose of it in a federally prescribed manner. And that suit costs about three thousand dollars. And you have to throw it away afterward. And we don't have the money for the suits. If we do manage to bust someone, three days later he's in another house up the street at it again.' Then the chief simply shrugs. He shrugs! That's where we are today, ladies and gentlemen, we're so frustrated, so immobilized by the absurdity of regulations, that we simply shrug. We've become a nation of *shruggers*."

I was getting worked up as I relayed the story and started going off-script.

"Well, I say, *screw the EPA*. You go in, grab the asshole by the neck, tell him to pick up his meth crap and put it in a Hefty bag, then we drive out to a farmer that will donate an old concrete silo that we can bury the stuff in. Then it's done! The EPA officials don't have to live next to these problems—we do! The EPA doesn't have to watch their daughters and sons live next to this—but we do!"

The audience applauded but I wasn't sure what I'd accomplished other than sounding like the news anchor from the movie *Network*. What I didn't tell them was that a week after that conversation with the Hillsboro police, I drove over to one of those drug houses, walked up to the front door and banged on it loudly. "Who is it?" a muffled voice inside said.

"Well, it's not the goddamn Welcome Wagon," I told him. This dude opened the door a crack and stared out. "I'm the mayor of Hillsboro and I know you're not selling Beanie Babies here."

"I don't know what you're talking about," he said as two separate cars pulled into the driveway and pulled right back out when they saw me standing there.

"Here's what I would like you to do. Move. Leave town. I don't care where you go. Jackson, Portsmouth, Sabina. Just get out of Hillsboro. If I have to come back here again it'll be with a lot of cops." Then I walked back to my car, fully expecting to hear the click of a shotgun or pistol hammer. Two days later, they were gone, never to be seen again.

The newspaper heard about it and referred to me as "Dirty Harry." Whatever. But I was just sick of it. All the *shrugging*.

The Hillsboro firemen were nervous. They had watched as we used the Jaws of Life to extricate ourselves from a longstanding series of bad deals with the townships and the writing was on the wall that they were headed for a different future. And the townships had let it be known they didn't care much for our firemen.

But our fire department had made their own bed. The Hillsboro firemen were widely known to attend the monthly city council meetings, lining up across the back of the room with their arms crossed in front of their chests, glaring at council members if they heard something they didn't like. During council meetings the firemen left their radio walkie-talkies turned on, which would erupt in jarring squawks. They could be an intimidating bunch and I knew it was going to be contentious from this point forward. In spring, we'd hired a Columbus law firm that specialized in labor issues. Our attorney, David Blaugrund, started sorting through the union agreements we had in place. Re-opening the contract to get concessions.

Overtime was a huge problem. I got an education in fire department sleight of hand when it came to wages. The IAFF had ingenious ways to screw taxpayers out of money. One of their most effective methods was *staffing*. By making the contract talks about staffing, it let the union rep tell the media, "This isn't about money, it's about staffing, and having the minimum staffing at the station for all shifts is essential to the public's safety." In contract negotiations, staffing talks go like this:

"We need a minimum of four people on a shift to adequately serve the community."

"Okay, I guess we can do four."

"Now we have to consider that some of them may call in sick or be otherwise absent, so we really require six."

"Six? That's a fifty percent increase over the minimum!"

"Yes. Now, once you get five or more people on a shift, we require a captain to be on duty to oversee and manage the others."

"What? We can't afford—"

"Then, when we multiply out the three shifts, adding up the personnel, we're over twenty people, so the union stipulates that we have a lieutenant to oversee the captains."

"What the hell—how much does a lieutenant make?"

"That's somewhat negotiable. Now we need to address equipment. Because the department has a new fire truck that is a ladder/pumper/rescue configuration, we are required to have a minimum of four personnel on the truck when it's called out on a run."

"Okay. Well we have four people already on the shift, so we're covered."

"No. We have to have the *firehouse* covered. If all of the shift people are on the fire truck, who is manning the station? If another call comes in, we have to have enough staff to answer *that* call so we'll need another two people per shift. Minimum."

"This is insanity! Can we use volunteers to fill in some of these positions?"

"Oh, I wish. But the union contract says volunteers can only be used after all the above staffing by IAFF firefighters are met."

I decided to hold a public town hall meeting on the fire department issues. These were unheard of in Hillsboro. I called Sam Stratman for his input.

"Are you fucking crazy? Rule Number One—elected officials should *never* willingly put themselves in front of large, angry groups of citizens. The firemen and their supporters will eat you alive!"

"Sam, comedians are used to speaking to and controlling large audiences. The public and the fire department need to see that I'm confident and not going to back down on the issue."

And so it transpired, one part Q&A, one part heckling.

Mayor Drew: "If we get no concessions from the department, we'll need to lay off firemen."

Firemen: "Well, that's only because you wouldn't cut a deal with the townships, which would have kept a large service area."

Mayor Drew: "But they didn't want to pay more and you guys make too much money."

Firemen: "We don't make too much money."

Mayor Drew: "The public says you do."

I walked off the stage happy with my performance and the next week we did our first round of layoffs.

The firemen's union took their predictably adversarial stance and fought every change we tried to implement, forcing costly, time-consuming arbitrations. As the year rolled on, more townships were joining the Paint Creek district. They were finally figuring out that I meant business, that their free ride was over. Then the city's firemen, seeing their service area (meal ticket) decline, got nasty. The next council meeting was overwhelmed by firefighters and their families, complete with firemen holding babies. A scummy tactic that a lot of people saw through, though they succeeded in intimidating some council members. Fortunately, there were other far less stressful events to look forward to.

A rainy day in mid-June was the most fun day I'd had since I took office. The city hosted an event for GOBA—the Great Ohio Bicycle Adventure. Six hundred cyclists from all over Ohio were riding into town for a psychedelic-themed, hippie fest billed "The Summer of Love."

"Deb, wouldn't it be cool if we could get mushrooms or acid for all these people?"

She looked up from her filing. "No, we don't have money in the budget for that. And there would be liability issues."

She had long since quit being shocked, though she never quite knew when I was being serious. Deb was around my age, had a great sense of humor, but was much more discreet and I never could figure out if she had a Past or not. But these are also the qualities that help make a great assistant.

A few days later, Deb stuck her head in. "They would like you to do a mass wedding for about two hundred couples."

"Now we're talkin'!" My old counterculture days were back—well, in spirit anyway.

When the riders hit town, they definitely had the vibe even though most were in their fifties and sixties. All looked like they'd been hippies since 1968 and had stayed true to the lifestyle. They rode expensive bikes and struck me as either academics from liberal arts colleges or directors of land conservancy non-profits.

"Give me an L!" "L!"

"Give me an O!" "O!"

"Give me a V!" "V!"

"Give me an E!" "E!"

We were all gathered in a huge barn at the fairgrounds. Paisley and flower-power everywhere. I wore a Nehru jacket and bellbottoms. For the mass wedding vows I used lyrics from my favorite '60s songs—Hendrix, Donovan, Joni Mitchell. The idea that I was the mayor of this city seemed surreal.

Back at my office, Sam, whom I'd made Economic Development consultant, was delighted. "That was gold!" he enthused. "An upscale, demographic with a high disposable income—we need to capture this group either via email or social media to convert them to similar-themed events thereby maximizing our impact on their brand of consumption. Of course, we'd design all events to appear as organic as possible."

I both agreed with his assessment and was horrified at the same time, and as he droned on I could once again hear Stevie Winwood's lyrics in my head: "The man in the suit has just bought a new car / From the profit he's made on your dreams."

One day in July, Deb looked up from her notes. "I heard that another township joined the district. I think they're finally getting it that we're ending service to them at the end of the year."

I'd been analyzing fire districts for months. They were an example of shared services; instead of every small community having its own fire department, a fire district is typically formed to serve residents over a large area, resulting in lower costs for all. A Costco approach.

176

"Holy shit, Deb. I've been looking at this thing all wrong. We've been trying to find all these ways to reduce our fire staffing, get concessions, and lower costs. Why not just *dissolve* our fire department and have Hillsboro join the Paint Creek District like these townships are doing?" The idea was so good and so simple that there had to be a catch. There was—it was getting the council members to go for it. *And it would not be easy.*

I spent the rest of the summer selling the idea to council people and went so far as creating a video to take the message straight to the public. Sitting in front of a camera with a script, I explained our fire department issue and why we should join a fire district. Mayors and municipal lawyers with the same hometown issues were watching this fight from around the state and wanted to see how it would end.

Meanwhile, our expensive but ruthlessly efficient labor attorney, David Blaugrund, started peeling back the layers on the onion that was our union contract and came up with a plan—maneuver them this way, corral them that way, cut off any escape paths. A good plan, but like everything in government, a maddeningly slow process. The union filed a complaint; we filed a counter complaint. Weeks went by. They'd file to go to arbitration. Another two months pass. The arbitrators wanted more info and scheduled still more arbitrations. Time dragged on. Arbitration found in favor of the union. Appeals were filed. Three more months. Our legal bills looked like a progressive slot machine that showed the jackpot steadily increasing as you pumped in quarters. The newspaper reported that $167,000 had been spent so far—*how much more?* they wailed. Money well spent but hard to swallow for a small town that was used to spending exactly zilch on outside attorneys. But as the adage goes, you had to spend money to make money. Victory would be ours only by having the best legal people doggedly grind the union down. And with all I had seen from these firemen, and how they'd raped the city, I had no compunction in dissolving their department.

Our fire department cost us $1.8 million annually. If we joined the fire district we'd pay $735,000. A no-brainer considering that our entire general fund budget was only about $4.5 million a year. One would think that our city council could see the obvious benefits. But as this fifty-seven-year-old politically naïve mayor was learning, people often don't do the right thing. City council didn't vote to fix the fire department issue for all of 2012 and half of 2013. It didn't matter that voting to join the fire district would allow the city to have a balanced budget, would enable street repairs, better policing, and better parks for the kids. If I was for it, they were against it. I could understand partisan politics, but a stance based on "I just don't like your fucking face" was something I hadn't felt since my bartending incident.

A special city council meeting to take a vote on dissolving our fire department and joining the Paint Creek District finally occurred in December 2012. The fire department came into the council meeting bullying council members, yelling, going over their allotted speaking time, and disparaging the firemen of the Paint Creek District. They were not going to yield an iota.

The council president called for a vote, the council members stared at their shoes. I reminded them of their duty, the importance, the huge budget cuts that would come if they voted no. Feeling behind them for their spines and not finding any, they voted it down. And so began the brutal budget cuts. The parks director. The code enforcement officer. Money for street repairs. And of course, fire department people. The coming year, 2013, was looking bleak already.

Laura had also resigned a few months earlier. She had been a huge help and would be missed. Then Sam left, taking a consulting job in DC. I couldn't blame them for wanting out. They were stunned by the relentless negativity present at every turn. It wore them down. It wore on me too, but I had a job to do.

Dealing with the cast of characters in Hillsboro's political scene often felt like visiting another planet. Yes, people here could be small-minded and ignorant—but I'd lived in urban areas most of my life and Urbans were just as ignorant and small-minded. And not everyone in rural towns was like that. I knew plenty of people that made small town living the great experience that it often was. But it was the opinion of most that there was something *different* about Hillsboro regarding its negativity, its mean streak.

Though the town's "anti" population was small, they were relentless, virulent. For them, Happy Hour lasted about six minutes—except there were no bars in Hillsboro. Maybe they were anti-nightlife as well.

My election coincided with people figuring out that social media could be used for more than posting pics of *the engagement ring he got me!* Facebook, along with a local, free weekly paper—the kind that gets thrown toward your driveway then lies there for a month because it's not worth fishing out of a ditch—became the mouthpiece for Hillsboro's Pissy Bunch. The paper's owner, man with a penchant for fixating on my every move, decided the best way to brand his flaccid weekly was to dedicate its focus to my demise. His online edition attracted the worst of the worst who posted comments non-stop.

"This mayor is after our beloved fire department because a fireman once spurned a homosexual advance made by him."

"His murky financial plans for Hillsboro will ruin us and make him rich!"

"This interloper is destroying what we once had and must be stopped by any means necessary."

My staff and I tried to ignore this crowd, except that this crowd would not be denied. From the day I took office until the day I left, they were ever present. We tried to refrain from reading their online vitriol and instead focused on the more garden variety pessimism of city council members. I was no Gandhi but I didn't have that kind of hate in me. My sense of optimism would never allow negativity of that caliber to infect my being. But these dealings with some of the council members and other elected officials would not be the first time I'd see this kind of visceral response to me, and before it was all over, I'd see far worse.

City Council started making the brutal, but needed cuts to the budget in the wake of their refusal to deal with the fire department. The fall of 2012 saw an ironic turn of events when the Paint Creek Fire District asked me to repair and then lease the old city fire department building to them, which I had purchased at auction after Mayor Zink and our fire department had vacated two years prior. The quickly growing district wanted to put a new station in Hillsboro. After conferring with the State Ethics board, it was decided that I could proceed. I informed Paint Creek that I could make improvements to render it habitable for about $75,000. When the newspaper got wind of this and reported, there was outrage.

The public was finally becoming aware of just how outrageous the big picture was. We warned council of a $630K deficit if layoffs and concessions from the firemen weren't forthcoming. Council members were angry, voicing their opinion that they had been maneuvered into this position of having to take action against the fire department, of slowly choking the viability out of the department, that I had planned it to go this way all along. I remained quiet in the face of their accusations, but inwardly I was becoming cautiously optimistic that I was going to accomplish what the voters had been asking for. This city council couldn't or wouldn't do what the citizens wanted.

Another township was meeting to consider joining the Paint Creek District. When the *Times Gazette* asked a vocal trustee about his vehement dislike of me, he responded angrily, "He's the man from nowhere!" Like some dangerous character from a western, riding into town seeking to set things right, this description of me stuck for a long time.

In November, Gary Abernathy, the publisher of the *Times Gazette* wrote in an editorial, "The Man from Nowhere makes progress." It was a dissection of my first year that I couldn't argue with. The article began, "Not everyone likes the mayor . . . his supporters outnumber his detractors . . . but chief among his critics are Hillsboro's more prominent citizens." Then, "After working many years around the most professional and accomplished of politicians, I find Hastings' complete lack of etiquette, finesse, or guile refreshing, not to mention often entertaining. The simplest of mayoral duties—like presenting a proclamation on the cause of the week—carries with it the hint of disaster, depending on what His Honor might do or say. The most annoying part of Hastings is that focusing on his foibles obscures his better qualities."

The most annoying part of Abernathy was that he knew me better than I knew myself. He went on to give a mostly flattering assessment of my first year—applauding my efforts with the still unsolved fire department issue, and going on to say that one of my best decisions was to hire Rick Giroux, a trained professional. Ironically, one week after this editorial, Abernathy would report that Giroux had just been arrested for a DUI when he drove home drunk from a local bar, and I ended up firing him.

At the end of the year we announced to the city council that we had cut $1.2 million from the previous year's budget, eliminating the huge deficit that we'd been facing just months before. The city council was shocked that we'd managed to turn the city's finances around in my first year in office. The Paint Creek District also opened their new fire station in uptown Hillsboro at the end of 2012. As Abernathy wrote in a December 13 editorial summing up the year, "It is apparent that the physical presence of the Paint Creek substation and its firefighters—many of them former Hillsboro firefighters—sitting in the middle of town has tamped down most of the anxiety that existed among some local residents about the potential loss of the Hillsboro Fire department."

All of this should have been evidence enough to convince Hillsboro's city council to disband the fire department and for the department itself to see the writing on the wall. But like almost all of municipal progress, it inched along throughout 2013 from grievance to appeal and back again, consuming my office and infecting my private life. I recalled a night backstage before a big show when I should've been thinking about what material I wanted to do onstage and in what order, but instead kept wondering how that federal mediator would decide on this latest issue of the fire department. Fire worries overrode most of my thoughts through most of the year until a night in mid-November at a city council meeting where we asked them to re-consider their stance on the fire issue and take a vote.

I was not hopeful—this thing had taken its toll on me. The room was packed with fireman, their families, and two former mayors. Betty Bishop, who had allowed the union to come in and take over the department, and Dick Zink, my predecessor, who arguably owed his political success to the firemen. Council voted. Yes. No. No. Yes. No. Yes. Not good—it was a tie and the deciding vote was on the seventh person, Pete Pence. The chambers got quiet. When he said, "Yes," there was a huge groan and angry screaming from the fire contingency. But all I heard was "Yes." Sonofabitch—he'd done the right thing in the face of a wall of hostility. I would be forever grateful for his vote. It still took months to take care of all the small details that make up huge changes, and finally on one nondescript morning, I sat down and signed the papers to contract with the Paint Creek Fire District, a ten-minute diversion from my day to sign documents in triplicate.

"Cheer up Drew, this is huge. It will probably be the biggest accomplishment of your time in office," Deb said. I had been accused by those aggrieved of engineering it all toward a predetermined outcome with no room for compromise. I now concede that was true, though it had to be that way. It's only in retrospect that I can see what a truly monumental accomplishment this was, a fundamental change for the better. Imagine owning a semi-truck that you used for your personal vehicle with all the accompanying costs and physical logistics of moving it around, and then one day you decided to get rid of it and simply take an Uber. Hillsboro's finances permanently improved, allowing money to be spent on streets, sidewalks, and recreational projects for the first time in decades. It streamlined and simplified the administration of the city by eliminating its largest and most high-maintenance department. Maybe most importantly, it let the citizens of Hillsboro and beyond see that things *could* change for the better if the will was there. I've been told that the dismantling of the Hillsboro Fire Department was the first time in Ohio history that an IAFF union fire department had ever been dissolved. At every mayors conference I attended over the eight years I was in office, fellow mayors pulled me aside—*How the hell did you manage to get that done?* All of those mayors were experienced enough to know that it couldn't be done. I gave them the same answer every time—*Because I was too naïve to know that it couldn't be.*

It was the hardest undertaking that I'd ever done. My first eight years in Hillsboro had been carefree—I farmed in the sun, performed shows for good money for adoring fans, and busied myself with fixing up old buildings. Then my entire first two years as mayor were immersed in this fire thing and suddenly I found myself hated by complete strangers. My face flushes remembering how much shit I had to take, how often I had to bite my tongue. I had maneuvered and guided all the players in the fire department project toward a new fate, and I myself seemed at times to be directed by some unseen hand as well. I am immensely proud of getting the problem solved. Of course, when I say "I," I mean We. There were many others that helped make it happen. And the ones that most made it happen were the citizens—the people that stopped me in the grocery store and the gas station, urging me to "keep fighting," "don't give up," "don't let them get you down." Had they not been there with those words, I think I might well have given up.

CHAPTER 19

Self-Awareness
and a Second Term

I t was late in 2015 and I was scrolling through my calendar. If a stranger were to have looked at it they would have thought that one man's calendar had been superimposed on another's. There was the busy schedule of an entertainment figure—shows, interviews, airline flights, and in-studio appearances—interwoven among the ambitious agenda of a mayor—council meetings, proclamations, and large-scale projects. And everything was Priority One. I operated with the fervor of a man with a terminal illness. Sidewalks were built where only dirt paths had been. Building standards were set where before there had been none. And we cleaned up a city long neglected. All of that was evidenced on my calendar. What was not evident was any indication of a personal life.

The frenetic pace of my office was offset by the maddeningly slow turning of municipal government, and this time-space discrepancy threw off my entire sense of chronology during my first four years in office—so much so that I had to scroll back through the calendar to see when I had actually gotten married. It turned out to be January of 2014, and it all started the day an old farmer named Murray died.

Back in the summer of 2012, I'd stopped at an estate sale. I loved auctions but seldom had time to go to them any longer.

"Next up is a box of six wristwatches. Looks like some work, some don't—who'll give me five dollars?"

I'd buy almost anything if it had some collectable or historic aspect. My house was slowly taking on a museum quality, my two extra bedrooms and barn filling up with oddities. "All of this will be passed down to my heirs," I'd say to myself, even though I had no heirs. I'd never wanted kids, yet I did want heirs—someone to pass down my personal history to—it was important that people knew of Drew Hastings, of course. All I had was my sister Karen and her kids—but my niece and nephew were suburbanites and didn't really like old stuff.

This estate sale was busy and was already underway. The old farmer—Mr. Murray—was widely known and I'd already missed half of the auction. So when the auctioneer said that they were going to offer up the entire contents of Mr. Murray's attic for one price because they were running behind, I jumped at it. A couple of us stuck our heads up through the small opening and peered in at the pile up there. I got it all for six hundred.

I went back out to the yard where there were long rows of knick-knacks being sold.

"Item 6221: a cigar box containing fifteen or so pocketknives—who'll start the bidding at ten dollars? Ten dollars—who'll give me ten?"

It hit me when the auctioneer got to the "six boxes of personal effects": *This is me.* This will be my life in fifteen or twenty years. Estate of Drew Hastings—my life distilled down to card tables stacked with collectables, suits hanging from garment racks in the front yard, and boxes of stuff. Everything special that I keep in pristine shape, that I take out to admire from time to time, will be pawed through by strangers looking for bargains. There'll be no one to oversee it. No one to advocate, "He would not have wanted to sell that." No one to tell eager bargain hunters, "People, have some respect, this was a man's life!"

I suddenly felt very alone. And I did not want to be there.

Often when people get married in Las Vegas it's because they just met and do it on impulse. Taryn Blanchard and I hadn't just met. I'd known her for maybe three years, though barely. Every nine months I played a comedy club in Peoria where she worked and we'd flirt. Went out for coffee and sushi a few times. After that estate sale things changed. I didn't want to flirt and laugh over coffees anymore. I started going out of my way after Midwest gigs to see her. She wouldn't let me meet her five-year-old daughter until she was convinced I was bona fide. Taryn was an unlikely pick. She was ruled by pattern and common sense. She was a mom. She had no dark sense of humor or cynicism. And even though she could get wild, she was *wholesomely* wild. Maybe it was all in the timing that made her unlikeliness suddenly likely.

I was fifty-nine. And though I was used to being alone it was the first time I *felt* alone—I was that estate sale waiting to happen. I'd moved to a small town made up of families, and my farm, even after a few years, seemed somehow barren. Farms are not meant for single men; they're a family effort. I thought of an African quote I'd written in my quote book long ago—"If you want to go fast, go alone. If you want to go far, go together." I was tired of going fast. Taryn and her daughter, Willow, had come along when I was finally open to someone coming along. Did I love *her*? Did I simply love what she *represented*? What I did know was that people get married for a lot of reasons and those reasons change over time and circumstance.

After we came back from A Little White Chapel on the Strip, Taryn went back to Peoria for six months to finish her schooling, and I to Hillsboro to finish what I was elected to do. We talked on the phone every night until she got to Hillsboro. Then she took a job as a physical therapist's assistant and, like me, was gone all day.

At first it seemed like a piece of cake. When you marry at sixty not much changes, it's not like you cut down on nightclubbing or running around with your buddies. No, not much changes and that was the problem. I'd been single for so long that I couldn't gauge how self-oriented I was. How disruptive these two people were to my neurotic routine. *That doesn't go there. Why are you doing it like that?* Taryn was obsessive in her own way, she just had far less experience at it than me. Most women had

185

never tried to change me—this one did. I took it so viscerally, that she was trying to *domesticate* me, but now I see that she only wanted to turn me from my feral, solo mindset into someone with *consideration for others.*

From the beginning, the dynamic was two plus one. Taryn and Willow, and then me. We weren't a family, though we would eventually become one. Instead, we were two sets of numbers: two, and one. Which equaled three but didn't make a family. We were a sum.

Six months after Taryn moved in, discord visited. And stayed. Our differences were bared. An unwillingness to compromise by two uncompromising people. A bluntly open personality versus a protective one. Value differences regarding attitudes about money, parenting. We had a thirty-year age difference that neither of us thought much about until now. At first it wasn't actual fighting. We started with sniping, which, like a gateway drug, led to bickering. Then we moved on to the harder stuff. Raised voices, fighting. And finally, screaming matches. These were disorienting, like when your car alarm goes off when you're standing next to it. All you can think is, *How do I turn this off, get it to shut up?* Drama at a hundred and ten decibels. It was so uncivilized. It was Mom and Marty, it was domestic violence.

When we can take the emotion out of this and have a rational conversation, we can try to talk again later. But the angry woman I was dealing with didn't want to hear that. She didn't know anyone in Hillsboro and often drove back to Illinois and I resented that. She came from a big loud Catholic family—all those extended relatives and family members just seemed so unnecessary and inefficient.

We were married barely a year when we started going to the marriage counselor. His name was Butch. What kind of expert in inter-personal dynamics was named Butch? We stopped going after a while because Taryn felt Butch was siding with me too often. Was he? *Or was I just right?* It makes you crazy—women, marriage, having to second guess your basic behaviors. I wanted to make this work. Had to make this work. I had been in a hundred relationships and had failed in most of them or they had failed me. *I was going to make this work if it killed me.* Which it felt like it was doing. Our disputes were mostly left unresolved as I lost myself in the work of the city which most of the time seemed no different than the dynamic at home.

For instance, sitting in a city council meeting in 2015 I listened as the council president ask those in attendance if there were any citizen comments and a man's hand quickly shot up—always a sure sign that I would be the target because they just couldn't wait to get up there and start in on me. He stood before the council, holding prepared notes in front of him. I noticed that his hands didn't shake. Most people, when they came up to address council, the moment they realized they were about to speak in public, it showed. It ranged from simply being fidgety all the way up to basket case. Many came off like the scarecrow in the Wizard of Oz. But not this guy. I respected that—even if he was an idiot, which I knew to be true having dealt with him before.

"Members of council, I come before you tonight to voice my complaint against this mayor."

The people that hated me always referred to me as "this" mayor, never "our" mayor, as if I was an unauthorized interloper. He continued.

"During a face-to-face meeting with the mayor in his office, he not only cussed, but also said some mean things to me." At this, he turned to look at me, before continuing. "You people on council are different. You talk nice to me." I tried not to let my eyes convey that I was gazing upon an imbecile. He droned on for a few more minutes which the council president was more than willing to accommodate. Clueless me had finally figured out that this smug prick of a council president not only was deliberately letting people go over their time limit to maximize their attempts at humiliating me, but that most of these citizens were recruited to do this. Like some kind of fake outrage. It felt like being heckled for five solid minutes at a comedy club and I wasn't allowed to respond. I just sat there expressionless—I was the mayor after all, setting a professional example.

"Don't stoop to their level," Taryn said, always urging me to take the high road. She was able to see my role clearly when I couldn't, the stature of my office that I needed to maintain. And Taryn knew I wanted to lash out, to call people cocksuckers and punch them. I could feel my old cynicism that Hollywood had created, the same cynicism that my new life on the farm had extinguished, but was now coming back.

187

Discord aside, there was much to admire about Taryn. She possessed a basic inner *goodness*. She had an uncluttered worldview and kept things positive when I unloaded on her at night about the day's inequities.

"I way underestimated how much time I'd be putting in as mayor—I hate what's happened to my standup—doing the same old material every show," I'd wail.

"Well, baby, can't you just write some new material?"

"I'm writing lots of new material—only now it's called *policy*."

A few days later I was sitting backstage in the green room in South Bend, Indiana, before the show. It felt good to be back with the same guys—comics that I worked with on the original *BOB & TOM Tour* a couple years earlier. It should have felt like old times but it didn't. There was a distance. It had been two years since I was elected. They all asked me the same thing, "Hastings, what's this whole mayor thing like?"

I had a hard time trying to describe exactly what I did on a day to day basis—I tried to formulate a succinct answer but when I looked up they were already scrolling through their phones. I should've been thinking about what material I wanted to do onstage, but mayoral worries kept interfering: *The new safety service director, Todd. I hope I didn't make a mistake hiring him—he's such a righteous do-gooder . . .*

"Ladies and gentlemen are you ready for your headliner tonight?" The emcee was whipping up the crowd—he introduced me as the "Mayor of Hillsboro, Ohio." He made it sound like I wasn't really a standup comedian anymore—but he wasn't entirely wrong, because somewhere along the line I've been elevated to the status of *public figure*, and it all felt a little schizophrenic.

One night Taryn, Willow, and I were having dinner.

"It dawned on me today why I get frustrated with my employees," I said. "I never get a sense of loyalty from them because they're not *my* employees. They're *city* employees—institutional employees beholden to whoever happens to be in the mayor's chair. Most of them have seen at least three mayors in this office before I got here. I'm just part of the institutional history to them."

"It's humbling, isn't it?" she said.

"That's one way to see it." After a moment I added, "Actually, you're right. You have the better perspective on it."

The look that we gave each other said that maybe we could make this work, after all. But it could all turn on a dime with us. Willow's bike left out in the yard overnight would set me off on *the utter disregard . . . the irresponsibility . . .*

"She's only nine."

Exactly—but if not now, when? I sounded like my mother.

In late spring, I took Taryn to meet my dad. He was living in a tiny house on Railroad Street in Barnesville, where he and my grandmother had both been born. It was a speck of a town twenty miles from Martins Ferry.

"Hi Dad, how's it going? This is Taryn." I had to talk loudly because he was losing his hearing.

"So, I understand you two got married!"

"Yes, yes."

It was a little awkward and I wasn't sure why. We chatted, had coffee, and went into the garage to see his motorcycle. He always had big, full-dressed motorcycles and had once ridden one out to my farm. We took a couple of pictures of him and us and left after about two hours.

"You and your dad look a lot alike," Taryn said after we left.

"Yeah, it's strange to look at him and wonder if that's what I'll look like when I'm eighty."

"Well, you can tell where you get your height, he's almost as tall as you."

"Yeah, I think he's about six-foot-three."

I wasn't sure why I'd taken her there. I guess to show her off a little. I think I just wanted someone else to know where I came from. We stopped at my grandparents' graves on the way back and I talked them up and couldn't help tearing up as I did. Then we went home.

We were heading toward the end of 2015 and my first term. No mayor wants one term, four years is too short to accomplish anything meaningful. It would be hard for me to do better than the fire department project. Running for a second term is expected, few would think twice about it. I did.

Taryn was helping me campaign for a second term. They were calling her the "First Lady of Hillsboro." Everyone who knew her liked her. Even my enemies didn't dare disparage her. She was so engaging and, well, so *good*.

"After all they keep throwing at him—I wouldn't blame him if he didn't run."

People around town were holding their breath. The vast majority wanted me to run again. The people that wanted me gone were praying that I'd throw in the towel. I remembered a morning in 2013 when Deb had walked into my office, holding up a copy of the day's newspaper. "State Attorney General Completes Investigation into Hastings' Residency." My reaction had been "'Completes'? I didn't even know one had started." One of our own police officers had gotten the state to initiate it, no less. The article went on to say that this had been done in an attempt to remove me from office, but that there was no evidence to pursue the matter further. When I had questioned my police chief whether he knew that his department was behind it he sounded like Inspector Renault from *Casablanca*: "I'm shocked—shocked I tell you!"

There'd been state ethics probes, thousands of bogus public records requests, and a finely honed small town gossip machine bent on my destruction. Everything they slung at me I met with a silent, *Is that all you got?* Of course, I would run again—I had work still to do. While my supporters breathed a sigh of relief, the other forces were preparing something nuclear. The month before the election the *Times Gazette* reported: "Ohio Democratic Party Gives $5000 to Hastings' Mayoral Opponent." The Dems at the state level wanted me out. I was flattered. It was unheard of for the state Democratic party to donate money to a small town mayoral race, let alone five thousand dollars. I was re-elected with 59 percent of the vote.

Times Gazette, December 7, 2015: "Hastings says, 'Blacks have all but formally declared war on whites.'" A Facebook post that I'd written giving a synopsis of America's cultural climate, and where we were headed, was all the talk around town. I'd long been outspoken, provocative—but this was different. Gary Abernathy, who was not just the publisher at the *Times Gazette* but a friend, did not agree with me on how to deal with it.

"You need to issue an apology," he said.

"No I don't. People are taking it out of context. Cherry-picking what they want to be offended by."

"Context is not going to matter."

Gary knew where this would go; me, I stubbornly stuck to the idea of context and critical thought, which had no place in the new arena of public discourse. Between Gary and Taryn, they convinced me to apologize. I issued an apology to the black community in Hillsboro and that seemed to settle it. Except that never settles it.

The next City Council meeting, a large contingent of very vocal black members of the community were in attendance. Another smaller, white contingent was made up of my recent mayoral opponent Ms. Limes, a past Democratic mayor, and other assorted members of Drew's Hate Squad. At least I was starting to see some actual faces of my enemies. The black attendees called for my resignation and with each speaker they became more inflamed. A woman pastor got quite excitable, her eyes rolled back in her head, and she pointed an accusatory finger at me declaring that I was Satan incarnate. The white group wildly applauded like they'd just seen a Barbara Streisand concert. I listened without comment as one after another came forth to voice their displeasure. Again I apologized but said I wouldn't be resigning over the issue. A day or so later, a council committee quickly drafted a Resolution of Disapproval: "... *the Honorable W. Drew Hastings, Mayor, has posted on social media certain missives that include commentary on white privilege, pejoratives for African-Americans, Muslims, Chinese, white supremacists, diversity, racism, affirmative action, sexual activity, workplace violence, queers, gay marriage, women, homophobes, transsexuals, gays, obesity, disabilities, and misogyny* ..." The clumsy writing and syntax errors made it hard to figure out what, exactly, I'd done, but I was impressed by their diligence. Apparently they'd scoured not only my social media posts, but every column I'd written and YouTube standup clip I'd ever posted. The resolution went on to affirm the council's abhorrence of my various communications and their desire to distance themselves from me.

"I told you an apology wouldn't end it," I told Abernathy. I was pissed that I'd apologized at all. I'd never apologized for anything I'd said on a standup stage, on social media, or from the mayor's pulpit.

191

Going into my second term, I was not the energetic, upbeat man of 2012. I was not good at the politics of the job, the required subtleties—the same problem I had at home. My immersion into marriage had been no different than my entry into mayoral life—neither were what I thought they'd be. In the mayor's office I'd slowly figured out how to compromise, when to back down. It was only a four-year commitment and if I managed to get eighty percent of the other players to see my way, it was a win. Marriage was harder. Only one other player, and they were for life. I dealt with issues and altercations at home like I did in the office—through sheer force of personality. I needed to find another way.

CHAPTER 20

Inquisition

M alfeasance. It was an odd-looking word. It looked like the name of a metal band—I pictured it printed on a black T-shirt with white gothic letters. I could hear a deep, gravelly voiced, rock radio announcer bringing them onstage at an arena: *"Are you ready for ... MALFEEEAAASANCE?"*

"It just never stops, does it?" Deb said.

"No, it does not." I said.

I was looking at a copy of a civil suit that had been filed against me just a week after beginning my second term. I was being charged with malfeasance—"improper or illegal conduct in office." There had been investigations into my qualifications for mayor since the day I'd taken office, but a lawsuit was different. Someone had to spend money to file a lawsuit and people had to make their identities known. This was a marked escalation. Filed by five citizens, the minimum required number in Ohio for filing against an elected official, I looked at the names: Ms. Limes, the mayoral opponent who'd just lost to me. Former mayor Bishop. Two former employees that had been terminated, and a local wag who owned a hair salon. They'd been armed with a document provided by the city auditor.

I got up and shut my office door and sat back down at my desk. An overwhelming sadness washed over me. Then the sadness left and I was just suddenly very tired. Why keep fighting these small town, small minded, pinheads? For *what*? To pave the streets, fix the finances, and better the prospects of a town I'd never even *heard* of a few years ago? My comedy career was suffering, my enviable hair was turning gray, and my marriage of two years was floundering. Maybe it was time to move on.

But the next morning, when I went to the grocery to get coffee, a lady in her seventies stopped me. "I'm sorry you have to deal with all this nonsense. Believe me when I tell you that a lot of people really appreciate what you're doing for Hillsboro."

"Thank you, I appreciate you saying that," I told her and hurried off toward the bread aisle. At the checkout, another old guy in a Korean War veteran's cap took me by the arm.

"You hang in there. You're doing a great job and I appreciate it."

Weird. How did these two elderly people know that I was at wits' end? And how did they know to be at Kroger this morning with their reassuring words? Suddenly, I wasn't tired anymore—I was angry. I thought about all those people who wanted me to bow out, who leveraged so much criticism and lies to make me back down. *Fuck these people*, I thought. *Fuck 'em*. I needed to get mad to shake myself out of my self-pitying defeatism. And I needed to get pumped up—it would be a long fight.

At the office, Deb had a look of relief on her face when she saw me. Maybe I was standing up straighter or something. She brought me a cup of coffee and I said, "Fuck these people, Deb."

She said, "That's right, and you know why? *Because you're the goddamn mayor.*"

I laughed. This was a favorite line of mine when I was joking around. "Yeah. Because I'm the goddamn mayor."

The good news that morning was that the civil suit had been dismissed. The bad news was that it was now a criminal investigation. The crime? Receiving a refund check. What was really fishy about this sudden investigation was that the refund check that I'd received occurred in June of

2015, seven months ago. Even fishier was that the city auditor—known for scrutinizing every expense that went through his office—had somehow missed this important transaction, though he'd personally signed for its approval. Fishier still, a month before the lawsuit and this investigation, an "anonymous party" had asked the city's law director, "How do you remove a mayor from office?" The answer: "He would need to be convicted of a felony." Then miraculously, not only does the auditor suddenly discover the old refund check, but the check then found its way into the hands of the people who filed the suit.

This criminal complaint alleged that I had improperly and illegally received a $500 refund check from the city for one of my vacant buildings uptown. Yes, I owned a vacant building; yes, I had registered it with the city and paid a required $500 fee. And then I had gone through the specified process of showing that it was no longer vacant. And then I had asked for my $500 back and a month or so later, the refund check was on my desk. So, when the newspaper called me for a comment I said, "It's ludicrous." A court appearance was scheduled and I needed an attorney. I wanted a high-powered attorney from Cincinnati but was told, "You want someone who is familiar to the courts here. A big, Cincinnati lawyer will be off-putting to the judges." One name kept coming up: Jim Boulger. I went to his office, over-explained my situation, and he took the case. It was the first time I'd ever hired a criminal attorney.

Meanwhile, the Highland County Sheriff's Department had come to our offices armed with search warrants. They seized files and documents and hard drives. Rumors were flying. We heard that the investigation was broadening to include allegations that I'd improperly dumped my personal trash into a city dumpster.

"Drew, the *Times Gazette*'s on the phone," Deb called out. Gary Abernathy wanted a comment.

"Can you hang on just a second, Gary?" I put him on hold so that I could think of a measured response and not say something half-cocked. I gave him a quote.

"I look forward to defending myself. Let's resolve this trashcan issue."

I started getting texts just hours later. Apparently, people were reading about this beyond Hillsboro. I was doing a show in Batesville, Indiana, the next night and the venue owner was texting me to ask if I was still coming.

"Of course. I'm not about to let a far reaching criminal investigation keep me from playing Batesville!" I had to keep a sense of humor about this.

At the end of January, Taryn, Willow, and I went to Sarasota for a vacation we'd planned. I didn't want to go, I felt duty-bound to stay and deal with the mess even though I couldn't really do anything. I was on the phone constantly, and the days on Lido Beach were spent switching the phone from one ear to the other periodically, the black iPhone baking hot from the sun. At dinnertime I'd lower the phone from my mouth only to say, "I'll have the grouper, please."

When I got back in the office the following week I tried to busy myself with the work piled in front of me—the current FOP union negotiations for the police department was a front burner issue—but I wasn't very focused so I passed it off to Todd Wilkin. He loved taking on responsibility so I freely gave it to him. *I sure am lucky to have him*, I thought.

I was scanning through my collection of quotes. It was all in a Word doc nowadays and I stopped at one attributed to Winston Churchill. "If you're going through Hell, keep going." He'd led an entire nation through far darker times than I was dealing with. I printed it out and taped it over my office door.

In January I read in the newspaper that the lead investigator at the sheriff's department was a Deputy Sanders, who just happened to be the son of Betty Bishop, the former mayor who had filed the suit against me. What kind of backwoods *In the Heat of the Night* justice was this? Thank God Abernathy had called them out on it and this Sanders was taken off the case.

Over the following weeks, things in our office got awkward. Todd—who ran the entire city day-to-day on my behalf—was now claiming that he hadn't authorized the refund to me and that his signature was *forged* on the refund request, inferring that the forgery came from within my office staff of three people—Deb, Ms. Collins, an assistant to Deb, or me. Todd now used this as a reason to run the city de facto on his own, ignoring me, and instead taking his orders directly from the Lord.

Around the first of February, Taryn, Willow and I were eating dinner at the farm. Someone was banging on the door and I opened it.

"Highland County Sheriff's Office. We have a search warrant."

"A search warrant? What *for*?"

"Can we come in?" the deputy said. There were three of them.

"Uh, sure. We're just eating dinner—what is this for?" I asked, not comprehending what they could possibly need a search warrant for.

"It's for your cell phone. We need your cell phone."

I gathered my wits about me. "Okay, well, if you have a search warrant I'd like to see it, please."

"Sure." A Deputy Bowen handed me the warrant, a three-page document. I started reading it over.

Taryn spoke up. "I don't mean any disrespect, but is it really necessary that you come over here late at night like this? You couldn't have come over during the day at a more appropriate time?"

I looked over at her. I didn't expect her to stand her ground like that, but I was glad she did.

Deputy Bowen said, "We just serve them when we serve them." Then he said to me again, "Can we have your phone?"

"Yeah, okay, just give me a minute to finish reading this."

I could not *believe* what I was reading. The deputy didn't realize that he hadn't handed me the search warrant—instead, he'd given me a copy of the sealed court order that was the basis for the warrant. This was testimony given by two of my trusted friends—Todd Wilkin and Sean M., a neighbor. I read it as fast as I could before Deputy Bowen realized his error. Being assured he would remain anonymous, Todd had testified that my cell phone contained incriminating evidence of some kind. Then he repeatedly asked for his name to be kept secret in the investigation because "I have a family to consider" and "am in fear for my life." Todd requesting a sealed search warrant because he was "afraid for his life" was crazy. He was 6'5", did Ironman events, was twenty years younger than me—the only exercise I was getting was mood swings. Todd didn't want his talks with the investigators made public because it would remind people of Judas.

No less shocking is that my friend Sean M., who I'd known for ten years—he often did work for me—had worn a wire for the sheriff's department. He'd worn this when we spoke on the phone just a day or so ago. He also wanted his name to remain secret.

On the bottom it was signed by a judge ordering this "sworn affidavit to be kept sealed by order of the court." I hand it back to Deputy Bowen. "I think you gave me the wrong papers. I wanted to read the *search warrant*."

Bowen took the papers from me, embarrassment coming over his face like a fast-moving red shadow. They dug the warrant out of their car, brought it in to me and I gave up my phone.

I was sick to my stomach. What were these guys trying to do to me? In Sean's case, they'd probably threatened him with charges if he didn't help. I tried to think back on the phone conversation we'd had a couple days before—he had sounded funny, not his normal speech pattern, like he was trying to get me to elaborate on something.

"The sheriff's department was at my place. They asked me if I worked for you and if I'd ever dumped any pieces of carpet or debris in the city dumpster. I told them I dumped some stuff there for you."

"Well it wasn't very much at all and it was only a couple times."

"Yes, but we're really guilty of this, Drew. Don't you think we're guilty of dumping the trash?"

"What the fuck are you talking about, dude?"

This whole trash thing was so minor, I couldn't understand why the investigators were making such a big deal out of it, trying to nail me on it.

Todd Wilkin was another matter. He was supposed to be a trusted and loyal employee. Whatever he was up to, it was likely because he'd been promised Big Things in some new power structure that the pinheads were plotting. The long leash I'd given him had gone to his head. Then again, maybe I was being overly paranoid—he may have simply been doing God's work by removing those of us that were tainted by sin.

The entire city building had quickly gone weird on me. I walked by the water department the morning after the search warrant and the two women who were conversing suddenly went quiet. Whenever I walked into the employee break room anyone who was in there suddenly left.

"The local prosecutor can't handle this case. She's turning it over to the state attorney general to prosecute," said Deb.

I was signing papers and looking over some planning commission items, trying to stay focused on anything but this surreal investigation.

Deb came back into my office an hour later. "Now it's moved from the attorney general to having a special prosecutor from the state auditor's office."

"Thanks, Deb. Make sure you don't interrupt me with any *good* news," I said, trying for humor but merely sounding cynical.

I went online to read the *Times Gazette* on this newest development. The man heading up the investigation was the deputy legal counsel for the state auditor. His office handled embezzlement and fraud committed by elected officials throughout Ohio. He had authored the state's computer crime and wiretap statutes and "specializes in prosecuting cases under the RICO statutes." I wondered how he planned to convict me of throwing my trash in a city dumpster under the RICO Act. This special prosecutor's name was Robert Smith. So utterly plain that it's slightly scary. A name that seemed coldly efficient, as if it had been assigned to him for a singular purpose. All I could think was that Agent Smith from *The Matrix* was coming for me.

The sheriff's department immediately got to work questioning my staff and seizing more hard drives for Mr. Smith's perusal. I left town, grateful to be doing shows in Evansville, Indiana. I spent the weekend writing my State of the City address for the following week, acutely aware that this was time not spent writing any new comedy material. I gave my State of the City address at the local Rotary Club luncheon by introducing myself: "What can you say about Drew Hastings that hasn't already been alleged?"

I wanted to lash out, rant. Name these idiots and the havoc they were wreaking and the cost to the community. But mayors had to set examples. *Keep your cool, remain above it all.* It had become my mantra because twenty-five years as a comedian had conditioned me to impromptu displays of emotion and passionate rants. Standup did not teach restraint.

I stuck to the speech and spoke about the need for a hotel in Hillsboro; I talked about our façade improvement program for uptown businesses. Last year, my State of the City address to this same Rotary group was an admonishment and a warning of what had now become reality. In that speech, I'd talked about attitude. "If the state of the city is about concrete and finance and its services, then the *state of mind* of the city is about its people. They are who make or break a city." A recent survey had shown that I wasn't alone—many business and professional people had cited *small mindedness* as a contributing problem for our local economic development. As I closed my remarks and asked, "How many of you sitting here today are carriers of this virus, spreading the contagion of sneering cynicism whenever you open your mouth?" I looked out and spotted no less than three of the people involved in the groundless effort to get me out of office sitting in the audience staring back at me.

In spite of all of this, a part of me still felt that this would just suddenly end—that these state investigators would see it for what it was. "Okay, we screwed up, this is just about a bunch people that don't like the mayor down there. Let's wrap this up."

February brought the first wedding of 2016. A young couple that were gaga for each other. They could barely keep their hands to themselves and giggled every five seconds like two animated chipmunks from a Disney movie. "You two are obviously on the same page—how long have you been a couple?" I asked.

They looked at each other for confirmation. "We're going on four— no—five weeks," the young man said, with just enough confidence in his voice to make his girlfriend beam.

"'Strike while the iron's hot,' as they say," and I proceeded with their vows.

Through February then March, I busied myself with ongoing projects, mainly an overhaul of Hillsboro's zoning laws, which had not changed in fifty years. This had been far more difficult since normally the safety service director would be working with me on a project this complex but he now had more nefarious items to attend to. Deb and I brainstormed the project since Todd's role as an inside informant for the state investigators made every interaction between us rather awkward. Whenever he came into my office for a meeting he secretly recorded everything that was said. I say "secretly" because he kept his cell phone in his shirt pocket, camera facing outward, his oversized phone making one side of his shirt sag in an unnatural and unstylish way.

I asked him, "Todd, are you recording our conversations?"

"I have the right to record any meeting, conversation, or interaction under Ohio Revised Code number blah blah blah, section blah blah, as long as one party in the conversation is aware of it, and in this case, I am the aware party."

It rolled off his tongue like he was reading scripture that he'd memorized from childhood. Deb and I looked at each other, trying to keep our disgust in check.

"A friend at the Board of Elections just called and said that the investigators were out there requesting information related to your residency," Deb announced a few days later.

This residency issue had been deemed a non-issue two years ago when my police department was driving around studying my nocturnal schedule. But Mr. Smith at the state was dredging it up once more.

A few days after that, Taryn called me, distraught. "There were investigators over at my work this morning demanding my work and personnel records from the HR lady. They'd never had anything like that happen there—they were freaked out and wondered what I was involved in."

I was fuming.

"Worse, Willow's principal called me and said that sheriff's department investigators had just been there at her school and wanted all of Willow's school records—attendance, family contacts, everything. The principal says Willow is really upset and I am beyond pissed about this."

"Okay. Meet me over at the school in twenty minutes and we'll get her."

Things were getting way out of control. I had bitten my tongue and said nothing as this fucking charade of an investigation had unfolded, but this was too much. Though Taryn and I still had our issues, the fighting all but stopped after that incident. We now had bigger things to worry about and we became closer by having a mutual enemy.

I wrote an open letter to the state auditor's office and sent it to the *Times Gazette*. Abernathy ran it. He'd followed this entire investigation closely, covering every aspect in his paper. Though he had no idea of my guilt or innocence, even he thought that they'd gone overboard and were primarily engaged in a witch hunt. My letter pulled no punches in berating both the Highland County Sheriff's Department and the state prosecutors. I wanted the public to know about the depths to which these people had stooped. "If the team of Special Prosecutors and Sheriff Donnie Barrera feel that going after a seven-year-old girl's elementary school records is pertinent to making their case against me, then they need to act. I will not allow my family to be swept up in this misguided prosecution," I wrote. The letter continued, essentially telling them, *either get a grand jury and indict me, or get out of my face.*

What they wanted from Willow's school records was something to prove that our residency was somewhere other than our uptown loft. But a glimmer of positivity emerged after the investigators went for our daughter's school records: the public was getting pissed. Willow went to a small Catholic school of fewer than sixty students, and the reactions were swift, shifting the public's perception of the entire investigation along with the opinion pieces Gary Abernathy had been writing. He reviewed documents and interviewed sources, started painting it as a circus of sorts. I was immensely grateful because no one else with his visibility and reach was standing up for me in this hellish affair. Investigation aside, I sometimes felt that he over-covered my time in office, until eventually I realized that though I knew I was an unlikely mayor, Abernathy's perspective made me see that I was even more out of place than I'd first imagined. He'd later go on to get an Associated Press First Place award for his coverage of my investigation and trial.

My father-in-law, Tim, came from Illinois for a couple days to visit. He was tired. He'd spent six hours driving from Peoria, had eaten dinner with us, and now just wanted to turn in. We were having him spend the night at our uptown loft and we were out at the farm. Late that night, a loud banging on the door woke him. There were shouts for him to "Open up." Understandably rattled, and somewhat frightened, he tried to call 911, then the Hillsboro Police Department, but the people outside were peering in and told him to put the phone down and open the door. My father-in-law called out, "Who is it?"

"The Highland County Sheriff's Department—we have a search warrant."

After they pounded on the door even more aggressively, and being afraid that they would break it down, Tim opened the door to three uniformed officers and two in plain clothes.

"Who are you?" they demand. He told them. They ordered him outside.

"I'm from out of town—I don't have anywhere else to go this time of night."

"Too bad. Get lost."

He called me and I was there twenty minutes later. A uniformed sheriff's deputy in a ski mask was guarding the door. "What the fuck are you doing?" I said to the officer in the black ski mask. "We are serving a war—and no one—is—"

"I can't understand what you're saying in that thing—could you please take the stupid mask off? Anyway, I know who you are because you're wearing your name badge."

A late night raid by five cops with a search warrant. Officers in ski masks. An observer might well have thought it was a murder investigation. I attempted to enter my loft but the unmasked man tried to keep me from going in. We had words and someone shoved a copy of the warrant at me.

Back at the farm, I read over the search warrant. The purpose was to, "photograph, video, view and document property, open, view, photograph any appliances, any dressers, any closets, any cabinets, any other locations that documents could be stored, view any appliance capable of holding water with purpose to record capabilities of said appliances, to seize and view any documents showing proof of residency."

An appliance capable of holding water?

For some reason, despite their "meticulous documentation," they didn't document a stack of bills sitting in plain sight, along with other mail—all addressed to us at 107 W. Beech Street—the loft. Also, a vase with a dozen red roses I'd sent to Taryn on the counter, complete with a card showing that delivery address. And let's not forget the fresh food in the fridge.

In their warrant it had said that they expected to find evidence of my non-residence, "by measuring the interior of the property, documenting the volume of water used by the toilet, and inspecting the property for furnishings appropriate to a family of three." It went on to say they'd "spent countless hours devoted to measuring how much water was used at various properties resided in or owned by Drew Hastings." Clearly my residency was now going to be a huge focus of the investigation.

The more surreal everything got the more time I spent in the grounded reality of my livestock. There was something peaceful about being in the company of cattle. They had no guile, no maliciousness. Willow thought that they were this way because they chose to be like this, because a cow knew that it wasn't right to be sneaky or hurtful. I told her that she watched too many Pixar animated movies and that cows were in fact very dumb and could not string even a basic sentence together. She thought I was mean. Regardless, there was still something calm-inducing about cattle as I watched them gathered around a hay ring in the early morning, steam billowing from their nostrils, and listened to the sound of them chewing hay and the plop, plop, plop of manure streaming out from behind them, a green purée identical to that apple/kale smoothie that Starbucks sells. When I tended to them, the mayor's office seemed very far away. Six calves would be born to these cattle in the next month. At least someone was getting something productive done.

"Deb where are we with the water rate changes—have we gotten any input from council members on this?"

"I haven't heard from any of them except one. They seem to be disengaged."

That exchange could have been about any number of topics. As the weeks then months dragged on, city council members were not giving us input on much of anything. It didn't help that the council president kept them in the dark. Nonetheless, we tried to keep the plates spinning as best we could, moving one project ahead, pivoting to another as needed. Then there were the regular duties of the office. Proclamations, weddings, and various commission meetings.

204

We had a large garbage problem in town. People tossed plastic trash bags in alleys if they didn't want to pay for a garbage pickup service. We were trying to get council to pass an ordinance requiring homeowners to have regular trash collection. City council was fighting it tooth and nail. "You can't tell people what to do with their property!" they'd scream. "It's called basic sanitation." I'd never seen any other city that didn't require garbage collection, either by a municipal trash collection department or via private collection. But such was reality in rural Appalachia.

More and more, life in my office became a waiting game. Almost all the other elected city officials weren't speaking to me and only the barest of city services were being fulfilled. *When was this investigation going to end*? I asked this, the public asked this, and Abernathy was asking regularly, writing opinion pieces castigating the state for spending hundreds of thousands of taxpayer dollars on a dubious investigation and not wrapping things up. It dragged on through spring and into summer.

More than four years in, and I still didn't quite get that I was a political figure, not a reformist-minded CEO. And that just because I refused to recognize—much less play the distasteful game of politics—didn't mean that others didn't revel in it. I refused to concede that this handful of malicious twats, this *confederacy of dunces*, could upend what was right and proper and legitimately won by a majority. Thus I completely ignored the fact that this whole affair could actually end badly for me. I simply kept following the Englishman's advice. "If you're going through Hell, *keep going.*"

I stayed busy with making plans for opening a coffeehouse called Insufficient Grounds. It's motto would be, "The only thing we're guilty of is good taste." I was genuinely excited about this prospect, trying to find the positive in some aspect of my life.

The most valuable person in a mayor's world is his administrative assistant, and any mayor from NYC to South Bend, Indiana, would likely agree. Admin assistants are part secretary, press agent, sounding board, friend, and confidante. They are the gatekeeper to your office, determining who gets an appointment or who is simply a return phone call. They schedule all your work activities and, often, much of your life in general. Your administrative assistant *is a version of you*. A better version, because they're a version of you without the ego. They are grounded, what you could be like if you had your shit together. They shadow you, represent you, act as you in your absence. They can often write a letter on your behalf that sounds more like you than if you'd written it yourself. And because the job of mayoring is often about having ideas or policy met with violent opposition, it tends to create a bunker mentality, an "us against them" bond that creates a fierce loyalty in both directions. Deb and I had that.

In April, the investigators with their warrants raided Deb's home. I was furious. Why the fuck were they dragging her into this? She hadn't dumped trash, didn't have a residency problem, or hadn't gotten a refund check. Word was that they'd decided that she was the one who had written a falsified refund letter with Todd's signature—or they'd decided that they could pressure her enough that she'd cave and be a witness against me.

In the meantime, we weren't about to let anything deter us from running the city and making improvements where possible—much less let anyone see that we were rattled.

"Damn, I love fried mush." I said. Having lunch with Deb at Bob Evans, we were catching up on the progress or lack of it in the city offices. The investigation had now dragged on for more than six months. City Council wasn't talking *to* me, the auditor was talking *about* me, and my safety service director was *recording* me. We were in the middle of lunch when I looked up and a Highland County Sheriff was standing over me.

"Hi, are you Drew Hastings?"

"Yes . . ."

He handed me a packet of papers. "This is a criminal indictment issued to you. You've been served." He turned and left.

I looked at the papers, looked at Deb, and said, "That is the fastest I've ever been served at a Bob Evans."

I felt relieved in an odd way. I now had some certainty in my life. No more conjecture or rumor. Any debate over whether I would actually be indicted was over. I was going to trial.

I was charged on four counts, all felonies: election falsification, theft in office, theft, tampering with records. The charges were not particularly easy to decipher. A lot of *did knowingly* and *with the purpose to defraud* were sprinkled throughout. The election falsification charge was how they were trying to get me on the residency issue. It appeared that the tampering with records charge was also related to the residency issue. The theft in office charge related to my improperly receiving the $500 refund check. The other theft charge pertained to my dumping of personal trash in a city-owned dumpster.

Sure I had dumped some stuff—a few times in fact—into a city-owned dumpster. Though my act could arguably be called improper, it paled at the transgressions of previous mayors—using on-duty city workers to perform personal work, awarding contracts to relatives, or lying to the public and creating a taxpayer expense to repay political favors. I refused to believe that someone would find me guilty of throwing debris into a dumpster even if it was the city's. And these other three charges leveled at me were simply preposterous—they were not only unfounded, but the evidence being used to indict me was such a stretch that it resembled a comedy sketch.

I left Deb and Bob Evans and headed over to a nearby strip center for a ribbon cutting at a new medical office. I stood, smiling, squinting into the sunlight with the other dignitaries, holding a giant pair of scissors, while we all froze in place for the photographer. The saying "Be careful what you wish for," came to mind.

"Hello?"

"Hi, Mayor Hastings? This is Kristin with the Highland County Sheriff's Office. I'm calling to tell you that you'll need to come in and get your mug shot taken. We take mug shots between nine and four daily."

There was no end to the weirdness of this case. I knew Kristin from when she worked at the Enterprise car rental. I was used to hearing her call to say, "Hi, you'll need to come in to pick up the rental you reserved with us. You can come in between nine and five." I waited until it was a good hair day, which was two days later, which didn't matter because I still took a horrid picture.

I read a newspaper article stating that the state prosecutor feared I "was a flight risk and would flee the area." Did Mr. Smith really think I'd disappear into the Matrix? *Over dumping trash?* The paper called me for a response. "Ludicrous. After the indictment was served, *I did a ribbon cutting*. I'm doing my job as usual for the city. I have multiple investments in this town—*my home is here*," I told Abernathy.

Over the next three months, I met with my attorney, read discovery documents, and got sick to my stomach. When people are being interviewed in criminal cases, they either forgot that you'll read their testimony or simply didn't care. "You know, he always seemed to be out of pens in the office—I often wondered if he might have been stealing them."

Many of my standup shows started getting cancelled, or failed to materialize in the first place. My wife was stressed; she started going to church much more often. I couldn't blame her. Me, I took the pharmaceutical route to find solace. My doctor put me on anti-depressants which killed the sense of urgency I normally had, so I wasn't getting any work done. I looked on the side of the pill bottle to see if one of the side effects was "going through the motions." It seemed like the only thing in my favor in the months leading up to the trial was the public's outrage. They were pissed about what they saw as a full-blown witch hunt.

My case was to be tried by an out of town judge, Judge Patricia Cosgrove, and in our preliminary court hearing she immediately placed a "pre-trial publicity order," which barred anyone remotely associated with the case, including witnesses, from commenting to the media or doing any social media postings. "There has been a lot of publicity about this trial. We are going to try this case in the courtroom." This gag order was due to the city auditor, a witness in the case, posting rants on Facebook that in essence claimed I was guilty. A month before the trial Michelle Truitt called. "Drew, they've arrested Bob Lambert."

"*Bob*? What the hell for?"

"Something to do with teenage boys."

"Great, just great," I said and hung up. I didn't know what to think about it. Except that if there was one thing I'd learned about everything surrounding me, there were no coincidences. Yes, Bob was gay, and yes, he liked younger guys, but this just seemed rather suspect. Though he had long been my best friend, I didn't know what to make of it but I had bigger problems right now.

My trial was set for November 7, 2016. The state asked my attorney if we wanted to plea bargain. No way. I wanted a trial to show the lunacy of this Inquisition.

Taryn had gone to bed and I was watching a movie, *Unforgiven*, for the third time. Near the end, Clint Eastwood, playing a bad guy, has Gene Hackman, who's playing a worse bad guy, cornered, about to shoot him. "I don't deserve this," Hackman wails. "Deserve's got nothin' to do with it," Eastwood replies, pulling the trigger.

Life's not fair.

Maybe I had this all wrong. Four years ago it sometimes felt like an invisible hand was pushing me forward to do good via this mayoral endeavor—a Joan of Arc-like quest propelled by an aroused, hopeful public and my own sense of righteous indignation. But maybe it was the opposite. Now, I couldn't help but feel that I was being punished somehow, that all of this was God's doing. Him showing me that not only did He exist but that He was punishing me for—*for what*? I was not a bad person, I was a pretty straight up guy. I had a decent moral code, though I would not have wanted my grandfather scrutinizing my life from Above, appraising all the years of sheer escapism and how often I was a shitty boyfriend. My remorse around these two chronic behaviors could have easily let me imagine that a punishing God might be at play here.

Yet I wasn't even sure there was a God. I was only sure that I was guilty of those things and that He might want to punish me for them if He did exist. I couldn't think straight. All I knew was that this was the hardest, most miserable, most trying time of my life and I couldn't point to anything else as being a cause other than that I had won a small town local election.

The prosecution was having a hard time finding a jury. The usual number of people in a jury pool in Highland County was fewer than forty, but the judge had ordered a minimum of a hundred because of pre-trial publicity and the difficulty of finding jurors who had not formed an opinion.

I heard they'd gone through closer to two hundred prospective jurors, unheard of around here.

On Tuesday, November 8, the actual trial got underway. My attorney thought it would only go two days. I should've been happy at this news but it seemed wrong that the past ten months of humiliation, stress, marital discord, uncertainty, and almost complete paralysis of city government was being distilled down to two days. The courtroom was filled but I didn't look back to see who was there. I didn't want to know. I knew Taryn sat behind me in the front row of seats along with my longtime friend, H.

My attorney always seemed like he was deep in thought. He and I sat in the courtroom at the large defendant's table. The surface and front edge of the table were well-worn and smooth, polished by damp and nervous hands, the murderers, thieves, and molesters of children. And now me.

There were opening arguments. The prosecutor explained the case he would lay out, the case that would convict me.

"The evidence will show *beyond all shadow of a doubt . . .*"

"The State *asserts . . .*"

"There was *no prior authorization . . .*"

"This case is about abuse of power and a mayor who thought the laws didn't apply to him."

"Any reasonable person must *conclude . . .*"

My attorney was low key and not at all like the passionate defense attorneys of television land. He was, as he opened with, "frankly, a little baffled why we're even here." He argued that "the evidence that the prosecution presents was long-ignored and only being used now as a political vendetta that began when Mr. Hastings won re-election."

Police Chief Todd Whited took the stand. He wasn't up there long. He testified that he was "tipped off to some two-by-four boards" that were left in a dumpster. When he was cross-examined by Mr. Boulger, he admitted that he pursued the theft charges against me after he and I had a disagreement about police department staffing when I'd turned down his request for more officers.

Todd Wilkin took the stand and Prosecutor Smith coaxed him along with his prepared testimony. Every time I looked at him I was reminded of the crazed, zealous preacher in the movie *There Will Be Blood*. He testified about the $500 refund that I requested, and that he had turned down. Then related that I was given the refund, but that on the letter that authorized said refund, he did not sign it but that instead someone had used his signature stamp on it. This was the crux of the Theft in Office and Tampering with Records charges even though the City Auditor had issued the check to me and no one could say if the refund letter was even forged. When Todd finished he looked pleased with himself and glanced around as if he might be rewarded with an ice cream cone. He stood to step down. "Just a couple of questions, if I may, Mr. Wilkin." My attorney questioned Todd, who became indignant that his truthfulness was being questioned. He tried getting cute with semantics. "Just answer the questions, Mr. Wilkin," the judge warned. Todd was rattled when he came down from the stand and did not look around for ice cream.

The entire proceeding was exhausting, listening to the language of law, a vocabulary devoid of warmth, each word and phrase, specific and impersonal, designed to get to the Truth. The prosecution had a witness list of twenty-seven people and we'd only heard from the two Todds. There were still various investigators from various agencies and a handful of city employees to come and I wondered briefly if there might be even more Todds.

Testimony was given. "Did you at any point . . . ?" "I cannot recall exactly." So much of it seemed to be an exercise in vagueness. One after another. People that I'd stood with in the office break room, laughing over a cup of coffee just a few months before, now testifying that they saw me throw used carpeting into a dumpster. Another testified that I tossed two-by-fours into the dumpster. The prosecutor had photos of broken boards piled in a heap inside of the dumpster. He thrust these lurid crime scene photos under the employee's nose: "Is this the lumber that Mayor Hastings disposed of?" A grim nod in the affirmative. More city workers were trotted out to confirm that there had been other times, other trash. My attorney cross-examined the first one.

"The walls of the dumpster go up over six feet high, and Mayor Hastings is throwing these two by fours over this wall. So, tell me how it is that you are so sure these are the boards he threw in if you *cannot even see into the dumpster?*"

"I—I—guess I can't be sure. I mean, a lot of two-by-fours look the same."

My attorney rubbed his temples as if trying to comprehend. "*A-lot-of-two-by-fours-look-the-same.* No more questions, your honor." Mr. Smith then brought up his star dumpster witness. "Mr. Pence, how many times would you say you witnessed Mayor Hastings dispose of debris into the city dumpster?" Mr. Pence, with a pleased look, sat straight up in his chair, as if getting ready to receive a First Place ribbon. "At least seven times." Mr. Smith wheeled around to face the jury. "*At least seven times!*—And those are just the ones *we know of,*" he exclaimed, as if trying to paint me in the same light as a serial killer. *Seven murdered prostitutes that we know of.* "I have no more questions, your honor," said Mr. Smith.

Mr. Pence, thinking he was done, stood up. "Just a second, Mr. Pence. I only have a question or two," said my attorney. Mr. Pence sat back down. "Mr. Pence, this dumpster—is it locked up during the day or is it accessible by the general public?"

"Uh, it's not locked up."

"Okay. Now, are there any signs either *on* this dumpster or *anywhere* in the vicinity that say, 'No dumping allowed,' or, 'Do not use'?"

"No, there are not."

"Okay. And doesn't the city have approximately *ten* dumpsters just like this, dotted around town?"

"Uh, yes."

"Last question—does the city have any policies about employees using the dumpsters or are there any ordinances that prohibit anyone from using a city dumpster?"

"Umm, no."

"No more questions."

Day Two. Mr. Smith started laying out for the jurors my residency—or lack of it—in Hillsboro. He had to prove that my residency was not my uptown loft, as I claimed, but instead the farm which was outside of the city limits, thus making me ineligible to be mayor. This was the first time in Ohio history that anyone had been charged criminally over a residency issue. During the now infamous search of our uptown loft, the investigators had documented everything by taking pictures. Photographs used in trials were called exhibits and they made me think of an art gallery. There were one hundred and ninety-four exhibits. "I would like to submit the following photographs as evidence, your honor," said Mr. Smith.

A picture of one of my suits, captioned, *Business suit with no matching shoes of a business nature.* A sock drawer titled, *A very small number of socks.* An eight by ten of Taryn's lingerie drawer titled, *Only one bra.* There was a photo of a toaster—*No crumbs present.* The concept of a loft as a place to live seemed to be beyond the comprehension of investigators since there was a large picture of the loft interior captioned, *There are no defined bedrooms of a traditional nature.* There were pictures of dishes, silverware, a photo of a bottle of dish detergent with a notation, *Almost entirely full.* Photos of our toilet complete with model and gallons per flush data and pictures of the hot water heater with close-ups of capacities. I had to remind myself that this wasn't a *Monty Python* sketch but felony charges.

My attorney had been baffled from the very onset by the state's insistence on pressing charges for residency. He knew what Ohio law said, which was that, in essence it presumed that your residency was where you planted your flag. By simply declaring your residency to be a certain location, that made it your residency. It didn't matter if you slept there six nights a year or three hundred. Mr. Boulger emphasized this to the jury, and we broke for lunch.

"The rest of the afternoon will most likely be you on the stand in your own defense. Stay calm. Don't let Mr. Smith get you angry or excitable. Tell the truth."

I sat on the witness stand and looked out toward the courtroom for the first time. It was mostly filled but I didn't see specific faces, only a crowd. I didn't want to recognize anyone mostly because I was ashamed to be there. Somehow, some way, I had allowed this to happen to me. I only took notice of my wife and occasionally looked her way.

Mr. Smith started in on me about my residence. "How many nights a year would you say that you spend at your loft, Mr. Hastings?"

"Objection, irrelevant."

Mr. Smith asked me numerous questions about my comings and goings from the loft and the farm. He had subpoenaed not only my water bills but the electric bills too, and had monthly statements spread out on a table.

"Mr. Hastings, it's obvious that you spend far more time residing at your farm than you do in your loft apartment, isn't that true?"

"Yes."

"So you'd agree that your lawful residence is, in fact the farm, am I right?"

"No. Our residence is the loft uptown, but I prefer to spend most nights at the farm. My farm is peaceful. It sits on a hill with a beautiful view. There are cattle to take care of. I think most people would want to stay there as opposed to a small uptown apartment. At least, I think so."

I looked at the jury, all of whom were from rural farm country. My answer to the prosecutor was probably the same answer that most of these jurors would have given, and so, an indictment of me was also an indictment of *them*. But Mr. Smith was from Columbus, and I don't know if he realized the significance of that exchange.

Mr. Smith moved on to the refund check issue. He made me recount the chronology and sequence of why and how I received a refund. He was trying to ascertain who, if anyone, had forged Todd Wilkin's signature, allowing my refund. And here, we had something in common. Because we were both baffled as to who may have forged his signature—or if his signature was even forged at all. I could not tell him.

We were getting into late afternoon and Mr. Smith was setting up an easel so that the jury could see the oversized photographs of dumpsters. There were arrows pointing to nondescript boards that lay amid plastic bags of trash. I was tired but I got the sense that Mr. Smith was tired too. He seemed to have lost some of the spring in his step. He played the tape-recorded call between me and my now former friend, Mahorney. I admitted to dumping stuff half a dozen times, though my attorney had already made the case that there was no law or ordinance making it illegal.

Mr. Smith made his closing arguments and Mr. Boulger made his.

"The prosecution rests."

"The defense rests."

Yet, no one in the room looked particularly rested. Least of all, me. Taryn and I and Mr. Boulger left to get dinner and the jury had food delivered while they deliberated.

It was early evening and the courtroom was empty except for me, my attorney, Taryn, my friend H, and Gary Abernathy, all waiting for the outcome. I was exhausted. I'd been up late the night before watching the presidential election results. It was a very different election than most: good old boy (or girl)—Clinton, in this case—versus a reform-minded outsider. When I'd finally gone to bed at three in the morning there were stunned news anchors muttering, "How did this happen? It wasn't supposed to be like this."

How could I not see the parallel? Though Trump's story was far bigger, our paths had been weirdly similar. Trump—businessman, show biz background—made a very unlikely play for political office. He too wanted to clean house, to govern with a businessman's perspective. Populist appeal, hated by elites. The difference was that I'd been in office five years and he had not yet seen his future.

I turned around and looked at Taryn, and tried to manage a smile. We'd only been married three years. She didn't sign up for this, didn't deserve this—having investigators go through her lingerie drawer counting her underwear, and watching detectives pore through our daughter's school records. I hadn't signed up for this either. It was worse than some peyote-induced bad dream. I was on trial for four felonies and if the jurors walked out of that jury room and voted for my guilt, I would immediately be removed from office, and very possibly be sentenced to jail.

When I'd first been indicted, a reporter had asked for a comment. "I am only guilty of trying to represent our citizens without the consent of an established political structure," I'd said. *That* was my true crime—it wasn't these trumped-up charges. For a long time I'd thought that these people had rained all of this down on me because I'd tried to make changes to their way of doing things, but I was wrong. My true crime was that *I simply was not one of them.*

When I ran for office, the residents had warned me about this, but I had stupidly thought of the good old boy system as a pest removal problem, like having rats or bedbugs. Except it turned out the rodents were well entrenched, and I was the one that needed to be exterminated. And now, over these last three very trying months, it was the residents, once again, that I was hearing from—at the grocery, the gas station, on the sidewalk: *This is nothing more than a witch hunt, you hang in there. This is BS, we're praying for you.* Hundreds of people from all over the county, along with

215

my wife's support, had helped keep me from saying, *fuck it*, and doing
something stupid. But at this moment, everyone's support and well-wishing
was a million miles away and not admissible as testimony. It was now just
my attorney and I sitting a defendant's table.

I was startled as the door to the jury room opened and the jurors filed
back into the courtroom, taking their seats. Then the judge entered the
room briskly, her long black robes swooshing behind her like some giant
bat, and the bailiff announced, "All rise . . ."

Of the four charges, I was acquitted of the first two—thrown out
without basis—and found not guilty of the other two. When the jury
foreman had read the first "not guilty," my wife, sitting behind me, had
burst into sobs and it broke my heart. I don't remember much else that day.
The slaps on the back, car horns honking around town, and congratulatory
phone calls were all blurred.

I still had three years left to serve as mayor. It was not going to be easy.
It wasn't my enemies that would make it difficult—of course they kept
fighting me, but they had lost the war. I got rid of my police chief. I fired
my safety service director. The city auditor quit his elected post and took
a job working under Todd Wilkin in a small town down the road. And our
city council president permanently lost his law license, got divorced, and I
occasionally saw him around town looking like a shadow of his formerly
shadowy self. Of all of them, I alone was left standing in the city building.
A line from a favorite poem, "Invictus," framed on my wall, came to mind:
"My head is bloody, but unbowed."

Things got smaller. Deb and I put our efforts into simpler but meaningful projects that would make a difference to the community, and there
were still the weddings, the ribbon cuttings, and meetings of the commissions. I went to the annual Ohio mayors conference in June of 2018 to
hang with other mayors and see what they were up to in their respective
towns. Decaying water and sewer infrastructure was the hot topic that
year, but like most things mayoral nowadays, I couldn't get that excited. I
left the conference a day early and detoured to see my dad. It was Father's
Day weekend and I figured I'd surprise him. I also felt like I wouldn't be
seeing him much more. He was now in an assisted living facility over in
Wheeling, across the river from Martins Ferry. He was sitting in the day

room in a wheelchair facing the window with his back to me and when I walked around in front of him he looked up.

"Hey Dad, how are you?"

He took a moment before he answered. "Ah—well, hey there!"

"I was on over at a mayors conference in Akron and thought I'd swing by and see you."

"Oh! My other son is a mayor too!"

I was thrown. For a second, I wondered if his other son had somehow become a mayor as well, but from what I knew about him that seemed extremely doubtful.

Then he added, "He also has a farm."

He was talking about me. He thought I was his other Drew. I didn't want him to be embarrassed by this mental lapse so before he realized his mistake, I quickly changed the subject. Beautiful. He'd only gotten to know me when I was fifty and he was already forgetting me at sixty-four.

"Happy Father's Day. I wanted to stop by before I went back to Hillsboro where I live. It'll be good to see my wife Taryn again." I was trying to make him realize who he was talking to and it seemed to work. He suddenly looked a tad startled and sheepish.

"I'm so glad you came! How is she? You still have the cattle herd out there?"

"Yes, yes."

We talked about his new quarters. He'd sold his home in Barnesville and moved into Peterson's Rehabilitation Hospital, a clean but depressing place. It was where you went when all you had was Medicaid. It didn't look like a place where people went to actually rehabilitate.

"They're really nice here but the food could be better."

"I'm sure, but people probably don't come here for the food."

We talked about trivial things. It was hard to look at him sitting there, aquarium tubing strapped to his face, doling out oxygen.

"I have to pee. Would you mind pushing me over to my room?"

I wheeled him over to the bathroom door in his room.

"No, just push me next to the bed. I'll be a few minutes so just wait out in the hall."

I walked over to the nurses' station.

"Hi, I'm Drew Hastings' son."

"We figured you were. You look alike."

"So, how's he doing?"

"He's not in too bad of shape. He can walk but he doesn't want to get out of his wheelchair. He can go outside if he wants but we can never get him to go. He sleeps a lot and reads a ton of books."

It sounded like me when I was in a bout of depression. I went back to check on him but he was still trying to get his pajama bottoms down so he could pee into a plastic bottle.

"Dad, you need my help with this?"

"No, no, I'll be out shortly." And he waved my away.

I came back three more times and he still wasn't done.

I sat in the day room resenting that what little time we spent together was near the end of his life, in this condition. It wasn't what you'd call quality time together.

My dad regularly talked about his two daughters but he seldom, if ever, mentioned his son, the other Drew. I'd been told he and my dad did not get along. I'd heard that he'd been in and out of trouble much of his life. I'd found enough on the internet about him to know that I didn't envy his life, certainly wouldn't trade places with him. For the first time, I wondered if maybe I'd been better off not having a father—at least this one. I felt guilty even entertaining the idea. I tried picturing my dad living in the house through all the years I was growing up—how different it would have been. I'd always just assumed life would have been much better, but was it possible it might have been worse? Not the living conditions or lifestyle, not the household dynamics that may have prevailed—but the end result. Me as a person, a man. I'd been told more than once that I had similar traits as my father, that I was like him in many ways. If that was true, then maybe just because he was not physically there, guiding me as I grew up, did not mean that he'd had no part in my life. His genetics had not only influenced me, but to some degree made me who I am today. So, from a strictly molecular level, he'd always been there for me. Fortunately, my father was done peeing and came wheeling into the room and disrupted my speculations.

"I'm sleepy. I didn't get enough sleep last night," he told me.

"I'm tired too. I don't like to sleep, I always fight it."

My father told me that he also has always fought going to sleep, stayed up late, and that my grandfather did too. "It runs in the family," he said.

He soon fell asleep in his wheelchair and I left. I just wanted to get home to my wife and the familiarity of my farm.

"I put a letter on your desk that you'll need to read today," Deb said.

But I knew what it was by the look on her face. I was beyond grateful that she had stayed as long as she did—most would've walked out long before. Deb had gone well beyond the call of duty and had become a good friend in the process. I think she knew better than I how unlikely a fit I was for this job and she was determined to see that I succeeded. I had. Her husband, Rick, had passed away less than a year earlier. Deb needed to take care of herself now and once she retired in late 2018, I felt a little like a ghost wandering the halls of the city building. Everyone I'd started with was gone. I was depressed, felt a little lost, and still had a year to go. I'd never quite feel about Hillsboro the way I once did. I would never quite trust it again. Like a partner that's cheated on you there would always be an underlying resentment. If it could happen once, well . . .

CHAPTER 21

The Making of a Man

I survived 2016, the darkest, most trying days of my life, and then spent the remaining three years of my last term fighting not my enemies, but myself, mostly trying to muster some semblance of the energy and sense of purpose that had brought me to a mayor's office in the first place, but never rising above the level of *semblance*. I operated in a PTSD-like state that would not allow me to envision my future as anything beyond *lacklus-ter*, and it was against this backdrop in July of 2019 that my son was born.

The arrival of one's first child is a momentous event in most men's lives. The arrival of one's first child when that man is sixty-five and had, up until age sixty-four, never wanted children, is even more noteworthy. When you hear couples talk about having children they don't quite convey the reality. "Your whole life changes—from that point on everything is about your child." What gets left out is, "Until he was born you had no clue what love was."

The part I did not expect was that after the *Overwhelmingly Immense Love* happened, it was immediately followed by terror—sheer terror that something could happen to the object of this love. That it could be killed or taken away, and now that was always present in me, lurking behind the love. For at least six months after he was born, every time I left the house I heard Harry Chapin's "Cat's in the Cradle" playing in my head and I'd fight the urge to turn around and drive back home. "And he said, I'm gonna be just like you Dad, / You know I'm gonna be like you." For the first year, when he tottered into my home office, I'd tear up when he came into view. Every single time.

One of my walls in my home office has what my wife calls my "Wall of Vanity." Maybe it is. But it's more. I've always thought of it as my record of achievements. Moments of pride. Framed picture of me on *The Tonight Show*. A blown-up poster of my Comedy Central special. There's a photo of me standing in front of the ruins of Tikal in Guatemala, and another of me on top of Machu Picchu in Peru. Then there's one of me on horseback, playing polo. One of my favorites is a huge thank you note from the first grade class at Hillsboro Elementary: "Dear Mayor Hastings. Thank you for coming to our class and reading stories to us . . ."

I'm sure my wife thinks me vain, maybe even shallow for having this Wall of Drew—all this emphasis on *me*. Back in the dark days of the Inquisition, when she was scared and our marriage was cracking under the strain of search warrants and lies, she began going to church, finding her faith, and has been a devout Catholic ever since. Thus she sees our lives on earth in a very different way than I do. I asked her what she thought that our purpose in life was about. "This life is lived for Jesus Christ. We love him. We worship him. We serve him."

That certainly doesn't leave much room for anything else, was my first thought. Then again, finding a balance between religious devotion and secular achievement has been a source of angst since the Dawn of Man—and that angst is probably proportional to the amount of doubt one has regarding what actually *caused* the Dawn of Man. And the appearance of "ILoveDrew" vanity plates at a specific moment in time would certainly contribute to that angst.

I think that my wife just sees a name—*Drew Hastings*—plastered across the wall. But unlike my old footlocker full of business cards, the Wall is not just a simple fixation. The Wall is where that name has been and what it's achieved. My name has had over a half century to justify its worth. *I am a man and I was here and I did things and just want to be remembered.* There have been moments when I looked at that wall in recent years and felt sheepish. "What is all of that for? When I die, it's all just a stack of photos on a table that someone is rummaging through—*bidding starts at $10.*"

But then my son appeared, and now my life will not end in a series of cardboard boxes scattered across the county in ten-dollar increments. Most of my adult life I'd been filling footlockers and saving memorabilia and displaying my pictorial history all in anticipation of having a child that I had never even consciously considered. I'd never once fantasized about having a child, never pictured myself playing with an imagined offspring. But it has happened and now I have an heir.

I've seen movies, usually set in medieval times, where the king gives a soliloquy or slumps down into his throne bemoaning the fact that he has no heir. *My family line dies with me—my kingdom for an heir!* I never quite understood the histrionics over this until I had a son. But it's very apparent now. It's how we live on.

He's twenty months old now and I've taken to planting trees. Boys love to climb trees and I buy sycamores that are of a size that, in ten years, they will be big enough for him to build a tree house in. For half a century I couldn't plan into next month, but now I plan decades into the future, planting trees on scrubby pasture land that will hopefully be a lush forest when he's a man. It takes hours to dig each hole in the rocky soil and I ache so badly I have to eat handfuls of ibuprofen and wait two days before I can resume. I wonder if he will appreciate what I'm doing but then I realize that I don't care if he ever does and that's because of the Overwhelming Immense Love.

When I look at my son, I cannot fathom how a father can walk away from his child. I'm sure that other fathers must feel the same but it wasn't enough to keep my dad in the picture. I know that lots of dads leave—relationships go bad, get toxic, hateful, and finally there's a tipping point, but I pray that I'm never tested with that consideration.

Two weeks after my son was born I got a call from my half-sister Jennifer telling me that my father had maybe a day or so to live. Initially, I'd told her to notify me when he passed, but I called her back early the next morning.

"How's he doing?"

"Okay. Asleep. Tossing and turning but he doesn't actually wake up."

"Have you made arrangements—you know, funeral home, casket."

"Oh, he doesn't want any service or funeral—*oh you know Dad!*—he wouldn't want all that ceremony. Actually, he sold his body to science. We're supposed to call an eight-hundred number once he's gone and within hours they come pick him up and take him to a lab in Philadelphia."

I heard her but my ears were still hearing her say, *"Oh, you know Dad!"* But I didn't know Dad. That was the whole point, kind of.

"Well, what about the cemetery—didn't he have a prior arrangement with a cemetery?" I asked.

"No, he never mentioned a cemetery that I know of."

What the hell? Did our arrangement, the whole "him and I being buried side-by-side," get lost in the commotion of my dad's final days? Or was that just some romantic notion he'd had and then never followed up on? He was fairly destitute, so I could easily imagine him selling off those plots in a moment of hardship. *Oh, I'll buy them again when my finances improve.*

"So, when he passes, a truck is coming to pick him up and that's it?"

"Yes. The lab said that three or four months after they're done with him—I don't think there are many parts left—then they cremate him and send ashes back to us."

When the lab is done with him. This was all way too non-traditional for my taste. When I die, I want one of those mausoleums—a little granite building all my own with an iron door and my name carved into the lintel above. A structure that causes passersby to exclaim, "Wow, who was *he*?" And I definitely want all my parts intact. I want my arms folded across my chest like a knight from the Crusades. No missing limbs in jars of formaldehyde that show up in some community college dissection class.

I decided to drive over there. I wasn't sure that I needed or wanted closure but I wasn't going to take a chance. He'd already left me once. I drove the three and a half hours to Wheeling, and pulled into the Peterson's assisted living facility. I asked Jennifer if her brother—the other Drew Hastings—had been notified and was coming.

"No, he and Dad haven't really talked for the last few years. Drew doesn't want to talk to Dad."

Oh, the irony. The kid that "replaced" me as a child, the one that got to have our dad as a father, had no interest in being here as he lay dying, and here I was, seeing him off. As I watched my dad in his hospital bed I was struck by how much he looked like my newborn son. He lay there, drawn up almost in a fetal position, limbs twitching, softly breathing, his skin baby soft.

We sat in his room talking—my two half-sisters and Jennifer's husband. They related random facts about our dad and told stories about him. They all said he was immensely curious about everything. Constantly read up on anything that he ran across—devoured information and facts. He had a huge interest in philosophy and metaphysics and history. I got the sense they were inferring that he was not cut out for family life, that though he was their father and a husband, he was not really a family man, that he was somewhat removed from day-to-day family matters in his pursuit of knowledge, or otherwise preoccupied in his thoughts. I think I knew what they were trying to say.

I found the night nurse. "How long can he go on like this?" I asked. He hadn't had water for two days and hadn't eaten in three. His kidneys were shutting down.

"He might last three hours or go sometime tomorrow."

I decided to leave and head home. I hadn't come to be there when he died, I had come to say goodbye. I asked to be alone with him and then sat there holding his cold hand. "I just came to say goodbye, Dad." I wanted him to open his eyes, recognize me, have a heart to heart moment with appropriate closure, but he just lay there softly breathing. I sat there for a few more minutes. It was the first time that I had ever felt really connected to him. I kissed his baby-soft face and sat there sobbing, mostly for me I guess. Then I went home.

I got a text the next morning. "Dad passed away at 6:38 a.m."

I went into my son's room to look in on him. Odd how things seemed to have gone from past to future overnight. My past, his future. My future will, from here out, always be in the service of my son's future, and I feel both insignificant and entirely significant. I'm jolted into an awareness that my significance is predicated on me remaining in his life. I worry about the regular marital fights that could snowball into divorce. But at sixty-six, I also worry about being dead. My first goal is to remain upright at least until he has conscious memories of me. Odds are decent I won't see him graduate high school, much less college, but my immediate concern is that we have enough time together to bond, to imprint, so that he remembers me, and doesn't just have some fuzzy awareness of a dad that he can't quite make out. I look down at him again. *How did this happen to me?* But now when I ask this question it's because I *marvel.* Yes, my son is very unlikely—and yet something about him seems so planned. His presence makes all of those inadvertent and unlikely turns that my life has taken, turns and scenarios that seemingly had no relation to each other, suddenly look like a convergence.

Then again, I could just be gaga about my boy, believing any romantic notion that pops into my head, like I used to do with women. *This is destiny! We were meant to be together!* I can't help but think of that church incident in Hollywood fifteen years back. It's crossed my mind a few times over the years but that's all it ever did—a brief, *What was that?* and then I'd move to other thoughts that were less uncomfortable and more easily answered. But too much has happened since that day in that parking lot and somehow the car with an "ILoveDrew" license plate seems almost undeniable.

I *have* to reconsider the church incident because my son is miraculous—not him per se, but his *presence* in my life, and the miracle is that I somehow moved in a direction that enabled him to come about. I've learned about family from my wife and stepdaughter but it has not been easy. Every day I fight my past. Too often, I remind myself of my stepfather, Marty, in my treatment of Willow. I often hear my own mother's voice, the critical part, the unapproving part, when dealing with both of them. It remains to be seen what part of me my son will see, but I'm hopeful. He's brought a joy into my life that all but shattered the pervasive cynicism in me. I am blown away by the radiance he exudes—innocence, love, an unconditional openness to anything in front of him. Was I ever like that?

I'm both ecstatic and terrified about being his dad, becoming *his* influence—and I no sooner type the words, *becoming his influence*, than their gravity hits home. My son—his name is Harrison—is not only the first person I've ever set out to influence, but I've never even practiced on anyone else. Hell, how does one actually go about influencing? I think back on those men that were my influences. Sometimes specific lessons were taught, but more often than not their habits or outlook just kind of rubbed off on me, good and bad. By my early-twenties, I'd taken all my influences and created a patchwork of manhood.

I don't want that for my son. I want to be the template he starts from. I think about how my half-sisters had described my father when we sat with him at the end, that he liked his solitude, that he had many interests, that maybe he wasn't a family man at heart. My impression of him matches what I know to be true about me. Marriage and family life for me feels like a construct that I am consciously aware of more often than I'd like to be. There are moments when I am organically immersed in my family-ness but, in general, I'm very aware of my otherness, standing over here looking at my family, aware that this is a role I'm in and it can suddenly all come crashing down. My wife and I still have our differences, and they're not small ones, and when we fight, the fragility of this construct is very apparent. My son's arrival has helped ensure that this family stays intact. I will never leave my son no matter how difficult my marriage. Maybe I say that as testament to how much I'm willing to endure for him. Maybe my son is teaching me a basic tenet of manhood. Men stay. But that also sounds smug, so ideologically unaware of the marital realities—the myriad of exceptions that make it so that fathers really do go away. And of course, there are the hypocrisies that troubled marriages, maybe all marriages, lay bare. But my son knows nothing of constructs or hypocrisy, he only knows *Dad is here*, or, *Dad went away*, and I will not allow him to remember what I had to remember. I'm the one that needs to show him what manhood is and isn't, what is worthwhile and what is energy wasted. Sometimes I wonder about all the time I wasted chasing Drew Hastings. But right now my son is sitting beside me and there's no reason to wonder about any of that.

Acknowledgements

I am indebted to my editor, John Knight, for his invaluable help in getting this book on the page. It would not have happened without him. Thank you, John. Also, a big thank you to Emily Gilbert for proofreading and formatting the book. Thanks to my friend Deb Sansone and my sister Karen for reading and re-reading all the incarnations this book went through. Most of all, thank you to my wife, Taryn, for giving me the time and the space I needed to make this a reality.